BEARS

BY THE NUMBERS

BEARS

BY THE NUMBERS

A Complete Team History of the Chicago Bears by Uniform Number

Lew Freedman

SPORTS
PUBLISHING

Sports Publishing books may be purchased in bulk at special discounts for sales promotion, corporate gifts, fund-raising, or educational purposes. Special editions can also be created to specifications. For details, contact the Special Sales Department, Sports Publishing, 307 West 36th Street, 11th Floor, New York, NY 10018 or sportspubbooks@skyhorsepublishing.com.

Sports Publishing® is a registered trademark of Skyhorse Publishing, Inc.®, a Delaware corporation.

Visit our website at www.sportspubbooks.com.

10 9 8 7 6 5 4 3 2 1

Library of Congress Cataloging-in-Publication Data is available on file.

Cover design by Tom Lau
Cover photo credit AP Images

Print ISBN: 978-1-68358-100-0
Ebook ISBN: 978-1-68358-104-8

Printed in the United States of America

Also by Lew Freedman

Game of My Life Chicago Cubs: Memorable Stories of Cubs Baseball
Game of My Life Chicago Bears: Memorable Stories of Bears Football
Game of My Life Cincinnati Reds: Memorable Stories of Reds Baseball
Clouds Over the Goalpost: Gambling, Assassination, and the NFL in 1963
A Summer to Remember: Bill Veeck, Lou Boudreau, Bob Feller, and the 1948 Cleveland Indians
Knuckleball: The History of the Unhittable Pitch
The Rise of the Seminoles: FSU Football Under Bobby Bowden
The Original Six: How the Canadiens, Bruins, Rangers, Blackhawks, Maple Leafs, and Red Wings Laid the Groundwork for Today's NHL

CONTENTS

INTRODUCTION

When it comes to the numbers professional football players wear, how they perform on the field and for how long is what makes the indelible impression on the fan. The greats make their marks with quantifiable statistics, how they carry themselves, and what their contributions are to championship teams.

Sometimes those stars become so identified with one specific number that the team's spectators begin referring to them as "Old 27" or the like, and everyone else knows who they are talking about.

The Chicago Bears were founded in 1920—along with the NFL itself—only initially they were the Decatur Staleys. During their long and frequently glorious history the Bears have sent some of the greatest players in the game onto the field to represent them.

When it comes to uniform numbers, there can be no greater honor than for a star player to have his number retired by his former team. It is a different, and often more personal recognition than even selection to the Pro Football Hall of Fame, although often the two canonizations overlap.

Fittingly, since the Bears are nearing completion of a full century of play, the team has a long list of jerseys taken out of circulation to honor past players and figures that made tremendous contributions to the club on and off the field.

These are the Bears' retired numbers:

3 Bronko Nagurski
5 George McAfee
7 George Halas
28 Willie Galimore
34 Walter Payton
40 Gale Sayers
41 Brian Piccolo

42 Sid Luckman
51 Dick Butkus
56 Bill Hewitt
61 Bill George
66 Clyde "Bulldog" Turner
77 Harold "Red" Grange
89 Mike Ditka

Now that is an all-star cast. The Bears have more Hall of Famers who have not had jersey numbers retired, too.

The National Football League has stricter rules about which player can wear which number than are on the books in Major League Baseball, the National Basketball Association, and the National Hockey League. The organization has categories of numbers based on position played on the field. That makes the NFL a bit different.

A rookie cannot just saunter up to the equipment manager of a pro football team and request any old number. A running back cannot ask for 87 because he wore that in high school. A quarterback cannot plead for 55 because it is his lucky number. A linebacker cannot bribe his way into number 4 because it is his favorite number and his brother, father, and grandfather all wore it when they were playing for their hometown team.

Nope. That's not how it works in the NFL, and every player and fan knows it. While it would be cool to be the first guy to wear number 100 in a game, it is not likely we will see that any time soon on *Monday Night Football*.

Under the rules of the game, players on NFL teams are permitted to wear jersey numbers from 1 to 99. Any player who is on the roster with a number between 50 and 79 is kind of in a no-man's land, or actually a no-offense land. Football players assigned those numbers are not permitted to touch the ball except under specific circumstances. There is the tackle-eligible play when a player comes off the bench and alerts the referee he may be in on a double secret play to fool the other side. The other exceptions stem from accidents.

An offensive lineman, not tackle eligible, can recover a fumble and can also make a quirky catch provided the ball is not aimed at him, but bounces off someone else and flies into the air. Otherwise, those disenfranchised fellows wearing 50–79 are out of luck in terms of canoodling with the ball.

This coupling of uniform numbers and positions played was introduced in college football in the 1930s and 1940s, and was informally adopted by the NFL beginning in 1952. This standardized numbering system became a formal rule in the National Football League in 1973 and so for more than forty years who wears what number (or at least the range) has been generally decided before a player even joins his team. So Chicago Bears who broke into the top level of the sport since that year fall into groups. No Bears quarterback coming aboard since Secretariat won the Triple Crown of horse racing or *The Godfather* won the Academy Award for best picture could wear 99, even if his heart tried to dictate it.

Under the NFL set-up in effect now, quarterbacks can wear a number between 1 and 19. So can punters and place kickers.

Although there is a policy exception for the preseason, when a team might have a large quantity around before trimming down to the final roster, running backs can outfit themselves in jersey numbers between 20 and 49.

Wide receivers can choose between numbers 10 and 19, as well as 80 to 89. Tight ends, or "H" backs, who are lumped in with them, can wear numbers between 40 and 49 and 80 and 89. Offensive linemen are slotted numbers ranging between 50 and 79, as are defensive linemen, although they can also choose between 90 and 99.

Linebackers must be assigned numbers between 40 and 59, or 90 to 99. Defensive backs' numbers must be between 20 and 49, except for the pre-season where the same rule and theory applies to them for 1 to 9 in case there are a glut of DBs in camp. Very clearly the number a player wears in the modern-day NFL is linked to the position he plays.

Interestingly, the numbering system was part of the discussion at the time of the merger between the National Football League and the American Football League in the late 1960s as the organizations moved toward accept-ance of a final deal.

At that time, future Hall of Fame center Jim Otto of the Oakland Raiders wore 00 because it so smoothly meshed with the spelling of his name. Also, wide receiver Ken Burrough wore 00. They were grandfathered in, allowed to keep wearing those off-beat numbers of their choice until retirement. Burrough, who retired from the Houston Oilers in 1981, was the last player to wear 00 in the NFL. The Bears have never suited up a player with 00 or 0.

For ten years in the 1950s and 1960s, fullback Johnny Olszewski, whose nickname was "Johnny O," wore 0. He played for the Washington Redskins, Detroit Lions, Chicago Cardinals (but not the Bears), and briefly the Denver Broncos. While he was No. 0 for the Bears, he wore 33 and 36 for the Cardinals.

During the 2016 season, the limit for carrying active players on an NFL roster was 53, and all of those guys needed numbers. Take away all of the Bears' retired numbers and it almost involves a little mathematical juggling to ensure everyone could have one with no duplicates.

In the formative years of the NFL, player numbers did not relate to the po-sitions they played. In those years NFL teams carried just 22 players. Most of them wore low numbers, with a very prominent exception being the Bears' Red Grange, who wore 77. Grange wore that number when he played for the University of Illinois in the 1920s and stuck with it. "The Galloping Ghost" was one of the first football stars to famously be identified with the number he wore on the gridiron.

Grange was one of the league's pioneers, all-time greats, and is an en-during legend. Would his stature be any different if he wore 17 rather than 77? Difficult to judge, but 77 possesses a certain cache and flavor that goes beyond the routine.

NO. 1: JIMMY CONZELMAN, HALL OF FAME PLAYER AND COACH

All Time No. 1 Roster	
Player	Years
Jim Conzelman*	(1920)
Paddy Driscoll*	(1920, 1926–29)
Jake Lanum	(1920–24)
Oscar Johnson	(1924)
Lee Artoe	(1940–45)
Jeff Jaeger	(1996–99)
Ryan Quigley	(2012)
* Hall of Fame	

One might think being No. 1 one would be something special, but only seven members of the Bears have ever worn that numbered jersey.

Of course, the first two men to do so set a pretty high standard. Before the Bears' first season was over as the Decatur Staleys two players flashed the No. 1 uniform and they both were ultimately selected for the Pro Football Hall of Fame.

Jimmy Conzelman was awarded the jersey first when the National Football League began play in 1920, which like the Bears/Staleys pretty much operated under a pseudonym for the 1920 and 1921 seasons. Not many fans remember the NFL was the American Professional Football Association when it was founded.

A friend of George Halas's from their playing days together at the Great Lakes Naval Station team during World War I, Conzelman was a short-timer with his pal, but for good reason. By 1921, when he was just twenty-three, Conzelman was offered the position of player-coach for the Rock Island Independents.

For Decatur, Conzelman was a quarterback (which mostly involved running at the time) and was even named to the NFL's All-Decade Team. He played nine of his seasons for other teams, none of which remained in existence beyond that first league decade.

Conzelman suited up for Rock Island, the Milwaukee Badgers, Detroit Panthers, and the Providence Steam Roller.

In college, Conzelman played for Washington University in St. Louis, his hometown. After observing team after team being waived out of business, Conzelman turned to coaching full time. He was successful leading his school to three Missouri Valley Conference championships before taking over the Chicago Cardinals for several seasons wrapped around World War II. In a display of versatility, Conzelman also worked as a team executive for the St. Browns of the American League during those 1943–45 war years. In 1944, the Browns won their only pennant in the half-century existence of the franchise.

While giving the commencement address at the University of Dayton in 1942, a time when the nation was at war, Conzelman said, "Courage is a mysterious quality, touching at times the strong and the weak, the rich and the poor, the wise and the fools in a bewildering method of selection." Present due to his football fame, Conzelman focused much more on the soldier than the athlete, naming a couple of heroes of battle who had never played football, boxed, or competed in other contact sports.

John "Paddy" Driscoll was another original Staley, who also excelled at quarterback and wore No. 1. His Chicago (and environs) links were many. He was born in Evanston, Illinois, just north of the city, attended Northwestern University, also in Evanston, played for the Staleys in 1920, resumed business with the cross-town Chicago Cardinals between 1920 and 1925, and returned to the Bears to play from 1926 to 1929. An all-around skilled athlete, Driscoll also played 13 games for the Chicago Cubs during his baseball career.

One of Driscoll's talents was mastering the dropkick. He once kicked a record four dropkick field goals in one game. Few of those living have seen that bygone skill performed in person.

Driscoll coached the Bears for two seasons, 1956 and 1957, during one of George Halas's hiatuses from the sidelines. He took the '56 Bears to the NFL title game, although they lost to the New York Giants.

Driscoll was an NFL All-Pro six times in the 1920s, the first time and the last two times while with the Bears, a period when he also switched around to other uniform numbers. Driscoll, a member of the pro and college halls of fame, once scored 27 points in an NFL game, but was playing for the Cardinals at the time.

Chosen for the Pro Football Hall of Fame in Canton, Ohio, Driscoll, who stood 5-foot-11 and weighed 161 pounds in his playing days, delivered an induction speech in 1965. In part, he seemed amazed by his own journey, saying, "It's inconceivable that a fellow like myself, weighing 128 pounds playing fullback in high school, would come up here to get these high honors."

No other successor wearing the No. 1 jersey could match the accomplishments of the first two Bears to wear it. Jake Lanum, a running back out of the University of Illinois, gained custody of the shirt before the end of the 1920 season and kept it through 1924. He did get on the field regularly, but scored just one touchdown. Oscar Johnson, who borrowed the number for just one game in 1924, may not even have gotten it dirty.

No. 1 went back into the closet for sixteen years after that, until Lee Artoe took over for four seasons between 1940 and 1945 with war-time off. Artoe, a tackle and kicker who attended Cal-Berkeley, was a rookie the year the Bears crushed the Washington Redskins, 73–0, in the NFL title game, the all-time league wipeout. Artoe started on the offensive line that day.

"He was a real tough guy, a real hitter," said Bears teammate Ken Kavanaugh.

Artoe had to be. With eight hip operations, broken jaws, and knocked-out teeth, he would otherwise have invented the disabled list.

No Bear wore No. 1 again until another kicker, Jeff Jaeger, took possession in 1996 and kept it hanging in his locker into 1999. He only played in seven games during those last four years of his career, but booted all but one extra point attempt and finished his playing days with 1,008 points.

Only one other time since has a Bear worn No. 1. Ryan Quigley wore No. 1 in 2012, but Quigley was down under on the Bears' roster. He never played in a Chicago regular-season game and has since been punting for the New York Jets and Arizona Cardinals.

NO. 2: DOUG FLUTIE, BELOVED BY ALL BUT THE BEARS

All Time No. 2 Roster	
Player	Years
Joe LeFleur	(1922–25)
Ralph King	(1925)
Link Lyman*	(1926–28, 1930–31, 1933–34)
Dick Nesbitt	(1930–33)
Billy Pollock	(1935–36)
Gary Famiglietti	(1938–45)
Doug Flutie	(1986)
Will Furrer	(1992)
Mike Horan	(1998)
Paul Edinger	(2000–04)
Jason Campbell	(2012)
Jordan Palmer	(2013)
Brian Hoyer	(2016)

Hall of Fame

Probably the best-known wearer of No. 2 for the modern football fan is Doug Flutie, Bears draft class of 1986. Flutie was a widely admired college star at Boston College, and won the Heisman Trophy. He is also one of the finest quarterbacks in Canadian Football League history.

But Flutie never won over Bears fans. In fact, he was loved by all *but* the Bears. He was brought in by coach Mike Ditka as a back-up to often-injured Jim McMahon following the Bears' Super Bowl triumph the year before, perhaps to add a little flair to Chicago's offense. However, Flutie hardly ever got off the bench.

Standing at only 5-foot-10, Flutie was deemed too small to make a difference in the NFL. But his game was certainly suited for the wide-open CFL where he threw for 6,619 yards in one season, was at the helm for three Grey Cup championship teams, and six times was chosen the league's outstanding player.

A national icon in college and a household name in Canada, Flutie appeared in just five games for the Bears. He did play for New England, Buffalo, and San Diego, and was chosen for the Pro Bowl in 1998 while with the Bills.

Flutie was a popular enough figure outside of Chicago that he had a cereal named for him—Flutie Flakes—and later appeared on *Dancing With The Stars*.

Link Lyman, who was a Hall-of-Fame lineman for the Bears in the 1920s and 1930s, is the most accomplished player to wear No. 2 for the Bears, but Lyman was not closely identified with the numeral because he kept changing numbers.

Few other Bears through the team history wore No. 2 with much distinction. Joe LaFleur (1922–25), a guard and fullback, was the first member of the team to display the number. Ralph King (1925) was a Bears guard for two games.

During some of the years Lyman was playing musical numbers but was still with the team, Dick Nesbitt (1930–33) wore No. 2. He was a five-year

NFL running back, bouncing around and was probably better known as a TV personality later in Minneapolis. Bill Pollock (1935–36) played in the offensive and defensive backfield and scored four touchdowns for the Bears.

Gary Famiglietti spent his time with Chicago between 1938 and 1945 at halfback and fullback. One season he rushed for as many as 503 yards and scored 20 touchdowns for the Bears before playing a last year with the Boston Yanks. He also dabbled in kicking for the Bears and on punt and kickoff returns.

A solid contributor, Famiglietti was three times chosen for the Pro Bowl and scored a touchdown in the Bears' NFL title game thrashing of the Washington Redskins in 1940.

For some reason, No. 2 remained on the sidelines from 1946 to '86, when Flutie briefly donned it and then again until 1992 when it was worn by Will Furrer during his solo year with the Bears. Furrer was a short-lived NFL back-up out of Virginia Tech.

Punter Mike Horan (1998) had a lengthy pro career, appearing in 205 games and averaging 42.2 yards per boot. He had many memorable moments, including a career-long 75-yard kick—just not many during his season with the Bears. He won a Super Bowl with the St. Louis Rams and kicked in other Super Bowls with the Denver Broncos.

Between 2000 and 2004, Paul Edinger was the Bears' place-kicker. He never missed an extra point in those five seasons and twice topped 100 points in a season for Chicago (112 and 105) before wrapping up his career with the Minnesota Vikings. Edinger hit two extra points and a field goal for the Bears in a 2001 playoff game, although it was a 33–19 loss to the Phila-delphia Eagles.

Chicago loaned No. 2 to quarterback Jason Campbell in 2012. A one-season backup, Campbell made it into six games, starting one, though he did complete 62.7 percent of his 51 pass attempts.

Jordan Palmer was another transient occupant of No. 2 during the 2013 season for the Bears. A quarterback, Palmer wore the uniform, but did not play in a game for the Bears.

Brian Hoyer is another quarterback who tried to improve on the luck of those wearing No. 2. A journeyman who showed flashes of being a possible regular starter, Hoyer played well for the Bears in 2016 as a replacement for the injured Jay Cutler. Before breaking his arm, Hoyer threw for more than 300 yards in a game four times for Chicago, including a career-high 397 yards. He was on a one-year contract at the time and when he healed jumped to the San Francisco 49ers.

NO. 3: BRONKO NAGURSKI, TOUGHEST OF THEM ALL

It took a few years after he retired for the Bears to retire Bronko Nagurski's No. 3 jersey. A few players wore it before him and a handful of players wore it after him, few with great note.

But in Bears lore when you talk No. 3 it is Bronko's number. If someone carved a Mount Rushmore of the National Football League, Nagurski would most certainly be one of those etched in stone. A true legend of the game, the bruising fullback-linebacker was said to be the strongest competitor of his era, mostly the 1930s with a bounce-back season in 1943.

When opposing players saw No. 3 coming at them, it was like trying to dodge a freight train. On offense, Nagurski gathered the ball to his belly and ran right through would-be tacklers. On defense, the 6-foot-2, 230-pounder often tossed blockers aside and racked up the ballcarrier with a bone-crushing hit.

Bronko may have been as wild on the field as a bucking bronco, but his given name was Bronislau. Born in Canada, but a long-time resident of International Falls, Minnesota, Nagurski gained his first football fame as an All-American at the University of Minnesota.

He joined the Bears in 1930 and retired for the first time in 1937. During Nagurski's tenure, he was a four-time, first-team All-Pro. When the Bears were short-handed during World War II, owner George Halas, himself off to join the Navy for a second time, recruited Nagurski to play again. He returned for the 1943 season, which enabled Nagurski to be part of a third NFL championship.

There are a mix of myths and legends surrounding Nagurski. Though all are good stories in the telling, not all are true. One such tale said Bronko was recruited by the Gophers after the coach got lost in his neighborhood. Supposedly Nagurski, who was plowing the field, raised the plow and pointed with it when asked for directions.

Nagurski followed his pro football days as a pro wrestling attraction. That career lasted longer, and he made more money from grappling than he ever did with the Bears.

One of the most revered and admired of NFL legends, Nagurski was always appreciated in his hometown. He ran businesses in International Falls and the nickname of the local high school athletic program is the Broncs, named in his honor.

Nagurski is not only a member of the College Football Hall of Fame, he was a member of the first class inducted into the Pro Football Hall of Fame when the building opened in 1963.

Before Nagurski came along to pull on the No. 3 jersey, a few other Bears wore it. Ed Sternaman, a member of the original Staleys, dressed in No. 3 during the first season of the club's existence and stuck with the team and the number into 1930.

Sternaman is not nearly as well-remembered as George Halas, but he, Halas, and Sternaman's younger brother, Joey, all played together at the University of Illinois. While Halas is regarded as the pioneer and league patriarch, Ed Sternman was a co-coach and co-owner of the Bears during the early years.

Sternaman, whose nickname was "Dutch," was wiped out by the Great Depression and had to sell his share of the Bears to Halas.

Meanwhile, during the 1920 and 1921 seasons, Robert Koehler also wore No. 3 when Sternaman did not. Koehler had an OK career as a fullback in the twenties, but the Bears sent him to the Chicago Cardinals during the 1921 season.

When the 1930 season began, Clifford Ashburn was given No. 3 after spending a year with the New York Giants, but he never played a game for the Bears. Nagurski was wearing the number before too long. A couple of other players with brief stays on the Bears wore No. 3 in between Nagurski's stints. Albert Johnson presumably tried on No. 3 in 1938, but didn't suit up for the Bears in any games. Also, while Nagurski was retired, Lewis Hamity was handed the number in 1941. He was college football's leading passer in 1938 for the University of Chicago, not long before the Maroons gave up big-time football. Hamity played one season for the Bears, but became a Marine fighter pilot during World War II after Pearl Harbor was bombed.

The Bears acquired running back Dante Magnani from the Cleveland Rams in 1943, but he turned over No. 3 to Nagurski when Bronko came out of retirement. In two other seasons with the Bears, 1946 and 1949, after World

War II and after Nagurski, Magnani wore No. 3. While Magnani was away at war, Jim Fordham, who attended the University of Georgia—not Fordham—played respectable ball for Chicago as a runner in 1944 and 1945. His nickname was "Flash."

Post-World War II, the Bears kept passing No. 3 around to short-timers: Eddie Allen in 1947 (16 yards rushing in 9 games) and Wally Dreyer in 1949. Dreyer was around for just that one season, although he played for Green Bay the following year.

Finally, the Bears front office decided enough was enough. Bronko Nagurski deserved the recognition of having his number retired and no one on the team has worn it since 1949.

The great Sammy Baugh once asked Nagurski why he did not get blocks from teammates when he ran through the line. Nagurski said, "I don't need one." Nagurski did not evade tacklers, he bulldozed them.

When Nagurski retired the first time in 1937 the reasons were two-fold: Halas's cheapness in refusing to pay him better, and his continuing allegiance to pro wrestling. Halas told Nagurski he was nuts to walk away from the gridiron.

"You're the best football player I've ever seen," Halas told Nagurski.

But at that point, money, not flattery, is what would have induced Nagurski to stay. Moving into a bare-chested sport, Bronko did not wear No. 3 in the ring.

NO. 4: JIM HARBAUGH, PUGNACIOUS EVEN THEN

All Time No. 4 Roster	
Player	Years
Pard Pearce	(1920–22)
Johnny Bryan	(1922–25)
Joe Sternaman	(1922–25, 1927–30)
Keith Molesworth	(1931–38)
Reino Nori	(1938)
Harry Clarke	(1940–43)
Dante Magnani	(1943, 1946, 1949)
Frank Mazicki	(1942)
Tip Mooney	(1944–46)
Nick Sacrinty	(1947)
John Roveto	(1982)
Steve Fuller	(1984–87)
Jim Harbaugh	(1987–93)
Steve Walsh	(1994–95)
Moses Moreno	(1998)
Brad Maynard	(2001–10)
Jay Feely	(2014)
Spencer Lanning	(2015)
Connor Barth	(2016)

These days, everyone who follows football knows Jim Harbaugh as the University of Michigan Wolverines coach with a snarl like . . . well . . . a wolverine. He was making a name for himself even before that on the sidelines with the San Francisco 49ers.

But Harbaugh was a pretty decent player, too, who as a quarterback, mostly with the Indianapolis Colts and the Bears, showed a lot of grit. It would not surprise anyone to hear Harbaugh would do anything to beat you.

Harbaugh played for Michigan, too, and was drafted by the Bears in 1987. He made the team that season, but spent much of the fall riding the bench. It took a couple more years before Harbaugh did much beyond appear in mop-up duty. By 1990, he was the team's starter.

While Harbaugh was not Mr. Fancy, he threw for 2,178 yards and 10 touchdowns in 14 games in leading Chicago to an 11–5 record. He simultaneously took a battering, being sacked 31 times, and was injured for the last two games of the regular season and playoffs.

He was a new man in 1991, throwing for 3,121 yards and starting all 16 games for the Bears. Harbaugh, perhaps foreshadowing his coaching chops, had a knack for inspiring his teammates. Again the Bears finished 11–5 and advanced to the playoffs. But that was a high point for Harbaugh in Chicago and the Bears behind his signal-calling. He gave up No. 4 after a 1988–93 stay.

However, the man who said, "Attack each day with an enthusiasm unknown to mankind," maintained that outlook.

Harbaugh is just one of 19 players who have worn No. 4 for the Bears. Going back to the beginning of the franchise, Pard Pearce debuted the numeral and kept it for the first three years of the team. Before that, seeking to keep his amateur football eligibility, Pearce played professional baseball in the minors under a fake name.

Johnny Bryan (1922–25) came next and became owner of the short-lived Milwaukee Badgers a few years later when his predecessor was forced by the league to relinquish the reins. Bryan then came back to the Bears. Joey Sternaman, part-owner Ed's brother, wore No. 4 and was the team quarterback ahead of Pearce, playing through 1930.

The multi-talented Keith Molesworth was a Bear from 1931 to 1938, a surprising make-good guy who weighed just 98 pounds in high school and was lucky his team gave him any uniform. Molesworth simultaneously played for the Bears and in minor league baseball and, in 1953, he coached the Baltimore Colts after significant experience gained elsewhere as an assistant coach.

Reino Nori was one game and done with the Bears in 1938. Harry Clarke (1940–43) was a war-time player. A big star at West Virginia, he scored two touchdowns in the Bears' 73–0 crunching of the Washington Redskins in the 1940 championship game. Clarke served in the navy and then played in the upstart All-America Football Conference.

No. 4 was one of the numbers Dante Magnani wore for the Bears. Frank Maznicki (1942) was nicknamed "Monk." Tip Mooney (1944–46), who gained 105 yards rushing in 17 carries in 1945, and Nick Sacrinty (1947) did not make many ripples wearing No. 4.

The number then went out for dry cleaning and wasn't returned to action for thirty-five years when kicker John Roveto (who wore number 9 in 1981) pulled on the jersey in 1982. Quarterback Steve Fuller was the Bears' back-up signal-caller on the 18–1 team that won the 1986 Super Bowl. Fuller only started 5 games and threw 107 passes during the Super Bowl season, but he did win a ring. It was Jim Harbaugh's turn in No. 4 next.

Steve Walsh (1994–95) had one pretty good year. Walsh threw for 2,078 yards and 10 touchdowns for the Bears in '94. That was better than Moses Moreno did in 1998. A star at Colorado State, Moreno was a Bears seventh-round draft pick and only appeared in two games.

Punter Brad Maynard formed a more permanent attachment to No. 4, holding onto it from 2001 to 2010. Maynard played 15 years in the NFL in all, the heart of his career in Chicago, kicking as many as 108 times in one season for the Bears. While that led the league, it was also a sign the 5–11 Bears could not move the ball in 2004. One year Maynard was voted the sexiest member of the team. It was a consolation prize for not ever being voted to the Pro Bowl.

Jay Feely (2014) was a just-passing-through kicker with four field-goal tries in four games. Spencer Lanning, a hopeful punter in 2015, played in one game. Next on the No. 4 list was Connor Barth, who booted 18 out of 23 field goals in 2016.

NO. 5: HALL OF FAMER GEORGE MCAFEE

All Time No. 5 Roster	
Player	Years
Charley Dressen	(1920)
Ken Huffine	(1921)
Carl Hanke	(1922)
George Bolan	(1921–24)
Laurie Walquist	(1922–31)
Bill Buckler	(1926–31)
George Corbett	(1932–38)
Anton Stolfa	(1939)
Robert MacLeod	(1939–40)
George McAfee**	(1940–50)
Billy Stone	(1951–54)

** Hall of Famer; Number Retired for McAfee

Even if you are not as well-known as the most famous of the Chicago Bears, if your name is permanently etched next to a number, then you know you did pretty well.

No. 5 was retired for George McAfee, who wore it in 1940–41, and 1945–50. McAfee was a halfback who could run the ball, return the ball, and catch the ball, the latter on offense and defense. He is a member of the College Football Hall of Fame, recognized for his performances at Duke, and the Pro Football Hall of Fame for his contributions to four Bears championship teams.

Besides taking handoffs and grabbing passes, McAfee was an accomplished defensive back with 25 interceptions. He also had a knack for wiggling free of tacklers while receiving punts and led the NFL in that category.

Red Grange, who had retired by then, and probably earned the same accolade from another observer a decade or so earlier, called McAfee "the most dangerous" player in the NFL with the football in his hands.

Although he did miss some playing time in the 1940s due to World War II, whenever McAfee was in the Bears lineup he was doing something spectacular. He led the league in rushing in 1941 and averaged 7.3 yards per carry. He also scored 9 touchdowns, which would be quite respectable in 2017—except McAfee did so in an 11-game season, not 16.

Considered very fast for his time, McAfee was clocked in 9.7 seconds for the 100-yard dash and won a college conference sprint title.

A *New York Times* columnist said McAfee compared favorably with the legendary Jim Thorpe as the finest ball-carrier of all time. His coach, George Halas, seemed to agree that he was the same caliber of player, saying, "The highest compliment you can pay any ball carrier is (to) just compare him with McAfee."

The first Bear to wear No. 5 for the team, during the initial Staleys campaign, was also quite a famous athletic figure—but not for football. Chuck

Dressen's hometown was Decatur, Illinois, which made him a natural candidate to play when the starch manufacturers suited up a team. Dressen was a quarterback who spent his lone season associated with the team in 1920, although he also put in two seasons with the Racine Legion.

However, Dressen was far better known for his days in Major League Baseball. He was already past thirty when he made his big-league debut in 1925 with the Cincinnati Reds. Dressen also played one season with the New York Giants, retiring in 1933. If that represented the entirety of his big-league connection, Dressen, who batted .272 lifetime, might not be well-remembered despite being a pro at the top level in two sports.

However, Dressen ended up winning 1,008 games as a major-league manager with the Reds, Brooklyn Dodgers, Washington Senators, Milwaukee Braves, and Detroit Tigers—and that didn't include coaching stints with the Brooklyn Dodgers, New York Yankees, and Los Angeles Dodgers. Although he did not win the World Series as a manager or player, Dressen earned two championship rings as a coach. Somewhat notoriously, Dressen was the manager of the 1951 Dodgers club that lost the National League pennant in a playoff game on Bobby Thomson's famous home run.

Take away Dressen and McAfee and the list of Bears players who also wore No. 5 is not terribly distinguished. Ken Huffine (1921) scored two touchdowns. Carl Hanke (1922) played two games. George Bolan (1921–24) also scored two touchdowns, in parts of four seasons.

Laurie Walquist (1922–31) had a lengthy Bears career, handling the punting and place kicking. Bill Buckler (1926–31), a guard who was around at the same time, is listed in Bears records as wearing No. 5 as well. But unless they traded the jersey back and forth between plays, most likely they used the number intermittently during their careers. Go figure.

After both Walquist and Buckler were gone, George Corbett (1932–38) inherited No. 5, perhaps because he could count to five. Corbett was a sometimes running back and a sometimes pass catcher. Quarterback Anton Stolfa (1939) was neither one and appeared in just one game.

Robert MacLeod (1939–40) wore No. 5 in the same season as Stolfa and in the same season as George McAfee. He was an All-American at Dartmouth and rushed for 88 yards as a bridge wearer of the number.

After McAfee retired, the Bears did not take the number out of circulation fast enough, giving it out one more time. Billy Stone wore No. 5 between 1951 and 1954 and during that time carried the ball well enough and caught

100 passes for the Bears. He out-did most of the No. 5s, but there was no mystery about it being retired for McAfee.

McAfee was inducted into the Pro Football Hall of Fame in 1966. As part of his acceptance speech, McAfee said, "I'll cherish this honor as long as I live." And he lived to be ninety.

NO. 6: JAY CUTLER, ALMOST GREAT QUARTERBACK

All Time No. 6 Roster	
Player	Years
Sid Gepford	(1920)
Jim Kendricks	(1924)
Hec Garvey	(1922–25)
Bill Senn	(1926–31)
Bernie Leahy	(1932)
Gene Ronzani	(1933–40)
John Siegal	(1939–43)
Don Kindt Sr.	(1947–56)
Hans Nielsen	(1981)
Kevin Butler	(1985–95)
Jay Cutler	(2009–16)

The best wearer of No. 6 in Chicago Bears history was shown the way out the door in March of 2017 after some serious highlight performances and other major disappointments.

Although just thirty-four, Jay Cutler, the former Vanderbilt quarterback who joined the Bears from the Denver Broncos in 2009, one season after being selected for the Pro Bowl, was contemplating retirement. At 6-foot-3 and 230 pounds, Cutler regularly flashed a strong arm and seemed to have a sturdy frame. However, often enough being banged around in the backfield brought physical consequences.

Too many sacks seemed to take a toll. Cutler played in just 10 games in 2011, 11 in 2013, and five in 2016. Although Cutler broke some of Sid Luckman's 60-year-old team records and had thrown for a career total of 208 touchdowns by the end of the 2016 season, he did not always please a demanding audience.

Cutler's lifetime pass-completion record was 61.9 percent, but the only category he ever led the NFL in was interceptions. That occurred twice. With Chicago, though, Cutler threw for more than 3,000 yards five times, including a high of 3,812 in 2014.

Born in Santa Claus, Indiana, Cutler could have used a few gifts from his teammates to keep him upright more often. Through 11 seasons, including time spent in Denver, Cutler had been sacked 302 times, a statistic not conducive to long-term health. In addition, in 2008, Cutler was diagnosed with type 1 diabetes and was forced to take insulin shots. He spent considerable time working with charities, especially those focused on helping young people.

It was not immediately apparent if Cutler would continue to play in the NFL. A shoulder injury in November of 2016 curtailed his last season with the Bears. The combination of a Bears team mired in the lower depths of the league and Cutler's injuries certainly indicated moving elsewhere for a fresh start could well be in his best interests if healthy enough. In 2017, Cutler retired and will be joining Fox Sports as an analyst for the upcoming NFL season.

Although Cutler often came off as immature and removed from circumstances during his earliest days with the team, by the time he left he impressed as a more mature man with the responsibilities of husband and father affecting his life more than ups and downs on the field.

"We all become a little wiser," Cutler admitted in a farewell interview with the *Chicago Tribune*. "Having kids helps you realize how selfish you can be as a person rather quickly." He admitted to the key improvement in maturity, saying, ". . . if you're not trying to get better in certain aspects of your life, you're just going to stay the same. I think we can all improve."

The next-most prominent No. 6 in Bears history rhymes with Cutler. Kevin Butler was the kicker for Chicago during its Super Bowl run, and spent 1985–95 with the club. During a 13-year NFL career, which concluded with a couple of years on the Arizona Cardinals, Butler scored 1,208 points in 184 games. That included 265 field goals. With 1,116 points, Butler left the Bears as the team's all-time leading scorer. Kicker Robbie Gould passed Butler twenty years later.

A University of Georgia player, Butler is a member of the College Football Hall of Fame and handles football radio broadcasts for his alma mater.

As a rookie, Butler kicked for 144 points, a record for a first-year player that lasted until 2014.

The first player to wear No. 6 was Sid Gepford, a Decatur Staley in 1920. He played just two games. Jim Kendricks (1924) lined up for the Bears at the same time he coached Centre College.

Hec Garvey (1922–25) hung around a little bit longer than the first two Bears to wear No. 6 and started 24 games as an end and guard. Bill Senn (1926–31) threw a few passes and made a few punts. Bernie Leahy (1932) played one game.

Things were different after Gene Ronzani pulled on No. 6. Ronzani stuck with Chicago from 1933 to 1945. Ronzani won nine letters in college at Marquette University. He was mostly a backup for the Bears, although one season he rushed for 485 yards, contributed some receptions, and was second-string behind Sid Luckman at quarterback.

Ronzani later turned to coaching and was an assistant at Notre Dame, a few years for the Bears, and in 1950 had the unenviable task of replacing Curly Lambeau as head man with the Green Bay Packers. Lambeau coached the team for more than thirty years, since its inception. Ronzani was the boss from 1950 to 1953.

John Siegal was a Bear from 1939 to 1943 and played both ways at end. That meant he caught some passes and made some tackles, more of the latter, three times being named All-Pro. When Siegal died at ninety-seven in 2015, he was the oldest living Bear.

Don Kindt Sr. made a living with the Bears from 1947 through 1956. A second-string halfback in addition to playing defensive back, Kindt gained as many as 266 yards rushing in a season. He often disagreed about strategy with coach George Halas, so it was surprising he lasted as long as he did in Chicago.

The No. 6 went to sleep for a long time following Kindt's career. No one on the Bears wore it until Hans Nielsen in 1981. He kicked in all of three games, though Nielsen made all eight of his extra-point tries.

After that came Butler and Cutler in No. 6.

NO. 7: THE FIRST CHICAGO BEAR TO WEAR NO. 7 WAS THE FIRST BEAR

All Time No. 7	
Player	Years
George Halas**	(1920–29)
Joseph Lintzenich	(1930–31)
John Sisk Sr.	(1932–36)
Ernest Rentner	(1936–37)
John Oelerich	(1938)
Edgar Manske	(1938–40)
Bill Geyer	(1942–43, 1946)
Ed Sprinkle	(1944–55)
John Huarte	(1972)
Bob Avellini	(1975–84)

* Hall of Famer; Number Retired for Halas

George Halas was the founder of the Bears (as the Decatur Staleys) when the National Football League began business in 1920. He was also the coach and a player. Over time, Halas was the team owner, general manager, and he probably sharpened the pencils in the office, unless he bossed around a secretary with the same bark he employed with his men on the gridiron.

When it comes to the Bears, Halas was Mr. Everything. He ran the show for sixty-three years, until 1983, made all of the key personnel moves, and as coach won seven NFL titles, the last one in 1963.

He earned the nickname "Papa Bear" and was regarded as nearly as important to the evolution of the league and its growth as he was to the Bears. He worked with legends, coaching legends, and in the end became a legend.

When Halas played between 1920 and 1929, there was no league-mandated rule dictating which players at which positions wore which numbers. However, in the earliest days of NFL play, the teams pretty much stuck with chronological order when handing the uniforms out. The teams started with No. 1 and worked their way up, indifferent to the player's assigned role on the team.

Rosters were also much smaller in the early days of the pro game than they are in the 2000s. As a direct result of this casual dispensing of numbers during the Staleys' first year of competition, no player in the first season wore a number higher than 24.

Halas could have ended up with any number, but wore No. 7. Many other Bears wore that number. Many of the players who wore No. 7 did so only briefly. The last Bear to wear No. 7 for the team was Bob Avellini in 1984.

It was only after Halas died that the club thought of retiring the number Halas wore as a player six decades earlier as a way to honor him.

When Halas retired as a player, it was not as if he zealously protected the No. 7 uniform jersey and forbade anyone else from wearing it. Such a sentimental thought was unlikely to cross his mind.

Promptly, in 1930, the number transferred to Joseph Lintzenich. Few long-term Bears fans instantly recall Lintzenich's contributions to the club during his two seasons in No. 7. However, although his career with the Bears and in the pros was short, some distinctive sports trivia attaches itself to his name—if not specifically his number.

In a game against the New York Giants on November 16, 1931, Lintzenich booted a punt that did not stop rolling for 94 yards beyond the line of scrimmage. That kick remained tied for the NFL record for thirty-eight years. It is still a Bears record eighty-six years later. Although this has nothing to do with Lintzenich's tenure with the Bears, he was also the father-in-law of famed sports broadcaster Jack Buck and the grandfather of current sports broadcaster Joe Buck. So although Lintzenich could not match Halas for renown, he did not pass through the landscape quietly, either.

John Sisk Sr., who next inherited No. 7, did not make much of a mark, but he did play from 1932 to 1936 and flaunted the nickname "Big Train," the same moniker applied to Hall of Fame baseball pitcher Walter Johnson. Sisk Sr. was a running back who was on the Bears 1933 team. In 2005, his championship ring from that season sold at auction for $8,120. In 1964, his son, John Sisk Jr., played three games for the Bears.

Ernest Rentner took over custody of No. 7 for the 1936 and 1937 seasons and proudly wore the number, as well as the nickname "Pug."

John Oelerich was less than one-and-done in 1938 and quickly passed No. 7 to Edgar Manske.

Manske, whose nickname was "Eggs," clutched the number to his chest from 1937 to 1940. The last college player to compete without a helmet, Manske did not transfer his bareheaded allegiance to the pros. Pictures show he was a good-looking guy—at least when he signed up with the Bears. Manske, who was a Bears regular and played in their 1940 championship-game 73–0 massacre of the Washington Redskins, is famous in Chicago for another reason. Halas traded Manske to the Pittsburgh Steelers in 1939 for their first-round draft pick. The Bears picked Hall of Famer Sid Luckman with the choice. Manske was then released by the Steelers and re-signed with the Bears. So, essentially, Chicago got Luckman for free.

Maybe the team should have retired No. 7 for Manske instead of Halas.

Although he played parts of three seasons (nine games counting as parts) in 1942, 1943, and 1946, Bill Geyer only wore No. 7 in 1942.

The No. 7 took the next year off, but starting in 1944 Ed Sprinkle displayed the number and he kept right on using it through 1955. Sprinkle's vitals were listed as 6-foot-1 and 206 pounds, but he played way tougher than that for 12 seasons. Before turning to wrecking offenses full time, Sprinkle played both ways and caught passes for his own offense.

Sprinkle featured a tackling method—an elbow to the throat which was legal at the time—called "The Claw," making him sound more like a professional wrestler than a football player. Citing an often-quoted line about Sprinkle, the *New York Times* included in its obituary that he was called "the meanest man in football" when he died at age ninety.

The No. 7 went into hibernation until 1972 after Sprinkle retired his Claw. Halas picked up John Huarte that year, hoping he could be a significant addition at quarterback. Huarte was a star at Notre Dame and won the Heisman Trophy in 1964, but had already passed through three teams.

A career backup in the American Football League and National Football League, Huarte was gone from Chicago after a single season and completed his pro career with the dearly departed Memphis Southmen of the World Football League.

By 1975, Halas had been looking for a long-term answer at quarterback for a quarter of a century, or since Luckman retired. Although Avellini, a sixth-round pick out of Maryland, remained with the Bears through the 1984 season, he was never a star. His best season was 1977 when he threw for 2,004 yards and 11 touchdowns.

Later in life Avellini had run-ins with the law over driving while intoxicated, worked in radio, and devoted time to charitable causes.

After Avellini surrendered No. 7, the number was given to George Halas for eternity.

George Halas

Several teams in several sports retire a number to honor a team founder or a long-time owner. The No. 1 is often chosen, unless there is a specific reason to choose a different numeral. That's how Halas ended up having No. 7 retired for him.

"Papa Bear" Halas, as he was often called during his sixty-three years at the helm of the Chicago Bears, was an unusual case. Halas not only helped to found the Bears, first known as the Decatur Staleys, but he was in on the ground floor organizing of the National Football League itself when it started business in 1920.

For decades, Halas served as coach, general manager, and president of the team that he owned. He wore more hats than a concessions vendor has at a ballpark.

However, little remembered except by the game's historians and trivia buffs (if anyone is still living who witnessed his other activity, the numbers are tiny) is that Halas also played. Indeed, he was a player first, naturally enough. Halas was born in 1895 and was a Chicago boy all of the way, graduating from Crane High School.

Halas then attended the University of Illinois where he was a three-sport athlete, competing on the football, basketball, and baseball teams. As a member of the 1918 Fighting Illini, Halas played for a Big Ten football champion.

The Rose Bowl is known as the granddaddy of all college football bowl games, and it was already going strong (without the later links specifically to the Big Ten and Pacific 8, 10, or 12 champions). As World War I was coming to an end, the powerhouse football teams in the land were military clubs. Halas was playing for the Great Lakes Navy Bluejackets, and that team defeated the Mare Island Marines in the Rose Bowl. The Most Valuable Player in the 17–0 Great Lakes victory was Halas.

Halas preferred a career in professional sports, but opportunities were limited and he accepted a job with the A.E. Staley Co. in Decatur, Illinois. The starch manufacturing company wished to start a football team and Halas was given authority over the plan to get it going. Thus, the Decatur Staleys were born. When the National Football League was jump-started, the Staleys were accepted into the fledgling league with Halas at the helm. The starch company swiftly lost interest in football and let Halas have the team and change the name to the Chicago Bears in 1922.

Standing 6 feet tall and weighing 182 pounds, Halas was a solid specimen for the times. Between 1920 and 1929, Halas was player-coach of the Staleys/Bears. He played end and wore No. 7 on the field. When he was thirty-three he turned to coaching full time.

There is no doubt that Halas, who led the Bears to a record of 318–148–31 in forty years, deserved to have some number retired in his honor. That can be a difficult choice in the case of a coach who pretty much worked in street clothes, but Halas's old-time connection on the field wearing No. 7 provided a logical selection for the Bears.

It should be noted that however briefly Halas played Major League Baseball with the New York Yankees—12 games in 1919—when he suited up he wore no number whatsoever on his back. His baseball jersey was blank on the back. The first year the Yankees wore numbers on their uniforms was 1929.

NO. 8: REX GROSSMAN TOOK BEARS TO A SUPER BOWL

While no one is ever going to put quarterback Rex Grossman in the same category as Sid Luckman or even Jay Cutler, you've got to give him this: When the Bears reached the Super Bowl in 2007 (only to lose to the Indianapolis Colts), Grossman was the man behind center.

That's as much as anyone who ever wore No. 8 for the Bears accomplished—and many tried. In fact, 21 players have worn No. 8 for Chicago, though almost none of them did much memorable and few wore it for very long. No. 8 is pretty much the musical chairs of numbers in the Bears roster history.

Grossman was a Bear from 2003 to 2008. Chicago made him a first-round draft pick out of the University of Florida, but he was bugged by injuries for parts of his first three seasons. When he got the chance to start, Grossman led the Bears to the Super Bowl. He threw for 3,193 yards and 23 touchdowns during the 2006 regular season. But he also threw tons of interceptions (20), and that was the only season in his 9-year career in which he played all 16 games.

It seemed Grossman was either injured, coming back from injury, or in the midst of a quarterback controversy for most of his career. But he can always say that he played in a Super Bowl.

Riding in the wayback machine, the first Bear to wear No. 8 was Leo Johnson in 1920, with the Decatur Staleys. If the name Leo Johnson is put into a Google search, his football career gets beat out by Leo Johnson, a fictional character from *Twin Peaks*. However, the real-life Johnson was an extraordinary track coach at the University of Illinois, winning three NCAA titles and 17 Big Ten championships. Not that it did the Bears any good.

Roy "Buck" White (1925, 1927–29) was a fullback who appeared in 46 games and scored 10 touchdowns. Pete Stinchcomb (1921–22), whose real name was Gaylord, was a shining enough All-American at Ohio State to be elected to the College Football Hall of Fame and was an All-Pro selection in both seasons with the Bears.

After his flirtation with No. 4, Johnny Bryan also wore No. 8. He was succeeded by Carl Brumbaugh (1930–37), who did some damage on the Bears' behalf as a quarterback pre-Luckman. Mostly, though, Brumbaugh was an insurance policy in the backfield. Al Moore (1932) played in two games. George Grosvenor (1935–36) carried the ball here and there and also threw it here and there. Charles Heileman (1939) was a former Iowa State end who got into two games.

Stanford All-American Hugh Gallarneau halted the No. 8 losing streak. With time off for World War II, he played five seasons between 1941 and 1947 and averaged 4.1 yards per rush. In 1941, Gallarneau scored eight touchdowns. He surpassed double figures in pass receptions in three separate years as well. Gallarneau also had a significant 81-yard punt return in a playoff game against the Green Bay Packers in 1941. This was all ironic because his father would not let him play football in high school and he concentrated on swimming, track, and other things.

Dante Magnani, one of many Bears who switched numbers while with the team, spent some time wearing No. 8 in the 1940s when Gallarneau wasn't. Bill Glenn wore No. 8 in 1944 and into 1945, but didn't even get the jersey sweaty, playing in just two games. James Canady (1948–49) was a backup runner.

Then the No. 8 got lost in the equipment room, not donned again until quarterback Vince Evans tried it on from 1977 to 1983. Evans was a star at Southern Cal, but a career backup in the NFL for 15 years. Only once, in 1981, did he play all 16 games and threw for 2,354 yards and 11 touchdowns for the Bears. But he also only completed 44.7 percent of his passes and tossed 20 interceptions, holding him back from ever receiving a star on the sidewalk outside of Soldier Field.

Maury Buford (1985–86, 1989–91) punted for several years. Mike Hohensee (1987) is a man who loves the sport. In addition to his one season as a quarterback with the Bears, he suited up for teams in Canada, the Arena Football League, and the United States Football League. He has been coaching steadily since 1990. Numerous football players only wish they had such a diverse and fascinating career even if Hohensee never had major success on-field in the NFL.

Pat O'Neill (1995) went from being a punter to a surgeon professionally. Carlos Huerta (1996) was small at 5-foot-7, with a big foot. Although he only got into a few games with the Bears, he led the University of Miami in scoring four straight years, and with the Las Vegas Posse of the Canadian league (during their short-lived US expansion) he scored 154 points in a season.

Cade McNown (1999–2000) was considered to be the Chicago quarterback of the future as a No. 1 draft pick out of UCLA. But next thing you knew, Rex Grossman was not only swiping his position, but his No. 8 uniform. This was just one of the innumerable Bears quarterback controversies, which pretty much date non-stop from Sid Luckman's retirement in 1950.

Adam Podlesh did an admirable job for the Bears as a punter between 2011 and 2013, (and that was after he beat cancer) and figured to be around longer. A four-time All-Conference player at Maryland, Podlesh was chosen for the Rochester, New York, Jewish Sports Hall of Fame.

Jimmy Clausen (2014–15) could have become a famous Bears quarterback, but he didn't, like so many of the others who came before him, after glittering college careers. Which is why the No. 8 was available for Connor Shaw in 2016. He hadn't become a famous Bears quarterback yet either as of the 2017 season, although he did have the same bald head as Hall of Famer Y. A. Tittle. Quarterback Mike Glennon will wear No. 8 for the Bears in 2017.

NO. 9: JIM MCMAHON, THE QUIRKIEST BEAR OF ALL

Somehow, No. 9 Jim McMahon parlayed being the boss of the offense on the Bears 1986 Super Bowl championship into being seen as a legendary figure.

And most fans would say it was worth it. McMahon, a one-time passing prodigy at Brigham Young University, was more leader than thrower for the mid-1980s Bears and he called the signals for one of the most famous teams of all.

No one lived larger than McMahon at the time. Everything he said, everything he did off the field, was magnified due to belonging to a team that went 18–1, won the Super Bowl, and made the remarkable "Super Bowl Shuffle" video. He was a star who at times outshone goings on at Soldier Field.

It was a crazy time to be a Bear no matter what number any player wore and no matter what position anybody played. McMahon even shook up the entire football world just by wearing a headband with a message. He also had about as strange an up-and-down career on the field, as he did life off of it.

McMahon made the Pro Bowl after the 1985 season with what would seem to be pedestrian statistics thirty years later: 2,392 yards gained with 15 touchdowns. He was injured so often he didn't even appear in all games in that special season.

Few fans even likely remember that McMahon actually won another Super Bowl ring—only it was as a backup with the Packers.

Unfortunately, in the years after retirement, McMahon ran into problems with drunk driving. Then he began suffering post-concussion syndrome symptoms and at times seemed to be a recluse. But no one more important ever wore No. 9 for the Bears.

However, it does seem that everyone and his cousin did model that uniform jersey, starting with Johnny Bryan (1922–25), who shuffled uniform numbers for the Bears the way that all-star cast shuffled in the video.

Roy White (1925, 1927–29) wore No. 9 for a few years. Clifford Lemon (1926) barely got the jersey dirty. Walter Holmer (1929–30) was marginally better known, but was better known later as coach of Boston University and Colby College. Paul Franklin (1930–34) was not more famous. Neither was John Bettridge (1937) who played only a few games for the Bears. Ray Buivid (1937–38) was a backup quarterback out of Marquette University.

Bill Osmanski (1939–45) was a far more significant Bears figure than his immediate predecessors who wore No. 9. His nickname at Holy Cross was "Bullet," and was Chicago's No. 1 draft pick in 1939, leading the NFL in rushing that year with 699 yards. Osmanski made the most of a fairly short career, playing for four league champions, even though he spent considerable time in the service during World War II.

Osmanski's 68-yard run early in the 1940 league title game started the deluge that began the Bears' 73–0 thrashing of the Washington Redskins in the worst beating ever delivered in NFL play.

Dick Flanagan (1948–49) played center, guard, and linebacker. Bob Williams (1951–53) was a minimally-used quarterback out of Notre Dame.

Bill Wade already made an All-Pro team for the Los Angeles Rams before the Bears acquired him in 1961 (and kept him through 1966). An all-around star athlete at Vanderbilt, Wade was the missing piece for the 1963 Chicago club that out-maneuvered the Green Bay Packers and New York Giants for the NFL title.

In retirement, Wade suffered from various health ailments, including going blind, but remained a Bears fan until his death in March of 2016. When a *Chicago Tribune* writer contacted him before the Bears 2007 Super Bowl appearance, Wade said he would have been at the game if he could have been, but did display a Bears cap to show his continuing allegiance.

Virgil Carter (1968–69, 1976), another quarterback, did not have Wade's success wearing No. 9. John Roveto (1981) was just passing through, but did kick a 51-yard field goal. He turned No. 9 over to Jim McMahon, who turned it over to Shane Matthews, another quarterback hopeful, between 1993 and 1996 and also between 1999 and 2001. A star at the University of Florida, Matthews spent 14 years in the NFL. His best year came with Chicago in 1999.

Chad Hutchinson's arrival was heralded when given a chance at QB, but his involvement in 2004 was limited, starting just five games. Even before that (2001), the 6-foot-5 240-pound Hutchinson reached the St. Louis Cardinals as a Major League right-handed pitcher. His big-league career encompassed just three appearances, however, and his record was 0–0 with a 24.75 earned run average.

In 2005, the Bears entrusted No. 9 to kicker Robbie Gould and that was well-placed trust. Gould kicked for Chicago through the 2015 season. He left Chicago as the team's all-time leading scorer with 1,207 points. Subsequently, he joined the New York Giants and San Francisco 49ers.

Gould made 12 game-winning kicks for the Bears and dismissed the pressure by comparing the role to Michael Jordan's with the Chicago Bulls. "Michael Jordan never said he didn't want the ball at the end of the game," Gould said.

David Fales (2014–16) was a quarterback hopeful, but played one game in Chicago and took his hope to Miami.

NO. 10: BOBBY DOUGLASS, THE QUARTERBACK WHO COULDN'T THROW

All Time No. 10.	
Player	Years
Burt Ingwerson	(1920–21)
Gus Fetz	(1923)
Oscar Johnson	(1924)
Milton Romney	(1925–29)
Leland Elnes	(1929)
Leo Jensveld	(1931)
Jack Manders	(1933–40)
Arthur Buss	(1934–35)
John Petty	(1942)
Noah Mullins	(1946–49)
Al Campana	(1950–53)
Tom O'Connell	(1953)
Rudy Bukich	(1958–59, 1963–68)
Bobby Douglass	(1969–75)
John Duvic	(1987)
Peter Tom Willis	(1990–93)
Anthony Brooks	(1993–94)
Mark Butterfield	(1996)
Jaret Holmes	(1999)
Louie Aguiar	(2000)
Henry Burris	(2002)
Kordell Stewart	(2003)
Doug Brien	(2005)
Richmond McGee	(2009–11)
Todd Collins	(2010)
Nathan Endelre	(2011)
Olindo Mare	(2012)
Marquess Wilson	(2013–16)

Bobby Douglass was Tim Tebow without the fanfare or the Heisman Trophy. He was a dangerous runner as a quarterback, but that was during a time period when quarterbacks were not expected to run unless they were being pursued by a stampede of wild bison.

Douglass, who played for Kansas in college where he starred, joined the Bears in 1969 and stuck around through 1975. The Bears really wanted him to succeed, but No. 10 was never quite the throwing leader the team needed. His lifetime completion percentage was 43 percent, and Douglass threw 36 touchdowns and 64 interceptions during his career.

Strongly built at 6-foot-4 and 225 pounds, Douglass was tough to bring down when he ran out of the pocket. As a rookie, he rushed for 408 yards. In 1972, Douglass rushed for 968 yards in 14 games, a single-season record for a quarterback for many years. Michael Vick owns the record now, with 1,039 yards in 2006.

Douglass's was a unique career. At the least he was a throwback to a time period when quarterbacks were asked to call plays, hand off, or carry the ball themselves rather than think pass-first.

A left-hander, Douglass actually played minor-league baseball as a pitcher in the Chicago White Sox organization after his football career ended.

Somehow it figures that one of the most unusual players in Bears history wore No. 10 because No. 10 has been shared by 27 players over the years, few of them ever heard of by any but the most discerning of historically-minded fans.

Burt Ingwersen started things off in 1920 and 1921 with the Decatur Staleys, but saw action only the first year. He later coached the University of Iowa.

Gus Fetz (1923), who scored one touchdown in one year, was actually a better golfer than football player in the 1920s and 1930s.

Oscar Johnson had a one-game cameo in 1924. Milton Romney wore No. 10 from 1925 to 1929 as a quarterback. This Romney's cousin was George Romney, former governor of Michigan and the namesake of former presidential candidate Mitt Romney, even though someone in the family missed by a letter or two.

Leland Elnes (1929) borrowed No. 10 for a couple of minutes. Leon Jensvold (1931) had it for a couple of minutes longer, appearing in one game.

Jack Manders (1933–40) was a for-real Bear, a key running back, punter, and kicker for the team during his tenure. His nickname was "Automatic Jack" for his kicking accuracy. Manders scored 72 points in 1934 and 67 in 1937. He was in the shadow of several Bears stars, but was an important part of the roster, playing on title teams twice.

It took around another quarter of a century before anyone else wearing No. 10 impacted Bears history so much. In between, Arthur Buss (1934–35), John Petty (1942), Noah Mullins (1946–49), Al Campana (1950–53), and Tom O'Connell (1953) authored short chapters in Bears lore.

Lineman Buss played in 45 games during his NFL career. Petty played fullback and was an All-Star. Mullins was a quarterback-defensive back who intercepted 19 passes. Campana gained 134 yards as a rookie and 12 more yards the rest of his NFL career. O'Connell, another limited-use QB, threw 67 passes in his only Bears season.

Rudy Bukich (1958–59, 1963–68) was not a big star, but he was a popular player who did some damage on the Bears behalf, actually having two stints with the team, the other being in 1958 and 1959.

The Most Valuable Player in the Rose Bowl in 1953, leading Southern Cal to victory, the 6-foot-1, 195-pound Bukich was nicknamed "Rudy The Rifle" because of his arm strength. He came along about thirty years too soon when his talent would have been better utilized. Bukich won a championship ring in 1963, but he was Bill Wade's backup.

In 1964, Bukich completed 61.9 percent of his passes in part-time work. In 1965, when he threw 20 touchdown passes against only nine interceptions, Bukich was an All-Star. As proof that Bukich possessed superior arm strength, Bears tight end Mike Ditka said he once saw this Rifleman throw a football 100 yards.

"I saw Rudy do it," Ditka said. "I was on the field that day." Other times, Ditka said, he watched Bukich attempt the feat and reach 95 or so yards.

Douglass followed Bukich in No. 10, and his arm strength was probably the opposite of Bukich's if such a thing could be measured.

No. 10 passed along quite quickly following Douglass's use. John Duvic (1987) was a kicker. Peter Tom Willis (1990–93) out of Florida State was a quarterback. Receiver Anthony Brooks (1993–94) out of Texas A&M-Commerce, never caught a pass. Mark Butterfield (1998) threw neither an interception, nor a touchdown pass. Jaret Holmes (1999) was a very short-term kicker. Louie Aguiar (2000) had a solid punting career, just not for the Bears, whom he reached at the end of the line.

Henry Burris (2002) had a cameo for the Bears, but an outstanding quarterback career in Canadian football. He was at the helm for three Grey Cup championships and twice was named Player of the Year in Canada. One season he threw for 4,647 yards and 30 touchdowns for the Saskatchewan Roughriders. Another year, Burris threw for 5,356 yards and 43 touchdowns for the Hamilton Tiger-Cats. He topped 50,000 yards throwing in Canada. Bears fans would have swooned if Burris could have recorded that type of production in Chicago.

A multi-talented weapon, Kordell Stewart was nicknamed "Slash" because he could. The best years of his NFL career were with the Pittsburgh Steelers, though.

Kicker Doug Brien (2005), punter Richmond McGee (2009–11), backup quarterback Todd Collins (2010), quarterback Nathan Enderle (2011), and kicker Olindo Mare (2012), who scored 25 points, handed off No. 10 so swiftly it was practically a blur.

Most recently, wide receiver Marquess Wilson (2013–2016) spent considerable time on injured reserve due to fracturing his foot three times.

NO. 11: LINK LYMAN, HALL OF FAMER OF MANY NUMBERS

All Time No. 11	
Player	Years
Andy Feichtinger	(1920–21)
Oscar Knop	(1923–28)
Link Lyman*	(1926–28, 1930–31, 1933–34)
Leland Elnes	(1929)
Lennon Blackman	(1930)
Harold Ely	(1932)
John Doehring	(1932–37)
Arthur Buss	(1934–35)
Joe Maniaci	(1938–41)
Frank Morris	(1942)
Bill Geyer	(1942–43, 1946)
Russ Reader	(1947)
Fred Evans	(1948)
Julie Rykovich	(1949–51)
Jim Haluska	(1956)
Jack Concannon	(1967–71)
Virgil Carter	(1968–69, 1976)
Greg Landry	(1984)
Kevin Brown	(1987)
Brian Gowins	(1999)
Mark Hartsell	(2000)
Jeff Blake	(2005)
Roy Williams	(2011)
Josh Bellamy	(2014–15)

Hall of Fame

William Roy "Link" Lyman was an early NFL great as a lineman, but he seemed to be determined to try out every number offered by the Bears during his 1926 to 1934 stay with the club. That was after turning pro in 1922 and suiting up for the Canton Bulldogs, the Cleveland Bulldogs, and the Frankford Yellow Jackets.

Lyman, who played college ball at Nebraska, was part of four league championship teams, but only his last, in 1933, was with the Bears.

A juggler of uniform numbers for Chicago, Lyman, who was chosen for the Pro Football Hall of Fame in 1964, wore No. 2, 11, 12, and 14. If he had come along later, no doubt Lyman would have worn jerseys in the 70s, 80s, and 90s, and might well have petitioned the league for the chance to wear No. 100.

At 6-foot-2 and 233 pounds, Lyman was a large lineman during his era and knew how to use his size. During his stay with the Bears, Lyman blocked for Red Grange, Bronko Nagurski, and Beattie Feathers, the first 1,000-yard rusher in league history.

Post-college Lyman initially had not thought of playing pro ball—it was not the lure it later became—but college chum Guy Chamberlin, also a pro Hall of Famer, talked him into it.

Lyman was the most distinguished Bear to wear No. 11. Generally, though, it was spread around pretty regularly.

Andy Feichtinger (1920–21) modeled the numeral first with the Decatur Staleys. The bulk of the career of Oscar Knop (1923–28) was spent with the Bears, but he also played for the Hammond Pros and Chicago Tigers. Knop once ran the wrong way with an interception, scoring for the opposition, but he did score seven touchdowns going the right way, too.

Leland Elnes (1929) perhaps borrowed the uniform for a minute or two. Lennon Blackman (1930) borrowed it back for a couple of minutes. While Lyman was trying on other numbers in 1932, Harold Ely, who was larger than Lyman at 268 pounds, tried on No. 11 and used it for six games.

John Doehring, a Bear between 1932 and 1937, also wore 11 that season temporarily—abeit temporarily. Doehring did not play much as a quarterback and completed just one touchdown pass during his Bears career, but possessed the rare skill of being able to throw the ball 50 yards downfield behind his back. That should have been worth something.

Arthur Buss (1934–35) picked up No. 11 when Doehring dropped it and was an under-sized tackle at 219 pounds. Joe Maniaci (1938–41) brought the number some honor. A fullback out of Fordham University in New York, Maniaci, who later coached at St. Louis University, saw plenty of playing time during the 1940 and 1941 Bears championship years. He made two Pro Bowls.

Frank Morris (1942) made a war-time cameo in No. 11. As did Bill Geyer (1942–43, 1946). Russ Reader (1947), Fred Evans (1948), Julie Rykovich (1949–51), and Jim Haluska (1956) occupied No. 11 for a while and then it was tucked into the equipment room for more than a decade. Evans spent a few seasons with teams in the old All-America Football Conference, as well as his brief stint with the Bears. In fact, he won a championship with the Cleveland Browns in 1946 under coach Paul Brown.

Jack Concannon (1967–71) had the name of a star quarterback and played pro ball for parts of 12 seasons with several teams, but while he wore No. 11, he never emerged as a No. 1 signal-caller. The Bears had clearly been hoping for more since they traded future Hall of Fame tight end Mike Ditka to the Philadelphia Eagles for Concannon. Concannon made appearances in the TV drama *Brian's Song* and the film *M*A*S*H*.

Virgil Carter (1968–69, 1976) was another quarterback hopeful who was a dazzling gunslinger at Brigham Young University, which became known as a cradle of quarterbacks. But his decade-long NFL and WFL tenure produced limited success.

Greg Landry (1984) accomplished many good things throwing the football, just not so much for the Bears. Landry made one Pro Bowl and was the NFL's Comeback Player of the Year in 1976 with the Detroit Lions. Later, Landry experienced a lengthy assistant coach career that included spending 1986 through 1992 with the Bears.

Kevin Brown (1987) punted for Chicago. Brian Gowins (1999) kicked. Mark Hartsell (2000) played one NFL game with Chicago and went 0–1 throwing. Jeff Blake (2005) made his final pro football stop in Chicago. Blake had some terrific moments in the pros, throwing for 134 touchdowns and more than 21,000 yards while making All-Pro once. But his No. 11 days with the Bears were fleeting.

Like Blake, most of the fine work put up as a receiver by Roy Williams (2011) occurred with other teams. His final season was with Chicago, and Williams caught 37 of his career 393 passes that year. Receiver Josh Bellamy has worn No. 11 since the 2014 season and he re-signed with the team for the 2017 season.

NO. 12: ERIK KRAMER, BEARS SHORT-TERM WONDER

While Erik Kramer played for the Chicago Bears from 1994 to 1998, he only had one terrific season in the mix and one other very good one. He only started for the team in 1995 and 1997. In '95 Kramer threw for a team record 3,838 yards, 29 touchdowns, and completed 60.3 percent of his passes.

The yardage and single-season touchdown highs remain team records. He definitely represented No. 12 well on the field.

He was a dream-come-true acquisition for a team that had been searching for a star thrower pretty much since the day Sid Luckman retired. Only Kramer promptly injured his neck and appeared in just four games in 1996. He bounced back to take charge of the Bears' offense again in 1997, and again threw for more than 3,000 yards. That was his last complete season with the Bears and in the NFL.

Kramer did pretty well for a guy who was not drafted coming out of North Carolina State in 1987. After retiring, he became a sports broadcaster. This was a typical career progression for a well-known player.

However, Kramer eventually took a very atypical turn with his life. He attempted to commit suicide by gunshot in 2015 after his oldest son died from a heroin overdose, his mother died, and he endured a romantic breakup. Kramer survived his suicide attempt. His former wife contended he had become a changed person from the man she married because he took too many hits to the head while playing football.

On the night he tried to kill himself, Kramer checked into a hotel room, climbed into bed, and shot himself in the head. He came close to dying from all the damage the bullet inflicted and doctors placed him in a medically induced coma for six weeks.

While depression was the reason he cited for his suicide attempt, Kramer did not blame football. He said he doubted concussions contributed to his situation.

"I've thought about that often, but nothing really stands out as connecting football to the sort of feeling I've had with depression," Kramer said in interviews. "It very well may be linked. It doesn't feel like it to me."

Emotionally revived, in 2017 Kramer was hoping to become a mentor of young quarterbacks.

The first player to wear No. 12 for the Bears/Staleys was Jerry Jones in 1920 and 1921. Not the Jerry Jones who owns the Dallas Cowboys. The older Jones met George Halas and other future Bears while serving in the Navy during World War I and they lured the offensive guard-kicker to Illinois.

Lou Usher (1921, 1923) was an offensive lineman who died young in 1927 in an automobile accident. Link Lyman wore this number, too. John "Sod" Ryan (1929) was a tackle.

There is some confusion over the timing of Abe Yourist going to the Bears. In the Bears media guide he is listed as wearing No. 12 in 1923. However, he did not graduate from high school until 1928 and then matriculated at Heidelberg University where he was a star all-around athlete. That school indicates Yourist was with the Bears for all of three games in 1932. Heidelberg U. is located in Tiffin, Ohio, and was founded in 1850—quite a bit before the Staleys or Bears.

A star center out of Loyola University of New Orleans, Frank Sullivan manned the position between 1935 and 1939 for the Bears. Anton Stolfa (1939) did a year in No. 12.

Hal Lahar (1941), later a coach at Colgate and Houston, moved on to World War II. Jim Benton (1943) was a star receiver out of Arkansas who caught 288 passes, 45 of them for touchdowns, but most of them for the Rams. He was the first end to catch passes for more than 300 yards in one game. He gained 303 yards on passes in a game against the Detroit Lions on Thanksgiving Day of 1945. The record stood for forty years.

Abe Croft (1944–45) played in 11 games for the Bears. Walter Lamb (1946) also appeared in 11 games. Coach George Halas wanted Zeke Bratkowski (1954–59) to become another Sid Luckman. Instead, he was the first Zeke Bratkowski, a player with a cool name who was a college All-American at Georgia, but primarily an NFL backup. Bratkowski earned two Super Bowl rings as Bart Starr's backup in Green Bay. He threw for 65 touchdowns and more than 10,000 yards in his career.

Dick Norman (1961–62) led the nation in passing yards and total yards at Stanford, but merely passed through the Bears. Larry Rakestraw (1964–67) threw for 407 yards for Georgia in the Orange Bowl, but was another Bears QB backup. More than twenty years passed before another Bear wore No. 12, perhaps because of the poor luck with passers.

Alas, Rusty Lisch (1984), another quarterback of brief duration, resumed the tradition. Steve Bradley (1987) played one game at quarterback for the Bears.

Erik Kramer arrived to provide dignity for No. 12 for a while. Brent Bartholomew (2000) couldn't be blamed for thinking Kramer brought some luck back to the numeral, but Bartholomew was here and gone in an instant. Quarterback Chris Chandler (2002–03) had the pedigree: a better-than-average career with 170 career touchdown passes and two Pro Bowl selections. But he was only a part-time player for the Bears near the end of his career.

Jonathan Quinn (2004) was called "The Mighty Quinn," but he wasn't during his short stint at quarterback. Justin Gage (2003–06) added flash to No. 12 because he wasn't a quarterback sitting on the bench. He was a perfectly fine wide receiver in Chicago and Tennessee, and caught 201 passes in his career.

It was back to backup quarterback life for No. 12 from 2008 to 2011 serving Caleb Hanie. Hanie came out of Colorado State and hustled his way onto the roster. He was a third-stringer who got to play because quarterbacks ahead of him on the roster kept getting hurt. Hanie even helped account for two touchdowns in the 2010 NFC Championship game.

Quarterback Josh McCown (2011–13) has played for many NFL teams, rarely starting for long unless someone else was injured, but in 2017 signed a one-year deal with the New York Jets at age thirty-seven. Quarterback David Fales (2014–15), who also wore No. 9, saw less action. In 2016, Matt Barkley inherited the Bears' starting quarterback job for seven games because those ahead of him on the depth chart were injured. He threw for 8 touchdowns and tossed 14 interceptions. A former Southern Cal star in college, Barkley signed on with the San Francisco 49ers leading up to the 2017 season.

NO. 13: THREE STRAIGHT HALL OF FAMERS

All Time No. 13	
Player	Years
Guy Chamberlin*	(1920–21)
George Trafton*	(1920–32)
Joe Stydahar*	(1936–46)
Monte Merkel	(1942–43)
Jake Sweeney	(1944)
Frank Ramsey	(1945)
Bob Snyder	(1945)
Thurman Garrett	(1947–48)
Jack Dugger	(1949)
Rick Mirer	(1997)
Johnny Knox	(2009–12)
Rashad Ross	(2014)
Kevin White	(2016)

* Hall of Fame

Many people view the No. 13 as unlucky, but when it comes to doling out the number for football players they might wish to reject the suggestion.

However, the first three Chicago Bears players to wear No. 13 all were inducted into the Pro Football Hall of Fame, so a different viewpoint might be to propose it is actually a lucky number for this team. All three were linemen, somewhat ironically, because linemen can no longer wear that low number due to NFL rule changes.

Chamberlin was an end, though in 1920 and 1921, his two seasons representing the Staleys, that pretty much meant playing both ways and blocking and tackling as opposed to catching passes. Chamberlin's given name was Berlin, his middle name Guy, and his nickname Champ. The 6-foot-2, 196-pound Chamberlin did not spend much time with the Bears/Staleys after playing college ball at Nebraska.

He spent more years playing for the Canton Bulldogs and Cleveland Bulldogs after the franchise relocated, and even the Chicago Cardinals at the end of his career. But Chamberlin was voted into both the College Football Hall of Fame and Pro Football Hall of Fame.

Chamberlin was both well-known and well-respected in the game, but his successor wearing No. 13 made a much larger impact on the Bears. George Trafton, a rugged lineman, played for Knute Rockne at Notre Dame and joined Chamberlin on the Staleys at first. However, he remained with Chicago through the 1932 season, manning the center position and making his style mark by becoming the first player to snap the football using only one hand. The 6-foot-2, 230-pound Trafton never played for a team other than the Bears during his pro career. As a two-time All-Pro who was much later selected as a member of the 1920s All-Decade team, Trafton earned his stripes for the Hall of Fame.

Trafton may have retired from football in 1932, but he never disappeared from the sports scene. He boxed for a couple of years near the end of his football playing days, but opened a prominent gym in Chicago and managed fighters with Chicago connections. Trafton also worked as an assistant football coach for the Green Bay Packers, the Winnipeg Blue Bombers in Canada, and with the Rams. He also coached for Northwestern University.

Trafton's boxing history added to his reputation as a tough guy on the line and opponents were wary of him because of that skill. Trafton actually had just five pro bouts, but one of them gained quite a bit of publicity.

Trafton made his pro debut in 1929 in a heralded fight against Art Shires of the Chicago White Sox. Star runner Red Grange was at a party with Trafton the night he decided to fight Shires. An early edition of a newspaper arrived and they discussed Shires's inclination to box. Trafton dismissed Shires, saying no baseball player could be as tough as a football player. Phone calls were made to arrange the bout. At a time when Trafton was being paid $100 a game to play football he made $1,000 for the fight.

Attended by 5,000 fans at the White City Arena (a vestige of the 1896 World's Fair), Trafton bested Shires on points in five rounds. Shires billed himself as "The Great," so Trafton billed himself as "The Super Great." Trafton's final boxing match was against future heavyweight champion Primo Carnera. Trafton also dabbled in professional wrestling and won his first eight professional matches.

Like almost all other players of the 1920s, Trafton played both ways, on offense and defense, for the Bears and never thought it should be any other way.

"You were hired to play a football game and you played it," Trafton said years later when NFL rosters had expanded to 33 players. "All 60 minutes of it, brother."

Joe Stydahar (1936–46) inherited No. 13 four years after Trafton retired. As a 6-foot-4, 233-pound No. 1 draft pick out of West Virginia, Stydahar was a six-time All-Pro selection who played on three Bears NFL championship teams in the 1940s.

Nicknamed "Jumbo Joe," Stydahar was as tough as any lineman out there. He also won another title as head coach of the Rams in 1951 before being enshrined in the Hall of Fame in 1977. The big dude from mining country was the first Chicago Bear ever taken in an NFL draft, the team's top pick in 1936 when the college draft was instituted. Bears owner-coach George Halas made that choice and never regretted it.

"Joe is something special for me," Halas said. "Joe Stydahar was a man of outstanding character and loyalty."

After Stydahar retired, No. 13 reverted to superstitious form for the Bears.

Monte Merkel (1942–43), a guard who appeared in one game, did not make the same kind of impact as his predecessors on the line. Neither did Jake Sweeney (1944), who played line for eight games for the Bears. The nine-game Bears tackle Frank Ramsey (1945) was not the same guy who was a basketball Hall of Famer for the Boston Celtics.

Bob Snyder (1945) wore other numbers in other years for the Bears, played for other teams, and spent decades coaching as an assistant in the NFL and in college and one year as boss of the Los Angeles Rams.

Thurman Garrett (1947–48) wore No. 13 a little bit longer than the others for Chicago as a lineman. Jack Dugger (1949), an All-American defensive lineman at Ohio State, played three years in the NFL, but only one of them with Chicago.

After that the Bears gave No. 13 a rest for nearly forty years, although it is not clear if everyone who had it offered to him wanted to stay away from the number. The next player to don it was quarterback Rick Mirer (1997). Mirer did a great job at Notre Dame and was the second player drafted in 1993 by the Seattle Seahawks. He bounced from team to team in the NFL as a backup for 11 years.

Johnny Knox (2009–12) flashed great potential with his speed as a kick returner and as a receiving hopeful for the Bears. Knox ran the 40-yard dash in a blistering 4.34 seconds. His first catch as a pro went for 68 yards. In 2009, Knox caught 45 passes before an ankle injury sidelined him. In 2011, a spinal cord injury led to the end of his NFL career.

It was a sad and unfortunate conclusion to his three-year Bears tenure.

"As an athlete, you don't want to give up, you want to keep on fighting. That's how I've always been," Knox said when he announced his retirement. "But it's been on my heart for a while. I know how my body feels, and I know I'm not going to be the same and perform at the ability that I used to."

Rashard Ross (2014) was in Chicago for less than a season. Kevin White (2016) caught 19 passes for the Bears, but a broken leg and sprained ankle suffered on the same play sidelined him as he was growing in importance to the offense.

NO. 14: DICK PLASMAN, THE LAST TO PLAY WITHOUT A HELMET

Although he played longer, when Dick Plasman showed up for the 1940 Chicago Bears-Washington Redskins championship game it marked the end of an era.

Plasman, a Bears running back wearing No. 14, was the last National Football League player to suit up without wearing a helmet in competition. Plasman spent eight years in the league between 1937 and 1947, with time off for World War II service, six of those seasons for the Bears.

While his contemporaries who had been around for some time were strapping on leather helmets, Plasman stuck with his bare noggin. Plasman was 6-foot-3 and weighed nearly 220 pounds. He played college ball for Vanderbilt and was part of two Bears championship teams, including the 73–0 massacre over the Washington Redskins. Plasman also made two All-Star teams in 1940 and 1941. After the war, he played for the Chicago Cardinals and was a member of the 1947 team which also won a title.

Plasman said he disliked hats. He did not solely harbor a prejudice against football helmets. His particular disdain for the helmets of the time revolved around him becoming exasperated with them being ill-fitting and drooping down over his eyes, which made it difficult to see passes headed his way.

Plasman, who did lose teeth playing football, said opponents rarely attempted to bash him on the head. One opponent for the Redskins, though, did so repeatedly and in retaliation after Plasman stepped on him between the legs.

Kile McWherter (1920) was the first team recipient of No. 14. J.R. Taylor (1921–22) followed. Fred Larsen wore No. 14 for part of 1922 as well. Then Link Lyman in his game of musical numbers took a turn. Harold Cunningham (1929), nicknamed "Cookie," was better known in college and the pro basketball world as opposed to his time in Chicago.

Frank Don Pauley (1930), Lloyd Burdick (1931–32), a Bears champ in '32 nicknamed "Shorty" despite standing 6-foot-4, and who died young in a train wreck, and Fred Crawford (1934–35) predated Plasman's usage of No. 14.

Chuck Drulis (1942, 1945–50) was another who had his career interrupted on the field by World War II. Drulis played for a short while and coached for some time, including briefly sharing the St. Louis Cardinals' head coaching duties in 1961. His wife Dale was an artist who created some original pieces for the Pro Football Hall of Fame in Canton, Ohio, when it first opened in 1963.

George Zorich (1943–44) was All-Big Ten for Northwestern and Ed Cifers (1947–48) won an NFL title with Washington before World War II service. They led up to Wayne Hansen (1950–59) in No. 14. Hansen was a linebacker and defensive captain most of his time in Chicago, and was an All-Pro selection three times.

Willie Thrower (1953) was a fascinating case. He was aptly named since he was a quarterback. African Americans were basically not welcome on big-time college teams or in the NFL at quarterback in the late 1940s and early 1950s. Although some credit Thrower as the first African American to play the position in the Big Ten at Michigan State and in the NFL, he was not the only pioneer of the period. Indiana's George Taliaferro predated Thrower in action for the Hoosiers, was the first African American drafted by the NFL as a quarterback, and, even though he first played in the All-America Football Conference, Taliaferro competed for the New York Yanks in the early 1950s prior to Thrower joining the Bears. Long before either Taliaferro or Thrower played, Fritz Pollard became the first African American NFL coach and played quarterback briefly in 1923.

Ken Gorgal (1955–56) was a bridge wearer of No. 14 before Rudy Bukich (1958–59, 1962) made more of his opportunities. Bobby Douglass (1969–75) did more running than throwing at QB. Buddy Lee (1971) stuck with the Bears in No. 14 as long as it took to add one and four. Jim Harbaugh (1987–93) had his moments in different numbers. Ben Bennett (1988) suited up for

13 pro teams in different leagues and worked in street clothes as a coach for nine. He is a member of the Arena Football League Hall of Fame.

The Bears had high hopes for Brian Griese (2006–07), son of the Hall of Famer Bob Griese, but he had a limited tenure in Chicago, making more of a mark elsewhere. In all, Griese threw for 119 touchdown passes and nearly 20,000 yards, won a Super Bowl ring in Denver (as a backup), and became a broadcaster for ESPN after his playing days were over.

Brett Basanez (2009) was from the Chicago area and was a star quarterback for Northwestern, but was mostly injured in his stop with the Bears. Eric Weems (2012–13) caught three passes in two seasons in Chicago. Santonio Holmes (2014) concluded his nine-year NFL career with the Bears after playing four seasons each with the Steelers and Jets. Deonte Thompson (2015–16) re-upped with the Bears for 2017 after catching 22 passes in 2016, the most excitement for a No. 14 since Plasman.

NO. 15: MIKE HOLOVAK, BOSTON PATRIOTS LEADER

All Time No. 15	
Player	Years
Jim Conzelman*	(1920)
Walter Veach	(1920)
Harry Englund	(1920–23)
Pat Flaherty	(1923)
Verne Mullen	(1923–25)
Bill Fleckenstein	(1925–30)
William Buckler	(1926–31)
Henry Hammond	(1937)
Al Matuza	(1941–45)
Forest Masterson	(1945)
Mike Holovak	(1947–48)
Curley Morrison	(1950–53)
Ed Brown	(1954–61)
Virgil Carter	(1968–69, 1976)
Mirro Roder	(1973–74)
Mike Phipps	(1977–81)
Dave Finzer	(1984)
Bryan Wagner	(1987–88)
Jim Miller	(1999–2002)
Josh McCown	(2011–13)
Brandon Marshall	(2012–14)

Hall of Fame

A fullback for the Chicago Bears for a few seasons, Mike Holovak found most of his fame as a star for Boston College before turning pro, and again in Boston with the new pro team of the 1960s well after he retired as a player.

Jimmy Conzelman, in 1920, was the first player for the franchise to wear No. 15, but that future Hall of Famer wore a few numbers for the Bears. In more recent years, No. 15 belonged to a series of backup quarterbacks.

Holovak had one of the more interesting football careers of those on the Bears roster who wore the number, even if the most interesting things that happened for him in the sport had nothing to do with the Bears.

Holovak was 6-foot-1 and 213 pounds and was an All-American runner for the BC Eagles, playing in the Orange Bowl in 1943. He finished college during World War II and was drafted by the Cleveland Rams, a team which had already announced the suspension of activities for the duration of the hostilities. Holovak then joined the navy.

After the war, Holovak spent one season with the resurrected Rams and the 1947 and 1948 seasons with the Bears. He rushed for 281 yards and 228 yards and caught the occasional pass for Chicago. That was the extent of his NFL career in uniform.

Soon enough, Holovak was back coaching the Boston College freshmen to undefeated seasons, took over as head coach at his alma mater, joined the Boston Patriots when the franchise began in the American Football League, and was head coach from 1961 to 1968 before working as an assistant coach for other teams around the NFL.

Besides Conzelman, Walter Veach (1920), Harry Englund (1920–23), Pat Flaherty (1923), and Vern Mullen (1923–25) passed around No. 15 for short periods. Veach got into two games. Englund hung around for two seasons.

Flaherty was not the same person of the same name who became a Hall of Fame coach. Mullen had better, championship days with the Canton Bulldogs.

Bill Fleckenstein (1925–30) was a guard who married actress Mildred Harris, one of Charlie Chaplin's ex-wives. Bill Buckler (1926–31) also wore other Bears numbers. Henry Hammond (1937), an end, did not. Al Matuza (1941–45) was only a war-time player who made the Pro Bowl one year as a center and intercepted four passes in his career.

Forest Masterson (1945) was a center out of Iowa. Mike Holovak wore No. 15 next. Fred "Curly" Morrison (1950–53) was the star of an Ohio State Rose Bowl champion, led the Bears in rushing two seasons and made one Pro Bowl later for the Cleveland Browns.

For most of the next fifty years with few exceptions, quarterbacks passed around No. 15 for the Bears. These included Ed Brown (1954–61), Virgil Carter (1968–69, 1976) Mike Phipps (1977–81), Jim Miller (1999–2002), and Josh McCown (2011).

On special teams, Mirro Roder (1973–74) was a kicker, Dave Finzer (1984) was a punter, and Bryan Wagner (1987–88) was a punter.

During a career that also included stops with the Pittsburgh Steelers and Baltimore Colts, Brown threw for 102 touchdowns. He was twice named to the Pro Bowl with the Bears, working his way past Zeke Bratkowski and George Blanda to become a starter. Brown led the Bears to the 1956 title game, a loss to the New York Giants, and was the team's punter for eight seasons. His lifetime punting average was 40.6 yards per kick.

Phipps was an All-American at Purdue, but could not quite wrest the starting quarterback job out of the hands of other Bears contenders.

Miller suited up for eight teams between 1994 and 2005, but he played his most important games for the 2001 Bears. Miller threw for 13 touchdowns, 2,299 yards, and completed 228 passes as Chicago surprised the football world by finishing 13–3 and winning the NFC Central Division. The season included five comeback wins, and the fans were very fond of No. 15 that year.

Although it did not last as long as hoped for, Brandon Marshall's 2012–14 residency in No. 15 as a wide receiver was remarkably exciting. He caught 118 passes in 2012, 100 in 2013, and 61 in 2014 before exiting for the New York Jets.

If he had stuck around a few more years Marshall could easily have been the all-time great for the Bears in No. 15.

NO. 16: HALL OF FAMER GEORGE MUSSO

They didn't call George Musso "Moose" for nothing. Musso sounded enough like moose for Bears teammates to slap the label on him, but he was also built like one. One of the first great linemen of size in the NFL, Musso was a 270-pound hard hitter at tackle and guard and on the defensive line.

A Hall of Famer who competed for four Bears championship teams, Musso would have been a 77 or a 99 if his career did not begin in 1933 and run through 1944 when linemen were still wearing any which number—like No. 16.

Musso was from the southern part of Illinois and his family was dependent on the coal industry. That's where Musso was headed, as well, once he graduated from high school. He talked his father into letting him extend his football education and he enrolled at Millikin University. Millikin was not much better known for producing star athletes just after the Depression than it is now as an NCAA Division III school, but Musso received a tryout from George Halas and agreed to a pittance of a salary of $90 per game.

A three-time Pro Bowl selection, Musso was captain of the Bears for nine seasons and played for four NFL champions. Teammate Red Grange said Musso was captain for so long due to the respect of the other players.

"The players wouldn't have anyone else," Grange said.

In a rather remarkable quirk as a trivia aside in Musso's career, Moose played in a college regular-season game against Ronald Reagan and in a college All-Star game against Gerald Ford, meaning he went up against two future presidents on the gridiron.

Musso pretty much had the wild animal field covered since he was adorned with a second nickname: Big Bear. Later in life he became a county sheriff in Illinois. When he was voted into the Pro Football Hall of Fame in Canton, Ohio, Musso said, "I didn't believe it."

Randolph Young (1920) was the first member of the No. 16 club for the Staleys. Russell Smith (1921–23, 1925) was a guard who won three NFL titles, though two of them for the Bulldogs. Offensive lineman Ed Healey (1922–27) joined the Bears after spending a few seasons with the Rock Island Independents. The 6-foot-1, 207-pound Healey packed a disproportionate wallop for his size when he blocked. A four-time All-Pro, Healey was inducted into the Pro Football Hall of Fame in 1964. He was part of the second class inducted. Bill Buckler (1926–31) switched numbers regularly. John Polisky (1929) was a guard for nine games. Harry Richman (1929) played in one. Henry Anderson (1931) was an All-American for Northwestern and a three-time NCAA pole vault champ.

Charles Braidwood (1932) did not play a game for the Bears. He died during World War II from a heart attack while serving as a Red Cross director. Although the team retired No. 3 in his honor, Bronko Nagurski also wore No. 16. Musso then wore the number for more than a decade. It can be argued that the jersey could well have been retired for Musso, but it never was.

It definitely wasn't going to be retired for Milt Vucinich (1945), who appeared in three games for the Bears. Rudy Mucha (1945–46) was an All-American center at the University of Washington and played a little guard for Chicago. Hank Norberg (1948) was a defensive end.

The great George Blanda (1949–58) was one of George Halas's biggest mistakes. He never appreciated the future Hall of Famer's talents at quarterback and did not take true advantage of his skills as a kicker before running him off the team. Blanda's greatest success came later with the Houston Oilers and Oakland Raiders after the American Football League formed in 1960. Except for two starting years, Blanda was mostly a bench-warmer in Chicago.

Ed Cody (1949–51) was a fullback and defensive back and later an assistant coach for the Bears (1965–70). Kent Nix (1970–71) gained as much attention for suing the team alleging misdiagnosis of a hand injury as he did at quarterback. His father, Emery, also played in the NFL with the New York Giants in the 1940s.

Kicker Bob Thomas (1975–84) booted 239 field goals in his 12-year NFL career, most of them for the Bears before ascending to a seat on the Illinois Supreme Court. He departed a teeny bit too soon since the Bears promptly won the Super Bowl with Kevin Butler kicking.

Tim Lashar (1987) kicked three field goals for the Bears. Todd Sauerbrun (1995–99) was Chicago's punter for five years. Craig Krenzel (2004) won a national championship as quarterback with Ohio State and his first three games with the Bears, but got injured and cut.

Mark Bradley (2005–08) was mostly a backup receiver, but turned in some worthwhile performances filling in for injured starters. His father Danny also played in the NFL for the Rams and Detroit Lions. Patrick O'Donnell (2014–16) is the Bears' punter.

NO. 17: RICHIE PETITBON

A defensive back who intercepted 50 passes during his NFL career, most of it spent with the Bears between 1959 and 1968, Richie Petitbon solidified his standing in team lore and as a notable wearer of No. 17 with one memorable play.

As the clock was running down in the 1963 title game vs. the New York Giants, and as the trailing team sought a last-gasp comeback, Petitbon sealed the deal with an interception off of Y. A. Tittle. End of Giants hopes.

Petitbon was selected to play in the Pro Bowl four times during his days with the Bears before ending his career with the Los Angeles Rams and Washington Redskins by 1972. In 1962, Petitbon returned an interception 101 yards for a touchdown, which remains the longest interception return in Bears history.

At 6-foot-3 and 206 pounds, Petitbon was a sturdily built defender. He had been an all-around athlete growing up in Louisiana and his older brother John also played in the NFL for the Browns and Packers after competing for Notre Dame's 1949 national championship team. He retired in 1957 before Richie came into the league.

Petitbon also ran back kickoffs and punts for a few years with the Bears.

In 1981, Petitbon began a long career as an assistant coach for the Washington Redskins. Renowned as a defensive coordinator, he won three Super Bowl rings in that job. He was the Redskins head coach for one season. Although his parting was somewhat bitter because of the short tenure of his time in charge, when Petitbon took over he was as enthusiastic as any coach in history.

"I really believe football is the best game in the world," Petitbon said. "It's more like life than life itself."

The first No. 17 for the franchise was Ross Petty (1920) with the Staleys, followed by Ralph Scott (1921–25). Scott jumped the Bears for the New York Yankees of the first American Football League, becoming the player-coach for the squad that included Red Grange after his famed national tour with the Bears and before he could agree to a contract with George Halas.

Fred Larson (1922) was an All-American end for the University of Minnesota and later coached the Winnipeg Blue Bombers of the Canadian Football League. Elmer Wynne (1928) also briefly played for the short-lived Dayton Triangles. George Lyon (1931), nicknamed Babe, played a long time for teams that went away, including the St. Louis Gunners and the Rochester Tigers.

Everett Nelson (1929) came out of the University of Illinois and quickly handed off jersey No. 17 to Milton Frump (1930), who handed it to Jim Pederson (1932), who also wore uniforms identified with the Minneapolis Red Jackets and the Frankford Yellow Jackets. Joe Zeller (1938) was another short-timer in No. 17, but the former Indiana University Most Valuable Player in football and basketball (in the same school year) actually spent six seasons with the Bears, wearing other numerals.

This was one of the numbers worn by Bob Snyder (1939–43), whose kicking helped the Bears win three NFL titles. Pete Gudauskas (1943–45) was a war years Bears player. No one else wore the number until Rich Petitbon and Cliff Hardy (1971) briefly took over. A 11th-round draft pick, Hardy played in one game as a defensive back. Ike Hill (1973–74) caught 17 passes for the Bears and 22 in his NFL career. Tom Barnhardt (1987) punted just one year for the Bears, but played in the NFL through 2000 and averaged 42.1 yards per kick.

Sean Payton's (1987) playing time was limited, but he is much better known now in the world of football as the long-time coach of the New Orleans Saints who helped bring a Super Bowl championship to that town after it was ravaged by Hurricane Katrina.

Quinton Smith (1990) caught two passes for the Bears. Chris Gardocki (1992–94) punted in the NFL for fifteen years and averaged 42.8 yards per boot. Dave Krieg (1996) has a much larger fan following for the good work he did for the Seattle Seahawks than he did wearing No. 17 for the Bears, a stay short enough to qualify as a drive-by. Injuries propelled Krieg into the starting lineup and Chicago went 6–6 on his watch.

Danny Wuerffel (2001) had a stunningly great college football career at the University of Florida where he won the Heisman Trophy, led the Gators to a national championship, and also won the Maxwell Award and Johnny Unitas Award. But his pro career fizzled, not just while wearing No. 17 for the Bears.

Cory Sauter (2002) bounced around with several teams, including the Barcelona Dragons overseas, but is now head coach at Southwest Minnesota State. Airese Currie (2008) was a track star who later tried Canada for football post-Bears. Juaquin Iglesias (2009) played one game for the Bears.

Alshon Jeffery (2012–16) brought 304 Bears catches to the Philadelphia Eagles for the 2017 season after his tenure wearing No. 17.

NO. 18: THE EVER-USEFUL HUNK ANDERSON

All Time No. 18	
Player	Years
J. L. Shank	(1920)
Richard Barker	(1921)
Heartley "Hunk" Anderson	(1922–27)
Ed Anderson	(1923)
Don Murry	(1924–31)
Edward Michaels	(1935)
Jim Mooney	(1935)
Joe Stydahar*	(1936–46)
Edgar Manske	(1937–40)
Alec Shellog	(1939)
Adolph Kissell	(1942)
Joe Osmanski	(1946–49)
Fred Negus	(1950)
Ron Knox	(1957)
Jerry Moore	(1971–72)
Mike Tomczak	(1985–90)
Steve Stenstrom	(1995–98)
Chris Boniol	(1999)
Kyle Orton	(2005–08)
Dane Sanzenbacher	(2011–12)
Michael Spurlock	(2014)
*Hall of Fame	

His real name was Heartley, but Hunk certainly sounded better for a football player. Only Mr. Anderson was not much of a hunk even as old-time football players went. He stood 5-foot-11 and weighed 170 pounds, which meant he did not even have to shop in the Big and Tall shop.

However, Anderson covered a lot of ground in the football world over many years. He played college football at Notre Dame for Knute Rockne, and then pro football for the Bears (1922–27) under George Halas. All of that was definitely glitter by association.

Anderson was a guard on offense and much later was given recognition as a member of the NFL's All-Decade Team of the 1920s. Before that decade was out, however, Anderson had turned to coaching. He was the head man for St. Louis University and then took over the reins of the storied program of his alma mater.

He later became an NFL coach and most importantly—more important than the impression he made wearing No. 18—Anderson was available as head coach for the Bears between 1942 and 1945. Halas had rejoined the navy for World War II and left the on-field operations of the team to Anderson.

Actually, Anderson shared the head coaching responsibilities with Luke Johnsos, another trusted Halas assistant. Anderson and Johnsos were in a difficult situation. They were minding the shop for a meticulous taskmaster at the same time they kept losing key Bears players to the service. Despite that handicap, they guided the Bears to a 1944 NFL crown.

Anderson was the third player to wear No. 18 for the franchise. In 1920, it belonged to J. L. Shank with the Staleys. Richard Barker, an Iowa State guard, wore it in 1921 before shifting to the Rock Island Independents. Don Murry wore the number briefly in 1924 while Hunk Anderson was still around, though the lineman played longer. Ed Michaels (1935) played for other teams during World War II, ruled 4-F because he was deaf.

Jim Mooney (1935) was killed in France during World War II. Hall of Famer Joe Stydahar also wore No. 18 for a while. Edgar Manske (1937–40) did, too, in that era of changing numbers. Alec Shellog (1939) was a Notre Dame guy who also served the U.S. during the war years. Adolph Kissell (1942) got into four games. Joe Osmanski (1946–49) was a running back who was solid when given the chance to carry the ball. He might have benefited from a slick nickname like Joey O. Fred Negus (1950) was a college star who was one of the many Bears to wear No. 18 during this stretch, but did little for the club to be remembered for it.

Ron Knox (1957) was the next wearer who didn't hold on to the number 18 long, either. Knox apparently had the ultimate Little League parent for a father who bugged his coaches. He became an actor after a period of some success at quarterback in Canadian football. Jerry Moore (1971–72) had his moments as a defensive back.

Mike Tomczak (1985–90) could play a little. Surprisingly undrafted after winning two Big Ten titles for Ohio State, Tomczak had a lengthy NFL career, part-starter, part-backup, and set a record at the time of winning his first 10 starts. Tomczak was the backup quarterback to Jim McMahon on the 1985 Bears Super Bowl team and even gained a part in the Super Bowl Shuffle video. You could say he went from backup quarterback to backup singer.

No. 18 seemed to become the province of backup quarterbacks with Steve Stenstrom (1995–98) next to wear the number. Stenstrom later became president of Professional Athletes Outreach, a Christian organization. Chris Boniol (1999) ended his kicking career with the Bears. Boniol once booted seven field goals in a game, although not for Chicago.

Kyle Orton (2005–08) was another quarterback who came closer than most Bears backups to making it big. He got chances to start, but couldn't carry the team to a satisfying full season and ended up playing out his days elsewhere.

Dane Sanzenbacher (2011–12) was a free agent out of Ohio State with potential and caught 27 passes as a Bears rookie. Michael Spurlock (2014) had a brief fling in No. 18 and unless he took the jersey with him it has been resting in team storage since.

NO. 19: GARY HUFF, ANOTHER QUARTERBACK WHO DID NOT CUT IT

Maybe it just seems that way, but the Chicago Bears appear to have run more quarterbacks through their rosters than any other team in the world. Whether they were draft picks or free agents, starters or second-stringers, the Bears seemed to change quarterbacks as quickly as some people change clothes.

In some ways, Gary Huff, another quarterback hopeful, is the most famous player to ever wear No. 19 for the Bears. That is another way of saying No. 19 may have been a jinx for anyone on the team who ever chose to wear it. Or it turned over so frequently the equipment manager always had it around to hand out to guys just passing by.

Huff was a 6-foot, 195-pound quarterback who starred at Florida State and was chosen by the Bears with a second-round draft pick in 1973.

Huff hung around the Bears, mostly on the sidelines, between 1973 and 1976, and then moved on to a few other teams. He never lit up scoreboards, concluding his NFL career with 16 touchdown passes and 50 interceptions thrown.

Never especially successful on the field, Huff served as an assistant coach in the pro and college game, and, after a second career in business, turned to athletic management and became the chief financial officer of the Los Angeles Raiders (1987–93).

Chester May (1920) was the first on the club to wear No. 19, doing so for the Staleys. Lineman Walter "Red" May succeeded him in the same season. George Bolan (1921–24) was a running back who died young at age forty-two. Frank Hanny (1922–26), who was once also a Providence Steam Roller, was the first player ever thrown out of an NFL game while with the Bears.

Earl Evans (1926–29) was a lineman. Lemon Blackmon (1930) wore more than one number during his tenure with the team.

Eugene Smith (1930) followed in No. 19. Latham Flanagan (1931), an end, got into two games for the Bears and two games for the Chicago Cardinals in his only NFL season. Charles Tackwell (1931–33) is listed on the Bears' all-time roster as wearing 19, but a sports website claims he wore No. 0. The Bears list no person ever wearing 0, however. Tackwell barely gained more than zero yards for the Bears, however.

Offensive lineman Dick Stahlman (1933) moved teams ten times between 1924 and 1933, his last season with the Bears. But he arrived at the right time because Chicago won the NFL title that year. Ed Kawal (1931–36) was a center. Lineman Lou Gordon (1938) was a University of Illinois All-American lineman. John Siegal (1939–43) also wore No. 6. Phil Martinovich (1940) won an NFL ring with the Bears in 1940.

Bill Hempel (1942) was a tackle during his sole NFL season with the Bears. Nick Kerasiotis (1942–44) appeared in 10 games for the Bears. Dominic Sigillo (1943–44) was a lineman and part of the Bears' 1943 championship team. Pete J. Perez (1945) was paid $150 a game for one season as a lineman. Don Perkins (1945–46) was a running back, same as the future, better-known Dallas Cowboys runner of the same name.

Defensive back Harper Davis (1950) later coached in college. After Davis, No. 19 took a lengthy break until being lent to Huff. Then the number took another long vacation before being handed to Ray Stachowicz in 1983, who was a punter for a few teams with a lifetime 40.2-yard average. Carl Ford (2005) played in 10 games. Devin Aromashodu (2009–10) might have had the most difficult name to say among No. 19s, but he never stuck around NFL teams long enough for people to learn it. He was on seven teams, including the Indianapolis Colts and the Bears twice each, if only on the practice squad for Chicago the second time in 2013.

Joe Anderson (2012–13), a wide receiver, had a fine career at Texas Southern, and was good enough for look-sees with NFL teams, but had trouble sticking on the main roster instead of practice squads. Josh Morgan (2014) caught 209 passes for three NFL teams, but only his last season was with the Bears.

Eddie Royal has been wearing No. 19 since the 2015 season. If he can stay healthy, the wide receiver with 408 catches on his resume entering the 2017 season, who also runs back kicks and punts, could become the best Bears player to wear that number.

NO. 20: PADDY DRISCOLL, HALL OF FAMER

All Time No. 20	
Player	Years
Paddy Driscoll*	(1920, 1926–29)
Jack Mintun	(1921–22)
Ted Drews	(1928)
Jules "Zuck" Carlson	(1929–36)
Fred Dreher	(1938)
Bob Nowaskey	(1940–42)
James Logan	(1942–43)
Fred Mundee	(1943–45)
Jim Keane	(1946–51)
Ray Gene Smith	(1954–57)
Pete Johnson	(1959)
Justin Rowland	(1960)
Bobby Jackson	(1961)
Joe Taylor	(1967–74)
Mike Adamle	(1975–76)
Reuben Henderson	(1981–82)
Kevin Potter	(1983–84)
Thomas Sanders	(1985–89)
Mark Carrier	(1990–96)
Corey Dowden	(1997)
James Allen	(1998–2001)
Roosevelt Williams	(2002)
Thomas Jones	(2004–06)
Adam Archuleta	(2007)
Craig Steltz	(2008–13)
Shaun Draughn	(2014)
Terrance Mitchell	(2014–15)

Hall of Fame

One of the greats from the first decade of the National Football League, John Leo "Paddy" Driscoll broke into the league when it was new, suiting up in No. 20 for the Decatur Staleys in his and their first year. He also played for the Bears again during the decade between 1926 and 1929.

Driscoll was a Chicago guy all the way. He was born in Evanston, Illinois, just beyond the city limits in 1895, and played college ball for Northwestern. Driscoll played part of 1920 with the Bears, then joined the Chicago Cardinals before the end of the season. He played for the Cardinals through 1925 and then rejoined the Bears.

A quarterback who measured just 5-foot-11 and 160 pounds, Driscoll was an eight-time first- or second-team All-Pro in the 1920s, adept at punting and drop kicking. He once made a 55-yard field goal. That achievement, among others, earned Driscoll a spot in the Pro Football Hall of Fame in 1965.

Initially, Driscoll believed his career lay in baseball and in 1917 he played 13 games for the Chicago Cubs, plus a bit more for Los Angeles of the AAA Pacific Coast League. In 1919, Driscoll competed in football for the Hammond Pros from Indiana, just as the NFL was starting up.

When Driscoll shifted from the Bears to the Cardinals in 1920, it was for the job of player-coach. He held the dual role through 1922. After retiring, Driscoll coached Marquette University and then was hand-picked by George Halas, his close confidante, to run the Bears in 1956 and 1957.

Driscoll was also selected for the College Football Hall of Fame, however, not the Baseball Hall of Fame since he hit .107 in limited at-bats.

When it comes to wearing No. 20, there is little competition with Driscoll for most famous player.

Jack Mintum (1921–22), at center for the Staleys, wore No. 20 while Driscoll was across town with the Cardinals. Ted Drews (1928) was a wide receiver with a two-season NFL career. Jules "Zuck" Carlson (1929–36) provided some longevity. An offensive lineman, Carlson played on two Bears championship teams.

Ferdinand Dreher (1938) took over No. 20 for one season, appearing in three games with three catches. Bob Nowaskey (1940–42) was an end who lasted eight years in the NFL. James Logan (1943) was a one-year guard, but was part of a championship team. Fred Mundee (1943–45) was a Notre Dame grad who also got in on the '43 title spoils.

Jim Keane (1946–51) was one of the best early Bears receivers. He grabbed as many as 64 passes in a season at a time when quarterbacks did not throw nearly as much as they do today. He led the team in catches four years in a row, collecting 206 in all for Chicago.

Ray Gene Smith (1954–57) was a four-season Bears defensive back. Pete Johnson (1959) got into seven games in his only Chicago season. Justin Rowland (1960) came out of Texas Christian and scratched the surface of three seasons in the NFL with three teams as a defensive back. Bobby Jackson (1961) lasted two years in the league as a defensive back.

Joe Taylor (1967–74) held on to No. 20 much longer than his recent predecessors. He also intercepted 15 passes for the Bears.

Mike Adamle (1975–76) was a star for Northwestern who had his stopover with the Bears, as well as with the New York Jets and Kansas City Chiefs. He became more widely known after retirement as a network sports broadcaster, host of *American Gladiators*, a station host in Chicago TV, and a pro wrestling administrator.

Now a doctor, Reuben Henderson (1981–82) spent four years in the NFL. Kevin Potter (1983–84) was a defensive back for nine games in Chicago. In five years with the Bears, Thomas Sanders (1985–89) rushed for as many as 332 yards in one season.

Mark Carrier (1990–96) was not as famous as Paddy Driscoll, but he was a worthy wearer of No. 20. Carrier was a terrific No. 1 draft pick for the Bears. A two-time All-American, Carrier won the Jim Thorpe Trophy as the nation's best defensive back while at Southern California. A three-time Pro Bowl safety selection, Carrier intercepted 10 passes as a rookie, making him the league's Defensive Rookie of the Year, and grabbed 32 in all. Carrier made 863 tackles during his career.

Corey Dowden (1997) did not keep No. 20 within his grasp for long post-Carrier. Dowden couldn't fill his shoes, either, in the defensive backfield, but had success in Canada, Arena Football, and won a Super Bowl ring with the Green Bay Packers.

James Allen (1998–2001) was a 5-foot-10, 215-pound running back out of Oklahoma, who at times definitely excited the fan base. Although his time in Chicago was short, Allen rushed for 1,120 yards in 2000 and helped the Bears to some startling comeback victories before losing his starting job to Anthony Thomas in 2001.

Roosevelt Williams (2002) had a few highlight moments as a defensive back, but was gone after one season. Thomas Jones (2004–06) rushed for over 1,000 yards in two of his three seasons in Chicago. Adam Archuleta (2007) starred in the defensive backfield for several years with the St. Louis Rams, but not so much with the Bears. Craig Steltz (2008–13) made his first mark with the Bears on special teams, but the Louisiana State All-American safety eventually proved out and was in on a lot of tackles for Chicago.

Shaun Draughn (2014) followed Steltz in No. 20 and was a blip on the screen in a well-traveled NFL career. Terrance Mitchell (2014–15) struggled to claim a spot in the defensive backfield and when he did he got hurt, then cut.

1920 Decatur Staleys

When the Chicago Bears, nee Decatur Staleys, were founded and joined the National Football League, nee American Professional Football Association, in 1920, the numbers for players were handed out pretty much on a first-come, first-served basis.

There were no rules governing the assigning of numbers by position as followed decades later, so the first players on the team to wear any numbers at all basically received the lowest numbers first and worked their way up consecutively.

This also meant members of the 1920 team were also the first players in team history to wear certain numbers.

These were the guys from the 1920 team and the numbers they wore:

1 – Jimmy Conzelman	5 – Charley Dressen
1 – Paddy Driscoll	6 – Sid Gepford
1 – Jake Lanum	7 – George Halas
3 – Ed Sternaman	8 – Leo Johnson
3 – Robert Koehler	9 – Johnny Bryan
4 – Pard Pearce	10 – Burt Ingwerson

Continued on next page

11 – Andy Feichtinger
12 – Jerry Jones
13 – Guy Chamberlin
14 – Kile MacWherter
15 – Jimmy Conzelman
15 – Walter Veach
15 – Pat Flaherty
16 – Randolph Young

17 – Ross Petty
18 – J.L. Shank
19 – Chester May
20 – Paddy Driscoll
21 – Hugh Blacklock
22 – Roy Adkins
23 – Guy Chamberlin
24 – Lennie High

No player wore a uniform number higher than 24 that first season. No one wore No. 2.

NO. 21: DOCTOR DAN FORTMANN, HALL OF FAME LINEMAN

All Time No. 21	
Player	Years
Hugh Blacklock	(1920–25)
Verne Mullen	(1924–26)
Dick Sturtridge	(1928–29)
Daniel McMullen	(1930–31)
Paul Engebretsen	(1932)
Wayland Becker	(1934)
Dan Fortmann*	(1936–43)
Chuck Drulis	(1942, 1945–50)
Bunny Figner	(1953)
Ron Drzewiecki	(1955, 1957)
Perry Jeter	(1956–57)
Jon Arnett	(1964–66)
Cecil Turner	(1968–73)
Dave Gagnon	(1974)
Nemiah Wilson	(1975)
Leslie Frazier	(1981–85)
Reggie Phillips	(1987)
Donnell Woolford	(1989–96)
Darnel Autry	(1987)
Terry Cousin	(1998–99)
R. W. McQuarters	(2000–04)
Rashied Davis	(2005–10)
Dante Wesley	(2006)
Corey Graham	(2007–11)
Major Wright	(2010–13)
Ryan Mundy	(2014)
Tracy Porter	(2015–16)

Hall of Fame

When it was time for Dan Fortmann to make the choice coming out of college at Colgate University, he wasn't sure what path to follow. He had been young, only sixteen, when he graduated from high school and was still nineteen when he completed his undergraduate degree.

His game plan for life was to study to become a doctor, but he also felt the tug of an alternative opportunity presented to him. The Chicago Bears wanted him to play pro football in the National Football League. They weren't begging him, but coach George Halas saw enough potential in the small-school star to draft him in the ninth round in 1936.

One rumor persisted through the years that Halas was out of ideas on who to take so late in the draft, but saw Fortmann's name and liked the sound of it. "I like that name, I'll take him," Halas supposedly said.

However, Fortmann had been publicized playing in some annual college All-Star games and, reportedly, Dick Hanley, who handled him in one, and was the former Northwestern coach, tipped Halas to Fortmann.

As Fortmann struggled with his decision, Halas made things easy for him. He suggested Fortmann go to medical school to become a surgeon and play ball, and he paid him money in advance of the season so he could enroll and get going on his studies.

Fortmann paid Halas back many times over by becoming a seven-time All-Pro guard and ultimately being selected for the Hall of Fame. Clearly, he was the greatest Bear to wear No. 21.

This was quite the achievement under any circumstances, but Fortmann was also an under-sized lineman, even for those times. He stood 6-feet tall and weighed 210 pounds. Fortmann would never dream of playing the position now, but would probably be shipped to the defensive backfield for a tryout.

Fortmann attended Rush Medical School in Chicago while playing eight seasons for the Bears and helped the club win three NFL titles during his tenure. Later, Fortmann was named to the NFL's 1930s All-Decade team. Fortmann's football career ended during World War II and he put his medical knowledge to use on a hospital ship in the South Pacific.

"I wanted to play pro football, but I was also determined to go to med school," Fortmann said. "George allowed me to miss two weeks of summer practice each year while I finished up in school."

The first Bear to wear No. 21 was Hugh Blacklock, who started with the Decatur Staleys and hung around from 1920 to 1925. Blacklock, an All-Pro in 1920, played all offensive line positions in a seven-year NFL career. Halfback Verne Mullen (1924–26) overlapped a little with Blacklock after winning a championship with the Canton Bulldogs in 1923.

Then came a parade of No. 21-wearers trading off the uniform with the seasons until Fortmann took over. Dick Sturtridge (1928–29) got into 10 games as a halfback in 1928, two the next year. Daniel McMullen (1930–31) was a star lineman out of Nebraska. Paul Engebretsen (1932) was a guard whose 10 extra points led the league his rookie season with the Bears. Wayland Becker (1934) played in two games for Chicago.

After Fortmann, Chuck Drulis (1942, 1945–49) held on to No. 21 for a while, though he wore 14 before World War II and 21 after he rejoined the Bears. Bunny Figner (1953) passed through quickly. Ron Drzewiecki (1955, 1957) was 11th overall pick who made the team in 1955 and missed the 1956 season due to Navy service. Perry Jeter (1956–57) squeezed in use of the jersey while Drzewiecki was out. A slightly built, 5-foot-7, 178-pound halfback, Jeter rushed for 327 yards in 16 games.

An All-American runner at Southern Cal, halfback Jon Arnett had his best years with the Los Angeles Rams, being named to the Pro Bowl five times, but played for the Bears between 1964 and 1966. Some say Arnett, nicknamed "Jaguar Jon," deserves a place in the Hall of Fame.

The next No. 21 in Chicago was Cecil Turner (1968–73). A small-college guy out of Cal Poly San Luis Obispo, Turner distinguished himself with a terrific 1970 season, running back four kickoffs for touchdowns, tying a league record. Dave Gagnon (1974) carried the ball once for 15 yards for Chicago. Nemiah Wilson (1975) was a one-time American Football League All Star.

Leslie Frazier (1981–85) was a much bigger name than almost all others who wore 21. As a cornerback, Frazier was a key member of the superb Bears' 1985 defense that led the team to its only Super Bowl victory. In a long college and pro coaching career, Frazier was head coach of the Minnesota Vikings and was on the staff at Indianapolis when the Colts beat the Bears in the 2007 Super Bowl. Most recently, Frazier became defensive coordinator of the Buffalo Bills.

Reggie Phillips (1987), who more often wore No. 48, was also a defensive back for the Bears in their Super Bowl victory over the New England Patriots, returning an interception for a touchdown in that game. Donnell Woolford (1989–96) wore 21 so long he probably wanted to take it with him as a pajama top. A first-round draft pick out of Clemson, Woolford kept playing a few more seasons elsewhere, and intercepted 36 passes for his career.

Running back Darnell Autry (1997) was a big star at nearby Northwestern, but his pro career was almost non-existent. Terry Cousin (1998–99) started with the Bears, but played for six more NFL teams through 2008 and amassed 371 career tackles as a cornerback.

R. W. McQuarters (2000–04) was a popular and colorful member of the Bears, who was a first-round draft pick by the San Francisco 49ers out of Oklahoma State where he played several positions well, as well as for the basketball team. R. W. (which stands for Robert William), won a Super Bowl with the New York Giants in 2007. McQuarters's distinguishing characteristic in Chicago was his hair, which he grew into long dreadlocks. He also wore cartoon-subject band-aids under his eyes where most players wear eye-black. In 2011, after his retirement, McQuarters was shot in Tulsa, Oklahoma, but not seriously harmed.

Wide receiver Rashied Davis (2005–10), who began with the Bears as a cornerback, never played football before high school and spent some time in the Arena Football League with the San Jose SabreCats before twice signing with the Bears. He actually wore No. 81 more than No. 21. A special teams regular, whose most productive year with the Bears was 2008 when he caught 35 balls, Davis was in the right spot for game-winning grabs and catches that aided Chicago in overtime games. Davis was often clutch, and not just on the football field. One year, he won the in-team NCAA men's basketball bracket prediction contest.

"I am a guy who goes with the punches, but I wanted to play wide receiver, anyway," Davis said when coach Lovie Smith moved him from defense to offense.

Cornerback Dante Wesley (2006) and free safety Corey Graham (2007–11) wore No. 21 after Davis switched to No. 81. Graham's best Bears year was 2008 when he was in on 91 tackles. Major Wright (2010–13) wore another number part of his time with the Bears. He participated in 100 tackles his last year in Chicago.

A high point for Ryan Mundy (2014) was a *Monday Night Football* game against the New York Jets. After Mundy ran an interception back for a touchdown, people called the appearance "Mundy Night Football." That season, Mundy was in on 108 tackles and grabbed four interceptions.

Cornerback Tracy Porter, who won a Super Bowl with the New Orleans Saints, wore No. 21 in 2015 and 2016 for the Bears, but was released in early 2017.

NO. 22: UNHAPPY ENDING FOR STAR DAVE DUERSON

Safety Dave Duerson was one of the kings of the gridiron. He excelled at Notre Dame and with the Bears, becoming a four-time All-Pro selection during his 1983–89 tenure with Chicago.

He also seemed like one of those football players destined for great things after leaving the game, and he accomplished plenty. A two-time All-American, Duerson recorded top grades in college and earned a degree in economics. He was a team MVP and captain of the football team at one of the most storied schools in the country.

As No. 22 for the Bears, Duerson was a member of the team's extraordinary defense as the club won the Super Bowl under Mike Ditka and defensive coordinator Buddy Ryan. In 1987, the 6-foot-1, 202-pound hard hitter was chosen the NFL's Man of the Year for his off-field work. Duerson picked up a second Super Bowl ring with the New York Giants in his post-Bears playing days. Even after his football career ended, Duerson remained prominent, serving four years as a member of the board of trustees at Notre Dame, not a common role for a football player.

Things began to go sour for Duerson in his forties and, on February 17, 2011, at the age of fifty, he died from a self-inflicted gunshot wound to the chest. Just before he committed suicide, Duerson, who had sensed he was no longer himself due to head injuries, notified his family members of his intentions and asked to have his brain donated to science for study. At that time, highly publicized efforts were underway seeking to find any links between football players' concussions and the early deterioration of brain function.

Duerson's brain was transferred to Boston University, where a well-known study of this subject was ongoing. It was determined Duerson suffered from chronic traumatic encephalopathy. Duerson was one of the highest-profile victims of CTE during this time period.

Later, after they were divorced, Duerson's ex-wife ruminated about how he played football. "Dave had one speed and that was full out," she said.

Duerson was one of the finest of all Bears players to wear No. 22, but he also had the saddest of endings.

Roy Adkins (1920–21) started No. 22s off with the Decatur Staleys, appearing in four games. Jim McMillen (1924–29) was an offensive lineman. Paul Schuette (1930–32) was another lineman who carried No. 22 into a new decade. William Karr (1933–38) was an end at a time when the Bears didn't throw much.

Saul Sherman (1939–40) was better known as Solly and, when he died at ninety-three in 2010, was the oldest living Bear. Sherman played for Clark Shaugnessy at the University of Chicago, so he was adept at the T-formation. He was not as talented as his friend Sid Luckman, but he was knowledgeable and helped Luckman learn the revolutionary offense. Although Sherman's career was short, he did play in the 1940 Bears' 73–0 massacre of the Washington Redskins in the NFL title game and threw a two-point conversion. When Sherman died, the *Chicago Tribune* speculated Luckman and Sherman may have constituted the only all-Jewish quarterback tandem in NFL history.

Norm Standlee (1941) led the Bears in rushing with 414 yards as a rookie and helped them win the NFL crown before entering the service during World War II. Running back Lloyd Reese (1946) was on a Bears title team and then won a Grey Cup championship with the Montreal Alouettes. The given name of Ed Ecker (1947) was Enrique, and at 6-foot-7 and 306 pounds, during his seven-year pro career in the 1940s and 1950s, the tackle was the biggest man in his sport.

It is hard to believe Hall of Famer Bobby Layne (1948) and Hall of Famer George Blanda (1949–58), both quarterbacks, wore No. 22 consecutively for the Bears, but were dismissed by George Halas as not good enough to be regular starting throwers.

Safety S. J. Whitman (1953–54) is not remembered nearly as well as his predecessors wearing No. 22. Jesse Castete (1956) played in eight Bears games. In the 1960s, the Bears actually had consecutive Billy Martins wearing No. 22. Billy Martin (1962–64) was a running back who rarely handled the ball. Billy Martin II (1964–65) was a tight end whose real name was Jake, but whose nickname was Billy. The first one was 5-foot-11, 197 pounds out of Chicago. The second one was 6-foot-4, 238 pounds out of Georgia.

Charlie Brown (1966–67) was a defensive back whose greatest football achievement was returning an interception 115 yards on the longer field in Canadian football. You won't catch anyone with the Bears or in the NFL matching that. Running back Ross Montgomery (1969–70) came out of Texas Christian. Cyril Pinder (1971–72) was supposed to be insurance for Gale Sayers after the Hall of Famer suffered one of his knee injuries. Clifton Taylor (1974) was a running back and kickoff returner from Memphis.

Johnny Musso (1975–77) was Walter Payton's backfield backup. Dave Williams (1979–81) started 12 games one season at fullback, blocking for Payton. Duerson followed in No. 22. Back Johnny Bailey (1990–91) won the Harlon Hill award three times at Texas A&I as the best player in NCAA Division II for his spectacular production, but his talent didn't translate to the NFL and he gained just 832 rushing yards total. Robert Green (1993–96) was another small-school running back out of William & Mary.

Ronnie Harmon (1997) had a very solid NFL career, just not with the Bears. Safety Shawn Wooden (2000) spent all but that season with the Miami Dolphins. Than Merrill (2001), whose first name looks like a typographical error (his given name is Nathaniel), made seven tackles for the Bears, but followed up with the Barcelona Dragons and the Amsterdam Admirals in NFL Europe. Merrill, who attended Yale, later became a successful businessman and appeared on the A&E show *Flip This House*.

Brock Williams (2003) played 10 games in No. 22 for Chicago after knee injuries at other NFL stops held him back. Alfonso Marshall (2004) made seven tackles in seven games. Tyler Everett (2006) had some brief shots with a few teams.

Matt Forte (2008–15) is the best player to ever wear No. 22 for the Bears, and many fans probably wish he was still in the lineup. The 6-foot-2, 218-pound running back did not have a big reputation coming out of Tulane when the Bears took him with a second-round pick. But he rushed for 123 yards in his first game and five times rushed for more than 1,000 yards for the team.

Forte was also a superb pass catcher coming out of the backfield and had 517 lifetime catches (though the last 30 were for the New York Jets after he became a free agent) as of the 2017 season. In all, Forte had accumulated 9,415 yards rushing and scored 72 touchdowns on the ground or through the air.

Although Forte has not been gone long, No. 22 was quickly inherited by cornerback Cre'von LeBlanc, who made 44 tackles for Chicago in 2016.

Defensive back Brandon Boykin signed with the Bears but was hurt for the season and spent 2016 on injured reserve, never appearing in a game.

NO. 23: DEVIN HESTER, GREATEST RETURN MAN

All Time No. 23	
Player	Years
Guy Chamberlin*	(1920–21)
Roy White	(1925, 1927–29)
Ernie Vick	(1927–28)
Ralph Maillard	(1929)
Lyle Drury	(1930–31)
Gilbert Bergerson	(1932–33)
Victor Zizak	(1934)
Ted Rosequist	(1934–36)
Verne Oech	(1936)
Ernest Rentner	(1937)
Aldo Forte	(1939–42)
Connie Berry	(1942–46)
Washington Serini	(1948–51)
Jerry Shipkey	(1953)
Dave Whitsell	(1961–66)
Al Dodd	(1967)
Clarence Childs	(1968)
Lee Calland	(1969)
Dick Daniels	(1969–70)
Joe Barnes	(1974)
Len Walterscheid	(1977–82)
Shaun Gayle	(1984–94)
Marty Carter	(1995–98)
Jerry Azumah	(1999–2005)
Devin Hester	(2006–13)
Kyle Fuller	(2014–15)

Hall of Fame

Danger was his middle name—or at least whenever Devin Hester got his hands on the football and tucked it under his arm. Chicago has never seen such a dynamic kickoff and punt returner, a more explosive practitioner of the return arts.

Kick the ball to Hester and you might get embarrassed when he exposed your coverage scheme. Sometimes it seemed Hester was so good he was a nuclear warhead aimed at soldiers carrying flintlock rifles.

Hester was plenty fast, with a 4.41-second 40 time, but a lot of guys are fast in a straight line who can't dance around would-be tacklers.

"It's really not any secret," Hester said. "It's just natural instinct. I'm a visual-type player who can see things before they happen."

For a time it was possible to believe Bears' No. 23 would be retired in Hester's honor. But special teams players, no matter how spectacular, don't obtain that type of recognitions. Still, Hester was a thrill-a-minute guy during his 2006–13 tenure with the Bears, one which Soldier Field fans hoped would never end. It seemed alien to watch Hester on the field in the uniform of another team, Atlanta, Baltimore, or Seattle, after his Bears days.

He was a guy who should always be a Bear and will always be remembered as a Bear for some of his most eye-opening feats.

The 5-foot-11, 190-pound Hester was born in Florida and attended the University of Miami. As a freshman, Hester returned a kickoff 98 yards for the Hurricanes, so foreshadowing was easy to interpret. The Bears made him a second-round pick—and he was underrated there. But boy, did that Chicago commitment pay off. A four-time Pro Bowl selection, Hester received far more attention than the usual kick returner and he repeatedly showed he deserved it.

During his rookie year, Hester was nearly unstoppable. He ran back six kicks for touchdowns, including a 108-yard return off a missed field goal. He could have kept running forever untouched by the defense. At the end of that successful Chicago season, the Bears met the Indianapolis Colts in the Super Bowl. Some of the pregame debate revolved around whether the Colts should kick the ball away from Hester so he couldn't hurt them. Sure enough, the game's opening kickoff came to Hester and he wiggled and ran, bursting free, running the ball all of the way back for a touchdown. It was the first opening kickoff taken to the house in Super Bowl history.

Forming the theory the best place to put the ball was in Hester's hands, the Bears turned Hester into a wide receiver. Although the experiment was not a huge success, Hester has 255 catches on his lifetime resume.

As Hester's career began winding down after the 2016 season he announced plans to retire at age thirty-four. He owned the NFL regular-season record for most kicks returned for touchdowns—20—14 of them on punts, five on kickoffs, plus that missed field goal. No recent player set off as many fireworks in the NFL or brought so much fun to the stadium.

Hall of Fame lineman Guy Chamberlain (1920–21) was the first Bear to wear No. 23, one of his numbers. Fullback Roy White (1925, 1927–29) followed. Ernie Vick (1927–28) was an all-around athlete who spent parts of a few seasons for the baseball St. Louis Cardinals, but did not appear in the 1926 World Series. Ralph Maillard (1929) appeared in four games. The nickname of Lyle Drury (1930–31) was "Hoot." He was only thirty-three when he died. Gilbert Bergerson (1932–33) was part of the Bears team that won the "Tom Thumb" NFL title game on a shortened indoor field in 1932.

Victor Zizak (1934) wasn't around long in 23 or in any number for Chicago. Ted Rosequist (1934–36) was a tackle. Verne Oech (1936–37) was a member of two University of Minnesota national champs. Ernest Rentner (1937) was nicknamed "Pug." Aldo Forte (1939–42), a lineman, made two all-star teams, but wasn't nearly as good as Matt Forte. Connie Mack Berry (1942–46) was a war-years lineman who also played pro basketball for Oshkosh (Wisconsin) of the National Basketball League and minor league baseball for the Chicago Cubs. Apparently his parents rooted for the Philadelphia Athletics.

Washington Serini (1948–51) was an offensive lineman who was an all-star in 1948. Jerry Shipkey (1953) was a six-year NFL linebacker, though most of his tenure was with the Steelers. Dave Whitsell (1961–66) was a reliable cornerback best remembered in Chicago as a veteran of the 1963 title team. He once intercepted 10 passes in a season, although for New Orleans. Al Dodd (1967) was a wide receiver with three teams and caught 111 NFL passes.

Clarence Childs (1968) was mostly on the taxi squad with the Bears after his prime seasons with the New York Giants. Lee Calland (1969) was a 10-year defensive back, just not for long with Chicago. Dick Daniels (1969–70) later became a scout. Joe Barnes (1974) was a Bear for just two games, but a star quarterback in Canada where he won a Grey Cup. Len Walterscheid (1977–82) was a safety. Shaun Gayle (1984–94) took over No. 23 for a decade, was part of the 1985 team's Super Bowl champion defense and the now-famous "Super Bowl Shuffle" video.

Marty Carter (1995–98) was another safety who collected more than 1,000 tackles with four teams. Jerry Azumah (1999–2005) brought some glitter to No. 23. An offensive star in college at New Hampshire with four 1,000-yard rushing seasons, defensive back Azumah is the son of immigrants from Ghana. Popular during his Chicago stay, Azumah led the NFL in average yards per kick return in 2003, and was named to the Pro Bowl.

Hester superseded Azumah at that position and eventually turned over No. 23 to Kyle Fuller (2014–15). Fuller was a defensive back who intercepted two passes in one game as a rookie.

NO. 24: JEFF FISHER, FUTURE NFL COACH

All Time No. 24	
Player	Years
Lennie High	(1920)
Heartley "Hunk" Anderson	(1922–27)
Chuck Kassel	(1927)
Reginald Russell	(1928)
Luke Johnsos	(1929–37)
Frank Bausch	(1937–40)
Billy Hughes	(1940–41)
Fred Davis	(1946–51)
Erich Barnes	(1958–60)
Roosevelt Taylor	(1961–69)
Don Shy	(1970–72)
Willie Roberts	(1973)
Virgil Livers	(1975–79)
Jeff Fisher	(1981–85)
Vestee Jackson	(1986–90)
Eric Jeffries	(1987)
Richard Fain	(1992)
Kevin Miniefield	(1993–96)
Terry Cousin	(1998–99)
Glyn Milburn	(1998–2001)
Reggie Austin	(2001–02)
Cameron Worrell	(2003–04, 2006, 2008)
Ricky Manning Jr.	(2006–07)
Marcus Hamilton	(2008)
Al Afalava	(2009)
Marion Barber	(2011)
Kelvin Hayden	(2012, 2014)
Montel Owens	(2014)
Teddy Williams	(2014)
Alan Ball	(2015)
Jordan Howard	(2016)

Once upon a time, Jeff Fisher was a player for the Chicago Bears. He wore No. 24 and played defensive back and was a sometimes kick returner between 1981 and 1985. Although an injury kept him off the field, Fisher did collect a Super Bowl ring from the 1985 team's championship.

That peculiar year, Fisher was a player who was inactive because of a broken leg, but worked as a defensive assistant coach. Those were the origins of his next career. Fisher is far better known as an NFL coach than he was as a player.

While his teams, the Oilers/Titans and Rams almost always made the playoffs, Fisher has not helmed a team that went all of the way. His playing career may have ended in an unsatisfactory way, but Fisher is the best-known wearer of No. 24 for the Bears.

No. 24's lifespan began with Lennie High (1920) of the Staleys. Hunk Anderson (1922–27) displayed it before he coached. End Chuck Kassel (1927) spent most of his NFL career elsewhere. Reginald Russell (1928) was around for just one season. Luke Johnsos (1929–37) made all-league as an end once, but he was better appreciated as a key assistant to George Halas.

Frank Bausch (1937–40) played center with the Bears, an example of how early linemen wore low numbers like 24 before the rule change forced them into high-numbered jerseys. Billy Hughes (1940–41) came out of the University of Texas to play guard. Fred Davis (1946–51) split his career as a defensive lineman between the Bears and Washington Redskins. Davis won one NFL championship with each team. Erich Barnes (1958–60) started his career in Chicago, but his glory days came later in the New York Giants' defensive backfield after being traded. A six-time Pro Bowler, Barnes intercepted 45 passes and ran one back 102 yards for a touchdown. At one point some considered that runback the best play in Giants history. The 6-foot-2, 201-pound Barnes also had good years for the Cleveland Browns.

Roosevelt Taylor (1961–69) had longevity in the defensive backfield and was a member of the 1963 Bears championship team. A two-time Pro Bowl player, Taylor came out of Grambling and is a member of that school's Hall of Fame. He led the league in interceptions with nine one year. Don Shy (1970–72) was a running back from San Diego State. A defensive back out of the University of Houston, Willie Roberts (1973) played in four games for Chicago.

Defensive back Virgil Livers (1975–79) kept No. 24 longer than most, and made 12 interceptions. Of all things, Livers is famous (sometimes in medical writings) for getting hit below the belt so hard his injury makes rankings lists for terrible injuries. As a caveat to young players, Livers was not wearing a protective cup and needed surgery. Simultaneously, his wife, who was nine months pregnant, was rushed to the hospital in labor. Whether this is a heroic statement, bragging, or politically diplomatic, Livers said his wife was in more pain than he was.

Jeff Fisher succeeded Livers in No. 24.

Vestee Jackson (1986–90) did OK for himself, starting by intercepting three passes as a rookie. He may not have been as famous as members of the Jackson Family singers, but he is probably going to be the only Vestee in NFL annals.

Defensive back Eric Jeffries (1987) was a one-game player. Richard Fain (1992) was another in the long line of cornerbacks who wore No. 24. In college, he once beat Alabama for Florida on a blocked punt return. Kevin Miniefield (1993–96) was only a 5-foot-9 cornerback. Terry Cousin (1997) also wore 21. Glyn Milburn (1998–2001) made No. 24 proud for a little while. A two-time Pro Bowler, Milburn held the Bears' kickoff yardage record before Devin Hester.

Reggie Austin (2001–02) was a cornerback who didn't get much playing time. Cameron Worrell (2003–04, 2006–08) was signed as a free agent out of Fresno State and was listed as a safety, but was busier on special teams. Ricky Manning Jr. (2006–07) was expected to make a bigger splash than he did before moving on. Marcus Hamilton (2008) borrowed No. 24 briefly in Chicago and won a title in the short-lived United Football League with the Las Vegas Locomotives.

A native of Hawaii, people liked Al Afalava's name during his 2009 Chicago stay. It seemed likely to last longer when he got in on 53 tackles and made two sacks. But he was waived in 2010. Aloha, Al. Marion Barber III (2011) is not Tiki Barber's twin brother (that was Ronde), but has two brothers, Dominique and Thomas, who both play football (With Dominique in the NFL and Thomas still in college). (Marion's father, also named Marion, played in the NFL with the New York Jets from 1982–88.). The running back gained 422 yards on the ground for the Bears in his sole season in Chicago.

Kelvin Hayden (2012, 2014) may have recovered two fumbles in one game for the Bears, but he spent more time with the Indianapolis Colts. In the 2007 Super Bowl he helped the Colts beat the Bears with an interception return for a TD. For a guy who was an undrafted free agent, Montel Owens (2014) did pretty well for himself, although not with the Bears. Representing Jacksonville, he was selected for two Pro Bowls.

Teddy Williams (2014) is not the Hall of Fame baseball player, but with a 4.31 clocking in the 40, he was faster. Alan Ball (2015) was on the one-year plan in No. 24 with the Bears. A fifth-round draft pick, the 6-foot, 222-pound Jordan Howard (2016) beat out the competition to win the running back job after Matt Forte's departure. He then rushed for 1,313 yards, caught 29 passes, and made the Pro Bowl. Howard, who finished second in the NFL in rushing, said he hopes to be No. 1 (in 24) in 2017.

NO. 25: J. C. CAROLINE, ONE OF THE 1963 GOOD GUYS

All Time No. 25	
Player	Years
Garland Grange	(1929–31)
Charles Malone	(1933)
Walter Kiesling	(1934)
Forest McPherson	(1935)
Ray Nolting	(1936–43)
Jackie Hunt	(1945)
Mike Jarmoluk	(1946–47)
Ed Macon	(1952–54)
JC Caroline	(1956–65)
Linzy Cole	(1970)
Ron Shanklin	(1975–76)
Art Best	(1977–78)
Lonnie Perrin	(1979)
Todd Bell	(1981–86)
Brad Muster	(1988–92)
Keshon Johnson	(1993–94)
Anthony Johnson	(1995)
Pat Eilers	(1995)
Chris Martin	(1996)
Tom Carter	(1997–99)
Thomas Smith	(2000)
Autry Denson	(2001)
Bobby Gray	(2002–04)
Derek Strait	(2006)
Garrett Wolfe	(2007–10)
Armando Allen	(2011–13)
Ka'Deem Carey	(2014–16)

The 1985 Chicago Bears that won the 1986 Super Bowl with perhaps the most dominant defense of all time, and possibly a world-record number of characters on the team, will almost surely remain No. 1 in the hearts of most Bears fans.

But the 1963 championship team, which was the middle man between two title droughts, is fondly remember for many reasons as well. The 1963 team interrupted the rival Green Bay Packers' dynasty, was the first Bears championship since 1946, and last until 1986.

It featured many famous players, but also many other solid ones who were likeable. And despite more than a half a century passing, many, many Bears rooters are still living who saw that team play.

J. C. Caroline was a southerner who attended the University of Illinois, and George Halas always knew who the prospects were coming out of his old school. Caroline was an offensive star as an All-American running back in college, but lost his eligibility for the Illini for academic reasons. So he detoured to Canada to play in Toronto and Montreal before finishing a degree at Florida A&M. He was drafted by the Bears in 1956, for whom he became a defensive back.

After retiring with 24 interceptions, Caroline returned to the central Illinois area of Champaign-Urbana and had a long career as a physical education teacher.

In the earliest days of the NFL, uniforms were handed out with everyone being given a low number, and when the team ran out of players who needed jerseys the wheel stopped. So it was that no Decatur Staleys or Chicago

Bears player ever wore No. 25 until the 1929 season, a decade into the team's existence.

The first player in No. 25 was Garland Grange (1929–31). If some notice the similarity to the name of the famed Red Grange, there is good reason for that. Garland was the younger brother of Red, just not quite as good a player. Worse, his nickname was "Pinky," yes, a pale version of Red.

Charles Malone (1933) was an end on his way to a much longer career with the Washington Redskins, a team he helped capture two NFL titles. Walter Kiesling (1934) was a first-rate offensive lineman, though mostly for other teams, including the Duluth Eskimos. Still, he was better known as a coach. Forrest McPherson (1935) played 10 years in the league, but didn't make it through one with the Bears before being traded.

Ray Nolting (1936–43) totaled 2,285 yards rushing for the Bears in a career where he helped Chicago win championships in 1940, 1941, and 1943. Jackie Hunt (1945) rushed one time for the Bears, but was a College Football Hall of Famer out of Marshall. Mike Jarmoluk (1946–47) made the Pro Bowl once as a tackle, but as a member of the Philadelphia Eagles in 1951.

His career with the Bears was limited to 324 yards rushing, but Ed Macon (1952–54) out of Pacific University was the first African American to suit up for the Chicago Bears. Not satisfied with the opportunities granted him by George Halas, Macon jumped to the Canadian Football League and spent several seasons with the Calgary Stampeders and the Hamilton Tiger-Cats. Halas roared like a bear, with fury, because Macon fled the team, so he sued his ex-player for $100,000 and engineered a boycott of him around the league. Macon never played in the NFL again but had a good career in Canada and played for the Oakland Raiders in 1960, the first year of the American Football League.

J. C. Caroline took over No. 25 post-Macon and kept it for a good while. Not true for Linzy Cole (1970) a half decade after Caroline gave it up. Cole was the first African American player for Texas Christian University and is in the school's Hall of Fame. In all, he played four seasons in the pros, including one in the World Football League. He caught three passes for the Bears.

Ron Shanklin (1975–76) won a Super Bowl with the Pittsburgh Steelers, made one Pro Bowl, and caught 168 passes in his NFL career, just two of them for the Bears. Art Best (1977–78) was a running back. Lonnie Perrin (1979) was an Illinois guy who played in the Super Bowl for Denver. Todd Bell (1981–86) was an All-Pro safety who made the greatest miscalculation of his career when he sat out in 1985 with a contract dispute. So Bell missed being part of the Super Bowl–winning defense. Then a broken leg ended his career early. He died young, at forty-six, of a heart attack.

Brad Muster (1988–92) was a bruising, 235-pound fullback who was forced to block more than run, leading to his departure for New Orleans. Keshon Johnson (1993–94) was a cornerback, not to be confused with the better-known receiver Keyshawn Johnson. Anthony Johnson (1995) was a journeyman who gained 2,996 yards on the ground, but only 30 of them for Chicago.

For a while during this period it seemed as if No. 25 had a new owner almost every season. Pat Eilers (1995) was a safety at the end of his career in Chicago. Chris Martin (1996) was a defensive back out of Northwestern. Tom Carter III (1997–99) provided some continuity at cornerback. He now works for the NFL Players Association. Thomas Smith (2000) was nearing the end of his career in Chicago. Autry Denson (2001) coaches running backs at Notre Dame, where he rushed for 4,448 yards and 46 touchdowns.

A safety, Bobby Gray (2002–04) made 88 tackles with one interception for the Bears. Derek Strait (2006) was a tremendous college defensive back and winner of the Jim Thorpe Award for Oklahoma, but toured the world in pro football. Besides lining up for the Bears, other stops included the Columbus Destroyers of the Arena Football League and a stretch as a practice player for the Winnipeg Blue Bombers in Canada.

Garrett Wolfe (2007–10) showed promise as a running back after a superb career at Northern Illinois University, but could never crack the first string regularly for Chicago. Armando Allen (2011–13) had a short NFL career after running for Notre Dame and is now an assistant coach at Texas Southern. Back Ka'Deem Carey (2014–16) is still around the Bears.

NO. 26: MATT SUHEY, UNSUNG BLOCKER

So much publicity and attention surrounded the 1985 Chicago Bears' dominating season and successful capture of a Super Bowl title that it is difficult to make the case anyone on the team was either underappreciated or overlooked.

That said, fullback Matt Suhey in No. 26, who was essentially star running back Walter Payton's right-hand support system, might have qualified. Suhey was neither as flamboyant as many members of the Bears' championship squad, nor were his key tasks contributing to the title run as noticeable.

A second-round draft pick out of Penn State in 1980, Suhey played a tough-guy position. He was 5-foot-11 and weighed 217 pounds and was the player who led the interference, as they so quaintly used to call it, coming out of the backfield. At Penn State, there have been four generations of Suhey family players dating back to Matt's grandfather and carrying through a son.

In Chicago, Suhey carried the ball once in a while when Payton did not. He was a power guy who totaled 2,946 yards rushing for the Bears between 1980 and 1989 in his secondary role. But he used his body as protection for Payton, the true star of the running game. Suhey was popular with fans who appreciated his workhorse style and dirty-work role.

The first Chicago player to wear No. 26 was Jim Kendrick in 1924. During his many travels within the NFL, the end out of Texas A&M managed to be part of two championship teams. Kendrick made stops with the Toledo Maroons, Louisville Brecks, and Canton Bulldogs, among other teams.

Harold Erickson wore the jersey in 1925 as part of the Bears' tour of America with Red Grange. It made sense for Erickson to surface with Chicago because he teamed with George Halas and Paddy Driscoll at Great

Lakes Naval Training Center before college. Everyone knew Erickson as "Swede," except he was Norwegian. That was a strange kind of rounding off.

John Mohardt (1925) played five games for the Detroit Tigers in 1922. Although listed in some Bears history documents as Henry Vick in No. 26, this was the same person as Ernie Vick who also wore No. 23. An offensive lineman, the real name of Bert Pearson (1929–34) was Madison. Center Milford Miller (1935) was nicknamed "Dub." Kay Bell (1937) was a part-time deep sea diver between appearances on the offensive line and was later a body double and stunt man in movies and television, his biggest claim to fame on that front was subbing for Victor Mature. Charles Apolskis (1938–39) was a defensive end.

Any fan raising a hand in response to whether or not he heard of the next group of Bears might be called a liar. Al Baisi (1940–42, 1946) was an offensive lineman out of West Virginia. Al Hoptowit (1941–45) wore No. 26 when Baisi wasn't around during World War II. Joe Abbey (1948–49) played in all 12 games in 1948, starting in just one. He caught 5 passes for 67 yards. Richard Barwegen (1950–51) was a four-time All-Pro lineman with the Bears and other teams.

Charles Sumner (1955, 1958–60) was a safety with 16 interceptions as a Bear who, in a long assistant coaching career, later won two Super Bowl rings. Defensive back Bennie McRae (1962–70) was part of the 1963 Bears' title victory and intercepted 27 passes for the team. Halfback Carl Garrett (1973–74) had his best years with the Boston/New England Patriots after coming out of New Mexico Highlands. He was named the *Sporting News* AFL Rookie of the Year in 1969.

Matt Suhey followed wearing No. 26 and kept it on his back longer than anyone. However, John Mangum (1990–98) came close to matching him during his time in the defensive backfield. Mangum's father, John Sr., and brother Kris also played in the NFL.

After No. 26 being on loan to just two players over eighteen years, the next borrower, Jermaine Jones, only wore it in 1999. Jones had a long pro football career at a number of places, including a lengthy stay with the Dallas Desperados in the Arena Football League. He is known for charitable works where he resides in Louisiana.

Todd McMillon (2000–04) was a defensive back in Chicago and then played for the Saskatchewan Roughriders in Canada. Later he beat back a prostate cancer threat. Daven Holly (2005) played just three games for the Bears. Trumaine McBride (2007–09) was a cornerback out of the University of Mississippi. DeAngelo Smith (2009) was a halfback just good enough to keep getting chances, but couldn't crack an NFL roster for long. Tim Jennings (2010–14) won a Super Bowl over the Bears with Indianapolis, and then joined Chicago. He intercepted passes in four straight games for the Bears and was a two-time Pro Bowl player.

Antrel Rolle (2015) won a Super Bowl with the Giants and was an All-Pro with the Arizona Cardinals before becoming a Bear. He signed a three-year, $11 million contract, but played only seven games before getting cut. Rolle was very bitter at the Bears when he was shoved out the door. Safety Deon Bush out of the University of Miami replaced Rolle, wearing No. 26 in 2016.

NO. 27: WHO ARE THESE GUYS?

All Time No. 27	
Player	Years
James Crawford	(1925)
Walter Voss	(1927–28)
Harvey Long	(1929)
John Polisky	(1929)
Ed Kawal	(1931–36)
Alvin Culver	(1932)
John Doehring	(1932–37)
Milt Trost	(1935–39)
Joe Mihal	(1940–41)
Edgar Jones	(1945)
Owen Goodnight	(1946)
John Sisk Jr.	(1964)
Randy Montgomery	(1974)
Bob Grim	(1975)
Mike Richardson	(1983–88)
Brian Taylor	(1989)
Lewis Tillman	(1994–95)
Walt Harris	(1996–2001)
Rabih Abdullah	(2002–03)
Jason Shivers	(2004)
Chris Thompson	(2005)
Marcus Maxey	(2006)
Nick Turnbull	(2008)
Kevin Jones	(2008–09)
Major Wright	(2010–13)
Sherrick McManis	(2012–16)

This may be the all-time Bears number for the least amount of star power, although there are definitely a few contenders. There are probably more Bears who wore No. 27 than any other that fans don't remember for any good reason.

Just about all of these players could show up at a costume party wearing a Chicago Bears No. 27 uniform, and almost nobody would be able to tell them apart. Management needs to go out and sign a superstar free agent and give him No. 27 so he can make even the most ardent fans and statisticians forget about everyone else. Of course, they probably already have.

The king of No. 27 wearers has to be Mike Richardson. However, that designation comes with an asterisk. The 6-foot, 187-pound cornerback was All-Pro in 1986 and won a Super Bowl ring with the Bears during his 1983–88 stay with the team. That's the good stuff, and Richardson would be pleasantly remembered for those highlights except they are balanced out by lowlights.

These days, if you do a Google search for Mike Richardson the immediate hits on his name also carry different types of statistics than the 20 interceptions he grabbed during his NFL career. They talk about a 13-year prison sentence. Richardson left the NFL in 1989 after adding one more season with the San Francisco 49ers. It is not clear if anyone besides the court system has kept track, but by 2008 when he was convicted on charges of possession of crack cocaine and methamphetamines it was his 21st drug conviction since retiring.

Bears friends, from ex-coach Mike Ditka and Hall of Fame defensive end Richard Dent, supported him and helped get Richardson's sentence changed to one year in prison with 12 more years of probation. He sought treatment and fought to turn his life around, staying clear of fresh visits to the justice system. Richardson began working with youths and giving advice to others who faced troubled situations and proclaimed himself a changed man.

The first No. 27 for the Bears was James Crawford (1925), a rookie lineman nicknamed "Mush" who played in three games. Lineman Walter Voss (1927–28) was nicknamed "Tillie," and played for 11 teams in nine NFL seasons. Harvey Long (1929) was a lineman not famed for much on the gridiron, but apparently was popular in his neighborhoods for making peanut butter pancakes for children. John "Bull" Polisky (1929) was a guard out of Notre Dame. Ed Kawal (1931–36) also wore No. 19. Alvin Culver (1932) split his one NFL season with Green Bay. John Doehring also wore No. 11.

Milt Trost (1935–39) was a tackle and end. Joe Mihal (1940–41) later played in the All-America Football Conference. Edgar Jones (1945) signed contracts both with the Bears and the Cleveland Browns of the All-America Conference, and ended up with the Browns after one game in Chicago. Edgar Jones (1945) was a running back nicknamed "Special Delivery."

Owen Goodnight (1946) picked up No. 27 after World War II. The jersey was then sent out for cleaning for eighteen years. John Sisk Jr. (1964) wore it for three games, then back into the bowels of the equipment room No. 27 went. It stayed there until 1974, when Randy Montgomery donned the number. After his stay with the Denver Broncos, Montgomery finished up with the Bears and made two interceptions. Bob Grim (1975) was a decade-long NFL player who made one Pro Bowl and competed in two Super Bowls with the Minnesota Vikings.

Mike Richardson was the next 27. Brian Taylor (1989) was a DB who made it into five Bears games. Running back Lewis Tillman (1994–95) had a phenomenal career at Jackson State, breaking Walter Payton's records, won a Super Bowl with the Giants, and finished his career with the Bears, leading the team in rushing in 1994. Walt Harris (1996–2001) gave the Bears six good years as a cornerback, including a 113-tackle rookie year. Rabih Abdullah (2002–03) was a long-shot runner out of Lehigh who just missed with a few teams. Jason Shivers (2004) left the Bears cold and then had more success in colder Canada.

Chris Thompson got in on the No. 27 sweepstakes in 2005 when he had 10 tackles and he also went north to the Canadian Football League. Marcus Maxey (2006) was only in Chicago for a few weeks and didn't get the jersey dirty. Nick Turnbull (2008) came and went quickly in Chicago and with other

NFL teams. Kevin Jones (2008–09) was a solid back out of Virginia Tech, but was mostly injured during his stay in Chicago. Major Wright (2010–13) also wore No. 21. Sherrick McManis (2012–16) has been an excellent special teams tackler for the Bears.

Mostly, No. 27 has been a merry-go-round for Chicago throughout its history.

NO. 28: THE TRAGEDY OF WILLIE GALIMORE

During his 1957 to 1963 career with the Bears, halfback Willie Galimore, wearing No. 28, rushed for 2,985 yards and 26 touchdowns, to go with 87 receptions during a time period where players coming out of the backfield were not as active as safety valves for quarterbacks.

The 6-foot-1, 187-pound Galimore was a fast galloper out of Florida A&M and only a fifth-round pick by Chicago. Galimore was known for his incredible acceleration and it was felt he was still improving when he reported to training camp for the 1964 season, the year after the Bears won the NFL title.

Gilmore was still only twenty-nine on the night of July 27, 1964, when he was killed in a one-car automobile accident with teammate John Farrington as they returned to their training-camp dorms in Rensselaer, Indiana, after an evening out. The shock of the players' demise was said to be so great it destroyed the Bears' season following their championship.

"For the Bears, the season was over before it began," said George Halas in his autobiography.

Halas, the distraught owner-coach, paid for Galimore's funeral expenses and kept providing financial assistance to his family and children so they could attend college. Galimore's young son, Ron, eventually became a seven-time national gymnastic champion and an Olympian. However, that was in 1980 when the U.S. boycotted the Summer Games in Moscow.

The Bears also retired No. 28 in Willie Galimore's name. The gesture was as much about what he had accomplished as his relationship with his teammates and the franchise as it was about what there might still have been to come.

The first Bear to wear No. 28 was Ed Garvey (1925), not to be confused with the future NFL Players Association head. Aldous Haddon (1928) was a Bear, a Panther, and a Steam Roller during his NFL career. Larry Steinbach (1930–31) was a tackle out of North Dakota. Fritz Febel (1935) was better known for coaching the University of Buffalo than time spent with the Bears.

Robert Allman (1936) played in one game. A College Football Hall of Fame guard from Ohio State, Gust Zarnas (1938) was Greek, and his full first name was actually Gustave.

Chet Chesney (1939–40) spent about the same amount of time with the Bears as he did serving one term in Congress as a Democrat representing Illinois. Bob Steuber (1942–43) was a halfback who played one game for Chicago, but excelled in college and later was a long-time sports announcer in Missouri. Lloyd Lowe (1953–1954) was a defensive back.

Upon further review, it may be the wearers of Bears No. 28 are the weakest crop of players to share a number. That even includes Galimore, whose career was sadly shortened.

NO. 29: THEY REMEMBER RUNNER RONNIE BULL

All Time No. 29	
Player	Years
Bill McElwain	(1925)
John Wallace	(1929)
Joe Kopcha	(1929–33)
Gus Mastrogany	(1931)
Russ Thompson	(1936–39)
Ed Kolman	(1940–44)
Douglas McEnulty	(1943–44)
Glenn Burgeis	(1945)
Jack Hoffman	(1949–56)
McNeil Moore	(1954–56)
Glen Shaw	(1960)
Ronnie Bull	(1962–70)
Bob Jeter	(1971–72)
Mike Morgan	(1978)
Vaughan Lusby	(1980)
Dennis Gentry	(1982–92)
Raymont Harris	(1994–97)
Frankie Smith	(1998–2001)
Adrian Peterson	(2002–09)
Chester Taylor	(2010)
Michael Bush	(2012–13)
Danny McCray	(2014)
Harold Jones-Quartey	(2015–16)

Ronnie Bull came out of Baylor and was a popular halfback for the Bears between 1962 and 1970, playing all but one season of his NFL career in Chicago. Bull gained all but a bit more than 300 of his 3,222 yards on the ground for the Bears, and was a member of the 1963 championship team.

Bull stood 6 feet tall and played at 200 pounds. Never a big star for Chicago, he was a steady presence, taking advantage of his opportunities to gain about 400 yards per season. No. 29 won rookie-of-the-year mention his first season.

The 1963 championship was the highlight of Bull's 10-year career. It was a frigid day when the Bears prevailed over the New York Giants. Some might say it would have been appropriate to wear gloves. But Bull said that was not in the cards for the Bears.

"And I didn't wear gloves," he said. "[George] Halas didn't want us wearing gloves. Once your adrenaline gets going, you don't notice it."

After Bull played his final season with the Philadelphia Eagles, he settled in the Chicago suburbs and became a businessman.

Even as a No. 1 draft pick, Halas was careful not to pay Bull too much in his first contract. The runner signed for $20,000 and when he asked for a new car to supplement the deal, Bull said Halas told him he was making enough that "you can buy your own friggin' car."

Bill McElwain (1925) was the first Bear to wear No. 29, but never played a game in that jersey. Apparently, equipment people gave it to him and took it back. John Wallace (1928) played 12 games for the Bears. Joe Kopcha (1929–33) used football to pay his way through the University of Chattanooga to become an obstetrician. Gus Mastrogany (1931) was another one-game wonder. Russ Thompson (1936–39) was a regular at tackle. Ed Kolman (1940–44) was a tackle out of Temple University. Douglas McEnulty (1943–44) was a halfback who gained 56 yards rushing in his career. Glenn

Burgeis (1945), who was part of an Orange Bowl champ for the University of Tulsa, was finished with the Bears after one season because of a knee injury.

Men who played all positions wore No. 29 over the decade, including Jack Hoffman (1949–56) who started out with that numeral and switched to No. 82 later when NFL rules changed. McNeil Moore (1954–56) was a defensive back, one of the positions included in the No. 29 range. Glenn Shaw (1960) was a fullback. Ronnie Bull took over from there. Bob Jeter (1971–72) was a bigger deal with the Green Bay Packers, being part of three NFL championship teams, including the first two Super Bowl winners, as a cornerback. His son, Rob, is a well-known college basketball coach.

Mike Morgan (1978) returned a handful of kicks in his one season in Chicago. Vaughn Lusby (1980) returned four punts for the Bears. Dennis Gentry (1982–92) might have been the most valuable Bear ever to don No. 29. He spent his entire 11-season NFL career with the Bears and caught 171 passes. Gentry won a Super Bowl ring and was part of the "Super Bowl Shuffle" video. He also led the NFL in kick returns in 1986 with a 28.8-yard average.

Raymont Harris (1994–97) was a starting fullback and, in 1997, he rushed for 1,033 yards and scored 10 touchdowns. That was a high, but after that Harris was sidelined by repeated injuries as he sought a new job. Frankie Smith (1998–2001) was a cornerback out of Baylor.

Adrian Peterson (2002–09) is not to be confused with the former Minnesota Vikings star runner of the same name. However, this Peterson was a huge star at Georgia Southern in Division I-AA, winning the Walter Payton Award as the top player in that division. He rushed for 9,145 yards in his college career. With the Bears, the 5-foot-10, 212-pound Peterson was mostly a special-teams specialist and a spot fill-in at running back during a lengthy career.

For a while, the Bears spent millions of dollars to put a body in No. 29, with limited returns. Chester Taylor (2010), also known as Che Tay, signed a rich contract with the Bears, but Matt Forte virtually ran him out of town by taking over the bulk of the work in the backfield. Michael Bush (2012–13) signed a big-money deal as Forte's supposed successor, but he got hurt and didn't last in Chicago. Safety Daniel McCray (2014) was more valuable on special teams, although he did grow out impressive dreadlocks. Harold Jones-Quartey (2015–16) is going on his third year wearing No. 29 in the defensive backfield.

NO. 30: GEORGE WILSON PARLAYED BEARS PLAY INTO COACHING SUCCESS

All Time No. 30	
Player	Years
Gerald Seibering	(1932)
Bob Dunlap	(1935)
George Wilson	(1937–46)
Allen Smith	(1947–48)
Herb Falkenberg	(1952)
Bobby Jack Floyd	(1953)
Chick Jagade	(1954–55)
Jimmy Gunn	(1970–75)
John Skibinski	(1978–91)
Jack Cameron	(1984)
George Duarte	(1987)
George Streeter	(1989)
James Rouse	(1990–91)
Tony Carter	(1994–97)
Ricky Bell	(1998)
Mike Brown	(2000–08)
D. J. Moore	(2009–12)
Demontre Hurst	(2014–16)

George Halas liked George Wilson, and George Wilson provided good effort for the dollar during his 1937–46 career as a Bear. The 6-foot-1, 190-pound end made three all-star teams and was part of the Bears' 1940s championship dynasty.

Wilson was born in Chicago and played college ball at Northwestern. He caught 111 passes for the Bears with 15 touchdowns, but he also did the job on defense as many players did in those days. Wilson caught a career-high 28 passes in 1945.

A solid player, if not spectacular, Wilson had a sharp eye and was a savvy player. It was natural for him to move into coaching. He paid his dues with two years as a Bears assistant and with a long, 1949–56 assistant coach tenure with Detroit before taking over as the Lions' head coach.

Wilson was at the helm when the Lions won the 1957 NFL title. That is the last time Detroit won the championship. He was the first winner of the Associated Press Coach of the Year Award for his leadership that season.

Detroit slumped after Wilson's debut season, but he rebuilt the Lions into a powerhouse by 1962, when they finished 11–3. However, Wilson's albatross was mostly the Green Bay Packers of the Vince Lombardi period. He just couldn't top the Packers. Also, in 1963, he couldn't beat the Bears when they interfered with the Packers dynasty.

Wilson quit the Lions after the 1964 season with a total record of 53–45–6. He spent a year as an assistant coach for the Washington Redskins and then became the first coach of the expansion Miami Dolphins in 1966. The Dolphins suffered through growing pains during his tenure, and Wilson gave up coaching after 1969.

His Bears years were his formative years.

Nobody wore No. 30 for the Bears until the 1932 season when Gerald Seibering tried it on. Bob Dunlap (1935) played 12 games in Chicago. Wilson came next. Allen Smith (1947–48) caught three passes for the Bears. There was no stampede for No. 30 and it was dormant for a while. Herb Falkenberg (1952) was a decathlon track star out of Trinity University in Texas, not so much with Chicago. Bobby Jack Floyd (1953) was a fullback. Chick Jagade (1954–55) was a two-time Pro Bowl player as a fullback with the kind of nickname people don't get these days.

Jimmy Gunn (1970–75) was an All-American linebacker out of Southern Cal. John Skibinski (1978–81), the son of another NFL player, Joe, didn't get much chance to carry the ball for the Bears. Wide receiver Jack Cameron (1984) he played in all 16 games and also had 26 kickoff returns. George Duarte (1987) made it into three games on defense. George Streeter (1989) recovered a fumble in his four-game Bears stay. Running back James Rouse (1990–91) gained 130 yards for the Bears. Tony Carter (1994–97) was a running back who played the first four seasons of his nine-year pro career in Chicago. Ricky Bell (1998) was not the star runner Ricky Bell. This Bell was a cornerback whose finest moment in pro football was probably winning a Grey Cup with Calgary in 2001.

One star displaying No. 30 was defensive back Mike Brown (2000–08). A two-time All-Pro safety, Brown made 518 tackles in a career that was 90 percent spent in Chicago and picked off 20 interceptions. In 2001, Brown turned in a couple of the most spectacular defensive plays in Bears history. Two weeks in a row he intercepted passes in overtime and ran both back for touchdowns to provide stunning Chicago victories.

D. J. Moore (2009–12) had his moments in the defensive backfield for Chicago. He intercepted a Donovan McNabb pass when he was with Washington and ran it back for a TD, and intercepted two Tony Romo passes in one game. Demontre Hurst (2014–16) was a free-agent cornerback out of Oklahoma.

Did He Play for the Bears?
Ronnie Harmon
Kinda sorta.

Ronnie Harmon appeared in just one game for the 1997 Chicago Bears, so fans cannot be blamed if they don't remember him suiting up for the hometown team wearing No. 22.

By the time Harmon signed with the Bears, the former Iowa college player had competed for the Buffalo Bills, San Diego Chargers, and Houston Oilers-Tennessee Titans. He had 582 catches on his resume, one visit to the Pro Bowl in 1992, and an appearance with the Chargers in a Super Bowl game.

Also, two brothers, Kevin and Derrick, played in the NFL.

Harmon was a running back, but did more damage through the air. He gained 2,774 yards rushing and 6,076 yards on catches during his career. His output for the Bears was two catches and two rushing attempts.

NO. 31: JOE FORTUNATO BELONGS IN THE HALL OF FAME

Somehow the honor of being selected to the Pro Football Hall of Fame in Canton, Ohio, has eluded Joe Fortunato, but there is no doubt he belongs in the Bears Number Hall of Fame for his achievements while wearing No. 31.

Just as an indicator of the injustice done to Fortunato in not having a bust in Canton, he is the only defensive member of the NFL's All-Decade 1950s team who is not enshrined. A five-time Pro Bowl pick who called the signals for the Bears' defense when it was one of the best in the game, including for the 1963 championship team, Fortunato had a notable 12-year career.

Fortunato loved telling the story of how the night before the showdown with the New York Giants for the title George Halas called him in his hotel room, seemingly asking for assurance that his defense would prevail. Fortunato seemed to indicate the Old Man was more nervous about the outcome than his linebacker.

The 6-foot-1, 225-pound Fortunato suited up between 1955 and 1966, appearing in 155 games. He intercepted 16 passes and recovered 22 fumbles while roaming the field, doing damage on all fronts. He far exceeded early expectations after being a seventh-round draft pick. A graduate of Mississippi State who later settled in Mississippi and operated the Big Joe Oil Company after his football days were over, Fortunato also spent two years as a Bears assistant coach after retiring.

Fortunato missed just one game during his long career and the fumble-recovery total is a team record for linebackers. For years he supervised the Joe Fortunato Celebrity Golf Classic to raise scholarship money for high school kids.

A friendly, outgoing man with a passion for fishing, but beset by late-in-life illnesses, it is a shame Fortunato has never been able to enjoy the same salutes to his abilities many of his contemporaries did.

The No. 31 was not worn by any Bears player until 1939 when Dick Schweidler pulled on the jersey and kept it through 1941, and then got it back again in 1946 after World War II. Len Akin (1942) played in 11 games. Paul Podmajersky (1944) had one of the strangest of football careers, transferring to a new school just about every year in college, playing for Michigan State, Iowa, and Wyoming. He was then helped with medical school expenses by George Halas. Stuart Clarkson (1946–50) also played in Canada. He died young, at thirty-eight, from a heart attack suffered on the sidelines during a high school game he was coaching. One of the league's early African American players, Emerson Cole (1952) passed through Chicago after a disappointing stay with the Cleveland Browns.

Joe Fortunato put the stranglehold on No. 31 for a while after that. Ross Brupbacher (1970–73, 1976) was a linebacker with 12 interceptions who had better success in the World Football League. Bill Knox (1974–76) was a 5-foot-9 defensive back who collected two interceptions. Anthony Hutchison (1983–84), who gained 52 yards rushing, later got in trouble with the law for hiring illegal aliens for landscaping. Ken Taylor (1985) was a defensive back.

Thomas Sanders (1985–89) was a backup running back for the Super Bowl champs and a good No. 31 representative. Eric Jeffries (1987) played one game. Bruce McCray (1987) was a defensive back. Greg Lasker (1988) was a safety. Mark Green (1989–92) gained 496 yards rushing and caught 22 passes and scored 7 touchdowns (one receiving and six rushing).

Rashaan Salaam (1995–97) won the Heisman Trophy at Colorado and as a Bears rookie ran for 1,074 yards and 10 touchdowns. He is the youngest player in NFL history to rush for 1,000 yards, but his career quickly declined after that and he moved from team to team and league to league before retiring in 2004. In late 2016, Salaam took his own life at forty-two, dying from a gunshot wound to the head.

Daimon Shelton (2001–02) was a fullback who played all over the map. Defensive back Nathan Vasher (2004–09) gave a boost to No. 31 fans everywhere. Although injuries cut short his Bears stay, Vasher had some great moments for the team. He made the Pro Bowl in 2005, and returned a missed field goal 108 yards for a touchdown. Also in 2005, he intercepted eight passes. Vasher may have wanted to play longer, but at least his memory bank was not cheated.

Joshua Moore (2010) played cornerback and made one tackle. Although he was a two-time all-star defensive back elsewhere, during his short stay in Chicago Brandon Meriweather (2011) received $45,000 in fines from the NFL for illegal hits. Isaiah Frey (2013–14) kept coming and going, waived and re-signed. Safety Chris Prosinski (2015–16) is hanging in with the Bears after playing high school ball in tiny Buffalo, Wyoming, college ball at the University of Wyoming, and marrying a former Miss Wyoming.

NO. 32: JOHNNY LUJACK QUARTERBACK STAR
FOR A FEW MINUTES

All Time No. 32	
Player	Years
Al Grygo	(1944–45)
Allen Smith	(1947–48)
Johnny Lujack	(1948–51)
Leon Campbell	(1952–54)
Lionel Taylor	(1959)
Ralph Kurek	(1965–70)
Charlie Ford	(1971–73)
Chris Brewer	(1987)
Garland Rivers	(1987)
Lemuel Stinson	(1988–92)
Dwayne Joseph	(1995–96)
Ricky Bell	(1997)
Edgar Bennett	(1998–99)
Marlon Barnes	(2000)
Leon Johnson	(2001–02)
Todd Johnson	(2003–06)
Cedric Benson	(2005–07)
Kahlil Bell	(2009–12)
Michael Ford	(2013)
Senorise Perry	(2014–16)
Deiondre' Hall	(2016)

Quarterback Johnny Lujack wore No. 32 in college for Notre Dame when he was making his name, and 32 with the Chicago Bears when he figured to extend his fame. However, in a relationship that went haywire, Lujack's 1948–51 stay with Chicago was over much too quickly.

At 6 feet tall and 186 pounds, Lujack was of typical size for a quarterback during his era. The winner of the 1947 Heisman Trophy, Lujack was so popular and well-known that he graced the cover of *LIFE* magazine and was also the subject of a radio show called *The Adventures of Johnny Lujack*. The radio deal was summer replacement for the *Jack Armstrong, All-American Boy* program. That showed how much esteem Lujack was held in by Americans.

From the coal country of McConnellsville, Pennsylvania, Lujack came of age for college during World War II. After his first two seasons at Notre Dame he joined the army and became an officer. He then returned to campus and resumed his football career, producing All-American credentials. The Fighting Irish won three national championships under his field leadership.

For nearly a decade, Sid Luckman had been the Bears' signal-caller, but owner-coach George Halas wanted to be prepared for the day when Luckman no longer ran the show. Lujack was drafted with the No. 1 pick in 1946, and at first played in the defensive backfield.

"I loved it when you played both ways," Lujack said years later of the offensive-defensive demands of his time. "If you made a mistake, you didn't have to go to the sideline to face the coach."

By Luckman's last year, 1950, roles had reversed and the old-timer was the backup and Lujack the first-stringer. He blossomed into a star and earned the first of two Pro Bowl mentions. It seemed the Bears were set for another decade in the most important position on the field.

There was only one problem. Lujack and Halas could not get along. It became more frustrating for Lujack with the passage of time and he abruptly quit the sport. During a time period when there was no free agency, Lujack did not have the option of playing for another team and Halas was just stubborn enough to keep him from doing so. Lujack, now in his ninetires, went into private business and also did some sports commentating. It was the Bears' and football's loss.

The No. 32 got a late start. The first Bears player to wear it was Al Grygo (1944–45), a running back with 420 total yards. Allen Smith (1947–48) also wore 30. Lujack followed him at 32. Fullback Leon Campbell (1952–54) got No. 32 when it unexpectedly came up for grabs. Lionel Taylor (1959) was the Broncos' near-legendary American Football League receiver whose talent went unrecognized in Chicago. The Bears used Taylor as a linebacker before he led the AFL in catches five times. Running back Ralph Kurek (1965–70) was a University of Wisconsin guy. Charlie Ford (1971–73) was a cornerback out of the University of Houston. Running back Chris Brewer (1987) played three games for the Bears after a stint with the Denver Dynamite of the Arena Football League, reviving No. 32 after a hiatus.

An All-American defensive back, Garland Rivers (1987) wore the number in the same year as Brewer and went on to Arena ball as well. Texas Tech defensive back Lemuel Stinson (1988–92) was listed on the roster at the ridiculously low weight of 159 pounds, but intercepted 16 passes for the Bears. Dwayne Joseph (1995–96) starred in the secondary at Syracuse and had some good moments with the Bears, though his longevity was derailed by injuries before moving into a second career in team administration. He is now player personnel director for the Philadelphia Eagles.

Ricky Bell also wore No. 30. Fullback Edgar Bennett (1998–99) had a fine career, topping 1,000 yards rushing one year and winning a Super Bowl with the Packers. Although most of the good stuff happened while in Green Bay, he did rush for over 600 yards for the Bears one season. Bennett is now the Packers' offensive coordinator.

Halfback Marlon Barnes (2000) ran through Chicago one season. Leon Johnson (2001–02) was better for the New York Jets before stopping in Chicago. Safety Todd Johnson (2003–06) had a 75-tackle season for the Bears. Power back Cedric Benson (2005–07) broke the string of Johnsons wearing No. 32. Benson was a No. 1 draft pick after becoming an All-American at

Texas and figured to be a long-term star in Chicago. Nope. Three 1,000-yard seasons lay in his future with the Cincinnati Bengals, but the most Benson gained in Chicago was 674 yards. A contract holdout and injury contributed to the disappointing relationship.

Given the strained departure of Benson, there was no pressure on Kahlil Bell (2009–12) when it became his turn to wear No. 32. Bell's debut was flashy: he ran 72 yards on his first carry. But contributions were a bit more limited after that. Louisiana State's Michael Ford (2013) hoped to become the Bears' go-to back, but had a better career in Canada afterward. Senorise Perry (2014–16) had an unusual first name, but the sun did not rise on him and his Bears experience pretty much was split between special teams and injured reserve.

Cornerback Deoindre' Hall was a fourth-round draft pick.

NO. 33: AN UNSUNG STAR AND HISTORICAL CONFUSION

All Time No. 33	
Player	Years
Denny Meyers	(1931)
Herb Joesting	(1931–32)
Bernie Masterson	(1934–40)
Ray Nolting	(1936–43)
George McAfee*	(1940–41, 1945–50)
Frank Martin	(1941)
Johnny Long	(1944–45)
Bill Johnson	(1946–47)
Jack Karwales	(1946–47)
Allen Lawler	(1948)
Bob Perina	(1949–50)
Wilford "Whizzer" White	(1951–52)
Jerry Shipkey	(1953)
Larry Morris	(1959–65)
Mike Hull	(1968–70)
Jim Grabowski	(1971)
Gary Kosins	(1972–74)
Ted Vactor	(1975)
Jack Deloplaine	(1979)
Calvin Thomas	(1982–87)
Lars Tate	(1990)
Darren Lewis	(1991–92)
Merril Hoge	(1994)
Tyrone Hughes	(1997)
Bam Morris	(1998)
Larry Whigham	(2001–02)
Charles Tillman	(2003–14)
Jeremy Langford	(2015–16)

Hall of Fame

Linebacker Larry Morris (1959–65) is right up there with the best Bears players to exhibit the No. 33 uniform—and maybe the truest Bear. Morris knew how to snarl and was a top-flight owner of a defensive starting position for a while, even if he was a bit overshadowed during his playing days. It was a mixed blessing. Morris could claim to be a member of the best linebacker trio in the game along with Bill George and Joe Fortunato, but they also received more acclaim and attention.

Still, the 6-foot-2, 226-pound Morris did OK for himself in a 12-year NFL career that included other stops after coming out of Georgia Tech as an All-American. That college reputation was enough to make Morris a first-round draft pick. He was chosen as a linebacker on the NFL's All-Decade team of the 1960s. Like Fortunato, though, Morris never got enough support for the Hall of Fame.

Morris won a national championship in college and an NFL title with the Bears in the pros. A 61-yard interception return was a major play in the victory over the New York Giants. The last years of his life were sad ones, though. Morris died at age seventy-nine in 2012 from complications of dementia. Before that, in 2007, he was one of the subjects in a national story in the *Sporting News* about football players with memory loss stemming from concussions suffered in the sport.

Overall, there is not a long line of really big Bears stars who wore No. 33, and that is a bit surprising because it is a flashy number that looks good on a jersey and one might think there would be a clamor to be assigned it.

One wearer of No. 33 for the Bears has a famous nickname, but it is unlikely many fans remember another "Whizzer" White.

Born in 1928 in Arizona, Wilford White (1951–52) became an all-around star athlete in football, basketball, and track and field, performing in the decathlon. White's football career took him from Arizona State to the Bears to Canada. Along the way, he was anointed "Whizzer," even though he was the second coming of a Whizzer.

The first and most prominent Whizzer White, Byron White was a 6-foot-1, 187-pound running back for Colorado. Although he did not play pro ball long, White led the NFL in rushing in 1938 and 1940 and was a three-time All-Pro. White was known for his shiftiness and his speed. Later, he became better known as a justice on the U.S. Supreme Court.

Another claim to fame by the Bears' Whizzer White, besides wearing No. 33, was his role as father of Dallas Cowboys quarterback Danny White. Also, this Whizzer White once pretty much set a record for running backwards. Under a heavy rush, he retreated from the line of scrimmage and kept going back, back, back, until he had fled 48 yards. Worse, then White fumbled on the one-yard line and the Los Angeles Rams recovered, converting the play into a touchdown.

Film of the play later indicted White on lists such as "The 13 Stupidest Plays in NFL History."

Denny Myers (1931) was the first Bear to model No. 33, playing two games at guard. Herb Joesting (1931–32) was a University of Minnesota All-American fullback. Bernie Masterson (1934–40) was the Chicago quarterback before Sid Luckman and threw for 34 touchdowns while playing in three title games. Masterson later coached the University of Nebraska. He hailed from that state and was a high school and college star athlete.

Ray Nolting (1936–43) also wore No. 25. Hall of Famer George McAfee (1940–41, 1945–50) also wore No. 5, and the Bears retired that number to honor him. Frank Martin (1941) was not the South Carolina basketball coach. Johnny Long (1944–45) was a quarterback who threw one interception and for one touchdown. Bill Johnson (1946–47) was one of the young players George Halas shipped to Akron as a sort of Bears farm team for a brief period. Although they were actually also named Bears, they were often referred to as Cubs.

Jack Karwales (1946–47) came out of the Air Force to sign with Chicago, but also spent time in Akron. Allen Lawler (1948) was a running back. Bob Perina (1949–50) played on five teams in five years in the NFL and All-America Football Conference. The faux Whizzer White used No. 33 next. Jerry Shipkey also wore No. 23.

After a six-year lull, No. 33 was resurrected for Larry Morris. Fullback Mike Hull (1968–70) was a No. 1 draft pick out of Southern Cal and was a frequent blocker for Gale Sayers. Jim Grabowski (1971) was supposed to be a stronger runner than Hull, but was at the end of the line after playing most of his career with Green Bay. A 6-foot-1, 215-pound back out of Dayton, Gary Kosins (1972–74) gained 100 yards rushing for Chicago.

Ted Vactor (1975) was a defensive back out of Nebraska. Jack Delo-plaine (1979) was a career backup running back, but collected two Super Bowl rings elsewhere. He had a funny nickname, called "Hydroplane" for its rhyming quality and his supposed ability to run well in wet field conditions. Running back Calvin Thomas (1982–87) was around for a while, but got only rare chances to carry the football. Lars Tate (1990) was not around long (three games) and only gained five yards in Chicago. Darren Lewis (1991–92) was an All-American who gained 382 yards with the Bears one season, but tested positive for drugs at the NFL combine and faced a domestic violence battery charge.

Future ESPN commentator Merrill Hoge (1994) retired following repeated concussion problems and ended up winning a $1.5 million judgment against a Bears doctor for the way a brain injury was handled. His situation, after gaining more than 3,000 yards rushing, brought early attention to the problem of football concussions.

A Pro Bowl defensive back and kick returner for the New Orleans Saints, nothing worked out for Tyrone Hughes (1997) when he signed a multi-million-dollar contract with the Bears. In between running into trouble with drug matters, running back Bam Morris (1998) played two games in Chicago. The 6-foot-2, 215-pound Larry Whigham (2001–02) excelled on special teams, twice being an all-star, but his career was nearly over when he signed with Chicago.

Nicknamed "Peanut," Charles Tillman (2003–14) had an excellent career for the Bears, being named to the Pro Bowl twice as a cornerback and doing No. 33 proud. Tillman was involved in 911 tackles and forced a huge number of fumbles—44—while grabbing 38 interceptions. Tillman also received the Walter Payton Man of the Year Award from the NFL in 2013 for his charity work. Tillman tacked on a final year with the Carolina Panthers where he added his last two interceptions.

Jeremy Langford (2015–16) has had as many as six touchdowns and 537 yards rushing in a season for Chicago.

NO. 34: WALTER PAYTON, WALTER PAYTON, WALTER PAYTON

All Time No. 34	
Player	Years
Jack Torrance	(1939)
John Federovitch	(1941–42)
John Dottley	(1951–53)
Joe Marconi	(1962–66)
Tim Casey	(1969)
Bill Tucker	(1971)
Norm Hodgins	(1974)
Walter Payton**	(1975–87)

** Hall of Fame, Retired for Payton

It's been thirty years since the great Walter Payton retired as the Chicago Bears' superback, and it's been that long since anyone on the Bears' roster has worn No. 34. The number, and the idea that anyone else can live up to wearing No. 34 again for this team, were both retired.

Famed coach Mike Ditka called Payton the greatest football player he had ever seen. That covers considerable ground for Iron Mike, himself a Hall of Fame tight end, and a man who coached numerous Hall of Famers. Note that he did not say running back; he said football player.

Ditka was closer to the real-live situation than most, and certainly other experts have their favorites, but he didn't get a lot of loud arguments against his position either. And a large body of opinion supports the notion that Payton might, at the very least, have been the greatest running back.

"You felt honored to tackle him," said ex-NFL linebacker Matt Millen, overlooking the point that many times he couldn't.

Payton was a 5-foot-11, 200-pound package of dynamite with a running style that saw him blast through would-be tacklers almost as often as he ran around them. He was no dancing back, but one who relished contact. He was "The Man" in the Bears' attack from 1975 through 1987, the king of the offense who could do anything asked of him. He rushed for 16,726 yards on a 4.4-per-carry average for his career, along with catching 492 passes out of the backfield. In all, Payton scored 110 rushing touchdowns and added 15 more on receptions. He gained at least 100 yards rushing in a game 77 times. He retired with the most yards for a career, and currently sits second behind Hall of Famer and Cowboy great Emmit Smith.

It is no surprise that the defenders Payton eluded and fooled respected him greatly.

"When God created a running back, he created Walter Payton," said defensive back Johnny Roland.

Payton was both spectacular and a purist, and was given the perfect nickname based on the plays he pulled off: Sweetness. One of the sweetest of all sights was watching Payton roll out and culminate the halfback option play with a touchdown pass—he completed eight of them. He was elected to the Hall of Fame in 1993.

The star once said, "When you are good at something, you'll tell everyone. When you're great, they'll tell you."

One of the greatest NFL players of all-time was born and grew up in Mississippi. It wasn't as if there was much doubt about Payton's talents coming out of high school. Living in the heart of Southeastern Conference territory, however, a league slow to integrate and even slower to expand its acceptance of multiple African American players, Payton was not offered a scholarship to any of the league's schools. He initially planned to attend NCAA Division I Kansas State, but then changed his mind, deciding instead to stay closer to home and enrolled in-state at Jackson State. Payton's older brother, Eddie, who later played in the NFL, though without making the same impact, also went to school there.

By the time Payton completed his eligibility, he was a hot commodity. The Bears made him their No. 1 selection, and he was taken fourth overall in the 1975 draft. The Bears were in rebuilding mode, and it took time and many other player acquisitions for them to reach their goals. Payton stayed around long enough to become a Super Bowl champ.

At times, Payton, who was known in the locker room as a prankster, could be soft-spoken, but those who knew him best credited him with being a marvelous human being. It came out much later that Payton had his share of family and other problems, as most people do.

He was well into retirement when one day Payton called a press conference in Chicago to announce that he was suffering from an incurable liver ailment. When he passed away at age forty-five in 1999, it was shocking to Bears teammates, as well as the legion of Bears fans and all Chicago residents. The city fell into deep mourning.

From 1970 on, the NFL awarded a Man of the Year Award to a giving player who devoted time and effort to charity and community work. Payton won the award in 1977. After he died, the league changed the name of the prestigious award to the Walter Payton Man of the Year Award.

The first No. 34 was worn for the Bears in 1939, when Jack Torrance pulled it on for the first of two seasons. The 6-foot-5, 285-pound tackle from Louisiana made the Pro Bowl in 1940 and was part of the Bears' title team that year. Torrance's pro football days followed his earlier career as a world-record-setting shot-putter and as a member of the 1936 U.S. Olympic team. He placed fifth in the shot in those Games.

John Federovitch (1941–42) was a two-year offensive lineman after coming from tiny Davis & Elkins College in West Virginia. John Dottley (1951–53) was a fullback with the nickname "Kayo." Joe Marconi (1962–66) was also a fullback, played on the 1963 title team, and went to the 1964 Pro Bowl. Tim Casey (1969) was a linebacker who played three games for Chicago. Fullback Bill Tucker (1971) spent most of his career with San Francisco. Norm Hodgins (1974) recovered three fumbles as a defensive back in his only Bears season.

It wouldn't have taken much for Walter Payton to out-shine all other wearers of No. 34, but once he shed the jersey it was never to be seen running up and down the field again.

NO. 35: RICK CASARES

One thing Rick Casares always relished was his 81-yard touchdown run during his rookie year. It pretty much established him in the NFL as the real deal. The only bad thing about it was that he never had a longer run in his career. Casares was a 6-foot-2, 226-pound bruiser and spent most of his career wearing No. 35 for the Bears between 1955 and 1964.

For a time, Casares looked like the best runner in Chicago history. He gained 5,797 yards on the ground, caught 191 passes, and scored 60 touchdowns during his Bears stay. Casares was a five-time Pro Bowl selection and was on the 1963 Bears title team. In 1956, Casares led the NFL in rushing with 1,126 yards, and was around for the 1956 championship game against the New York Giants, though the Bears lost.

"He was the toughest guy I ever played with," said Mike Ditka, a Bears teammate in the 1960s.

Ditka said he remembered Casares playing on a broken ankle, but that injury actually forced Casares to the sidelines for the 1963 championship victory.

Casares came from Tampa, Florida, and spent most of his life in that area after retiring from football. But he also said, "The best years of my life were in Chicago."

Dick Bassi (1938–39) broke in No. 35 for the Bears and was a one-time all-star (for the Eagles). Lee Artoe (1940–42, 1945) was a tough two-way tackle and kicker, and a three-time Pro Bowl selection. He made numerous memorable plays, often involving contact with opponents, but also scored a touchdown on a 50-yard fumble recovery in the 1942 championship game versus the Washington Redskins. It was the Bears' only touchdown.

Bill Steinkemper (1943) was a Bears tackle for just one season, but was part of a title team. Fred Hartman (1947) was a tackle who appeared in 11 games. Paul Stenn (1948–51) played tackle. Rick Casares took over No. 35 after Stenn.

Jim Harrison (1971–74) rushed for 1,099 yards in his career. Roland Harper (1975–82) was a very dependable fullback, opening holes for Walter Payton and even rushing for 992 yards in one season. He did later get into some trouble with the law as a businessman. Mike Hintz (1987) briefly made the grade as a defensive back out of NCAA Division III Wisconsin-Platteville.

Neal Anderson was a No. 1 draft choice drafted out of the University of Florida to replace Walter Payton. Of course nobody could replace Walter Payton, but the 5-foot-11, 210-pounder was an all-around excellent player for the Bears between 1986 and 1993. Anderson made four Pro Bowls and scored 71 touchdowns, 51 of them on the ground while gaining 6,166 yards rushing. He also caught 302 passes. Anderson topped 1,000 yards rushing in a season three times. Darned fine totals. When Anderson signed a four-year contract extension, he said he planned to retire after eight years as a back with the team. Still, he might have played longer except for injuries, which essentially made the retirement decision for him.

James Burton (1994–97) was a defensive back out of Fresno State. The 6-foot-2, 221-pound Anthony Thomas had the makings of a long-term star running back for the Bears when he arrived in 2001 . . . but he was done with Chicago after 2004, despite turning in some terrific showings. Known as the "A-Train," Thomas was the NFC Offensive Rookie of the Year when he ran for 1,183 yards that season. It coincided with a surprising Bears 13–3 season no one saw coming, and Thomas was a big part of that success. He then rushed for 721 yards and 1,024 over the next two years, but lost his job and moved on from Chicago to Dallas.

Todd Johnson also was decked out in 32. Ade Jimoh (2007) was a cornerback and special teams guy who broke his collarbone before the end of his sole season with the Bears.

Zackary Bowman (2008–11) was one of a small number of pro football players to come out of Anchorage, Alaska, and did some good work for the Bears. Bowman got his chance to move up from the taxi squad when three cornerbacks were injured going into a game. He took advantage of his chance. While Bowman's best years were with the Bears, he also saw time with a couple of other franchises. In all he intercepted 13 passes and was in on 200 tackles.

Runner Jacquizz Rodgers (2015) got into only five games before breaking his arm. Raheem Mostert (2016) is a running back currently with the San Francisco 49ers. Johnthan Banks (2016) is a cornerback.

NO. 36: AT LEAST YOU HEARD OF MAURICE DOUGLASS

Bears fans may not know that safety Maurice Douglass spells his last name with a double 's,' but at least they remember his name from his 1986–94 stay with the team. That is probably not so for almost every other Bear that ever pulled on No. 36. Let's just say it has not been a Hall of Fame position.

Douglass is from Muncie, Indiana, and played college ball at Kentucky. Chicago made him an eighth-round draft choice in 1986. He played all but his final two seasons in the NFL with the Bears, moving on to the New York Giants to wrap up his pro career.

In college, Douglass intercepted a pass for the Wildcats on his first play, the equivalent of a running back scoring a touchdown on his first carry. Douglass was one of a herd of defensive backs brought in his rookie year and, although coach Mike Ditka liked him, for his first few years Douglass had to scrap and hustle constantly to find a place on the roster. One thing he was known for during his Bears days was dressing in a flashy style.

Despite his slow start, Douglass played 139 games in the league. In a nice, symmetrical story, Douglass returned to coach his high school football team in 2001.

You practically have to be George Halas, or one of the greatest Bears students of all time, to recall much about the other players combined who have worn No. 36 for the team.

Stuart Clarkson (1942) was the first Bear to display the number, but he also wore No. 31. Bill Steinkemper (1942–43) also wore No. 35. Fred Mundee (1943–45) was a center who stuck around for three years. John Morton (1945) was a linebacker. Tom Farris (1946–47) was born in Casper, Wyoming, came out of the University of Wisconsin, and played quarterback for the Bears, throwing one touchdown pass in his career. Bill DeCorrevont (1948–49) was a famous Chicago high school star who participated in a highly hyped Christmas charity game in 1937 that drew an astounding 120,000 people to Soldier Field. He also played for Northwestern and won an NFL title with the Chicago Cardinals in 1947, but had limited opportunities with the Bears at the end of his pro career.

Merrill Douglas (1958–60) played for several teams and rushed for 213 yards. He later spent 11 years as an NFL official. Running back J. D. Smith (1961) got into three games. Apparently no one wanted No. 36 for a while after that, because Ron Copeland (1969), eight years later, was the next guy to wear it. He died at age twenty-eight of heart disease.

Then followed a period where most of the No. 36 players handed it off almost annually. Roger Lawson (1972–73) was a running back. Perry Williams (1974) was a star at Purdue and most of his pro career was with Green Bay, only coming through Chicago at the end. Tom Donchez (1975) was a running back. Larry Schreiber (1976) spent most of his time at running back for the San Francisco 49ers. Wentford Gaines (1978–80) was a defensive back and return man who constantly battled injuries with the Steelers and Bears. Maurice Douglass came in and held on to No. 36 longer than anyone else. Running back Frank Harris (1987) was not Franco Harris, gaining only 23 yards.

The defensive back career of Markus Paul (1989–93) had him starting 15 games for the Bears. However, as a multi-team strength coach from 1998 to the present, Paul has worked with five Super Bowl champions. Cornerback Anthony Marshall (1994–97) managed five years in the big leagues with three teams, plus a cameo with the Memphis Maniax of the XFL. Ray Austin (1998–99) was another defensive back who played four years in the NFL and a year in the XFL.

Stanley Pritchett (2001–03) squeezed out nine seasons in the NFL as a fullback. Jerrell Pippens (2004) was a cornerback and went on to acting. Brandon McGowan (2005–08) also played for Bears in college—the Maine Black Bears. In 2007 he was in on 80 tackles for the Chicago Bears and then played for the New England Patriots. Josh Bullocks (2009–10) had better performances in New Orleans. Josh's twin brother Daniel also played in the NFL.

Sean Cattouse (2013) was a safety. Ahmad Dixon (2014) managed to sign five times with four teams in one season as a safety, including the Bears, Miami Dolphins, Dallas Cowboys, and Minnesota Vikings (twice). He was cut by Dallas after being late to team meetings twice. The Bears signed Dixon off the Vikings' practice squad, but did not keep him long either.

Sherrod Martin (2015) did much better with the Carolina Panthers. Safety DeAndre Houston-Carson (2016) is trying to get his career started.

What kind of prize might be offered to a person who could identify every one of the Bears players who wore No. 36?

NO. 37: TONY PARRISH AND JASON MCKIE

In a wasteland of Bears stars who have worn No. 37, only two players really stand out. Put it this way: No. 37 is not going to be retired any time soon in Chicago. There is actually a good chance that fellow members of the club of wearers of 37 haven't heard of each other. Lot of one-and-dones here.

Tony Parrish did some damage at safety between 1998 and 2001. It's just that he did much more of it with other teams. The 6 foot, 210-pound Parrish was a star at the University of Washington, and the Bears jump-started his pro career. He did good work for Chicago, but shined even more with the San Francisco 49ers.

Parrish was not only respected by his teammates, winning the Bears' Brian Piccolo Award, but made 111 tackles as a rookie. He topped 100 tackles a year for his first three seasons in Chicago and made as many as 14 tackles in a single game. During his career, Parrish was in on 719 tackles, grabbed 30 interceptions, and forced 11 fumbles. He was known around the league as a dude who hit hard.

Injuries slowed Parrish at the end of his NFL career, but demonstrating his passion for the game he made a 2009 comeback with the Las Vegas Locomotives of the United Football League. It was no mere cameo appearance, either, with Parrish being one of the most visible players on the club and a key figure on a championship team.

Fullback Jason McKie's use of No. 37 occurred between 2003 and 2009. McKie was an undrafted free agent let go by both the Philadelphia Eagles and Dallas Cowboys when he found a home in Chicago. A 5-foot-11, 247-pound battering ram in the backfield, McKie came along at a time when fullbacks hardly ever touched the ball on a handoff and were relied on chiefly as blockers. That's why he only had 29 carries in his entire career. But he was a rock.

During his years in the league and in retirement, McKie has been widely appreciated for his community service. He started the Jason McKie Foundation, which provides educational and health services to those connected to the military.

Take away Parrish and McKie, and No. 37 has not had such a glorious past.

The first season anyone wore No. 37 for the Bears was 1934, when Ed Aspatore borrowed it. An offensive lineman, he didn't keep it long. The real first name of Young Bussey (1940–41) was Ruey. As a youth he excelled in a laundry list of sports, including water polo and wrestling. A member of the 1941 Bears championship team as a backup quarterback, Bussey was killed in action in the Philippines during World War II as a member of the navy.

James Logan (1942–43) was a lightweight (190 pounds) guard who was part of the 1943 title team. Bernie Digris (1943) played two games as a lineman. The Bears squeezed Bob Steuber (1943) into one game at halfback. Bob Masters (1943–44) was a running back. Edgar Jones (1945) also wore No. 27. Charles Mitchell (1945) was a defensive back out of the University of Tulsa. Broughton Williams (1947) was an end who signed with the Bears after starring for the University of Florida and gaining the nickname "Brute."

John O'Quinn (1950–51) was nicknamed "Red" and intercepted three passes in his first season in Chicago after being drafted out of Wake Forest. He later was a huge receiving star for Montreal in the Canadian Football League, grabbing 499 balls. O'Quinn ended up becoming general manager of two teams in the North.

George Youngblood (1969) was a defensive back. Rich Coady (1970–74) was a center who dabbled at tight end and whose son, Rich Jr., also played in the NFL. Conrad Graham (1973) was a Bears draft pick who hardly played because of injuries. Cid Edwards (1975) was a running back. A star running back at Georgia, Willie McClendon (1979–82) rushed for 369 yards total in Chicago.

Darryl Clark (1987) gained 11 yards rushing in three games. Maurice Douglass (1986–94) snuck in there and wore No. 37 when he wasn't wearing No. 36. Pat Eilers (1995) also wore No. 25. Keshon Johnson (1995) also wore No. 25. Tony Parrish followed in No. 37. Damon Moore (2002) was a safety out of Ohio State who made bad news for abandoning a puppy. Jason McKie followed him. Anthony Walters (2011–13) was twice a Bear, but part of the time was on the practice squad. Bryce Callahan (2015–16) is a cornerback out of Rice.

NO. 38: DANIEAL MANNING

Everyone got along pretty well with Danieal Manning in Chicago as soon as they figured out how to spell his first name. No. 38 also did well on the field in Chicago as a hard-hitting defensive back and a sometimes-spectacular return man.

Manning (2006–10) was from Texas, and he came to the Bears as a second-round draft pick out of Abilene Christian. The best years of Manning's career were with the Bears, although he also signed with the Houston Texans twice—that Texas thing.

Overall, Manning was involved in 552 tackles during his NFL career and ripped off 11 interceptions. In 2017, he returned to Abilene Christian as a coach.

The first player to wear No. 38 for the Bears was Roger Ashmore in 1927, at a time when few numbers ran higher than the 20s. Ashmore, whose real first name was Marion, was an offensive lineman who actually won a championship with Green Bay in 1929. Sam Francis (1937–38) was a powerful runner at Nebraska, took fourth in the Olympic shot put in 1936, and was the NFL's No. 1 draft pick in 1937 by Philadelphia. He coached Kansas State one season, but finished 0–10.

Charles Apolskis (1938–39) also wore No. 26. Bill Milner (1947–49) was an offensive lineman. Guard Ed Bradley (1950, 1952) stood 6 feet tall and weighed 212 pounds out of Wake Forest. Bill Brown (1961) became an outstanding fullback with the Minnesota Vikings. Ray Ogden (1969–71) was at the end of his career when he joined the Bears as a wide receiver. Dave Juenger (1973) played one game. Running back Lakei Heimuli (1987) may have gone to high school in Hawaii, but he was the first Tongan to play in the NFL.

John Hardy (1991) was a defensive back who played in four games. Running back Tim Worley (1993–94) recorded more notable stats in Pittsburgh. Mike Faulkerson Dulaney (1995–97) was a 237-pound fullback.

The 252-pound Robert Chancey (1998) played minor league baseball instead of going to college and hadn't played football since high school when the San Diego Chargers signed him. Chancey showed up for his cousin's pro day and ran some drills.

Eric Joyce (2002) was a defensive back. Danieal Manning took over No. 38 and then passed it to Zack Bowman, who also wore No. 35. Adrian Amos (2015–16) is a safety out of Penn State.

NO. 39: CURTIS ENIS

All Time No. 39	
Player	Years
George Gulyanics	(1947–52)
Pete Perini	(1953–54)
J. D. Smith	(1956)
Ralph Anderson	(1958)
John Adams	(1959–62)
Phil Clark	(1970)
Reggie Sanderson	(1973)
Robin Earl	(1977–82)
Al Wolden	(1987)
Jeremy Lincoln	(1992–95)
Curtis Enis	(1998–2000)
Reggie Austin	(2000–02)
Travis Coleman	(2002–03)
Lousaka Polite	(2007)
Derrick Martin	(2013)
Al Louis-Jean	(2014)
Jacoby Glenn	(2015)

Man, were the Bears excited when they selected Curtis Enis with their No. 1 pick, fifth overall, in the 1998 NFL Draft. Enis was such a star at Penn State that the Bears had to think their running game was set for a decade. Instead, it sadly turned out it wasn't even set for 10 minutes, nevermind 10 years.

Enis was a Parade All-American in high school in Ohio, and an All-American in college for Penn State where, in his third season, he rushed for 1,363 yards and 19 touchdowns. Who wouldn't have been excited about adding the widely admired player to the roster?

Only things went wrong from the start. Enis held out for a richer contract in negotiations, a process that meant he missed nearly a month of training camp. Then, as soon as he reported, he injured a knee. That was foreshadowing. Enis was with the Bears from 1998 to 2000, but he was rarely at 100 percent. He retired with just 1,497 yards gained on the ground on a puny 3.3 yards gained per carry average.

No one wore No. 39 for the Bears until 1947, when George Gulyanics obtained its use and kept it until 1952. Gulyanics had a fascinating life. He was from Indiana and is in his Mishawaka High School Hall of Fame. He was a Golden Gloves fighter in Indiana, winning a welterweight title and then attended Alabama, playing football there before serving in World War II.

Gulyanics spent six seasons with the Bears as a running back and punter. He gained 2,081 yards and scored 19 touchdowns, compiling a 4.1-yard average per carry. Gulyanics so impressed onlookers that he was called "Little Bronko" after the revered Bronko Nagurski. But he truly excelled in the kicking game, averaging 44.5 yards per boot. Back in Mishawaka, Gulyanics was elected town assessor and the job became his second career. He retained the position for thirty-two years.

Pete Perini (1953–54), a fullback from Ohio State, inherited No. 39 from Gulyanics. J. D. Smith played six games in 1956 and later played for the San

Francisco 49ers and Dallas Cowboys. Offensive end Ralph Anderson (1958) was in Chicago briefly, found success with the Los Angeles Chargers, and died tragically due to diabetes at age twenty-three. Anderson had jumped to the new American Football League team and caught 44 passes. An angry George Halas felt he was in breach of contract and sued the Chargers for $300,000, claiming they "induced" Anderson to jump. John Adams (1959–62) was a backup running back.

Phil Clark (1970) was a safety out of Northwestern. Reggie Sanderson (1973) had three carries in two games. Robin Earl (1977–82) was a fullback-blocker and tight end who occasionally thrust himself into the limelight with five touchdowns. After retirement, Earl was active as a broadcaster while working as a financial consultant. Al Wolden (1987) was a 6-foot-3, 223-pound running back who played in just three games. Jeremy Lincoln (1992–95) made it through eight years as an NFL defensive back after a highlight film moment in college at the University of Tennessee when he blocked a Notre Dame field-goal try with his rear end.

Lincoln passed No. 39 to Curtis Enis, who was succeeded by Reggie Austin (2000–02). Austin was a backup cornerback who intercepted two passes. Travis Coleman (2002–03) kept coming close to a breakthrough with the Bears, but spent most of his football time seeing the world for such squads as the Berlin Thunder in NFL Europe and with the New Orleans Voodoo in the Arena Football League.

Lousaka Polite (2007) played five games for the Bears. Derrick Martin (2013) gained notice at the University of Wyoming, but has been bounced from team to team as a special teams guy or backup. He only got into seven games, but had a tackle for each appearance. Somehow, though, Martin was fortunate enough to land with other teams at the right time and he has two Super Bowl rings. Al Louis-Jean (2014) was barely active with the Bears or other NFL teams, so he joined Ottawa in the Canadian Football League. The light, 6-foot, 176-pound cornerback Jacoby Glenn (2015) intercepted one pass for Chicago.

No. 39 is still looking for greatness.

NO. 40: THE GREAT GALE SAYERS

Gale Sayers dazzled.

The way he ran, the way he saw the field, the way he made things happen with his smarts, instinct, and speed, he produced riveting theatre. Sayers was the type of player who yanked people out of their seats in spontaneous gestures of excitement. When the fans saw No. 40 break into the clear, they were drawn to him, ached to see the next move a little bit better. They wanted to get closer.

Yes, Sayers dazzled. Until he could not do so any more.

The wonder of Gale Sayers was his brilliance on the field. The tragedy of Gale Sayers was how swiftly his brilliance dimmed because his knees were wrecked. People sometimes mention Sayers was the youngest player ever inducted into the Pro Football Hall of Fame as if it is some special achievement. No. The reason Sayers was inducted at thirty-four, at such a young age, is that he was eligible. He was eligible because he had to give up pro football at a younger age: twenty-nine.

Sayers's body of work was so impressive in such a short time that he was selected even though he did not play nearly as long as many of the other stars. If he had played at full strength for perhaps twelve years, then he would likely still be acclaimed the greatest halfback of all time. Given his limited time in the spotlight he still makes the discussion, but loses out on longevity to the Walter Paytons and Emmitt Smiths. Fullback Jim Brown is a topic for another day.

Born in Wichita, Kansas, Sayers went to high school in Omaha, Nebraska. His college days were spent at Kansas and the 6-foot, 198-pound running back was chosen by the Bears with their No. 1 pick in 1965. The entirety of Sayers's pro career was encapsulated between 1965 and 1971 and he wasn't even healthy for that limited period.

Certainly, though, Sayers was at his finest as a rookie in 1965 when he won the NFL's Rookie of the Year honor. That was the first of his five straight All-Pro selections as well. Sayers scored 22 touchdowns that rookie season, at the time a league record. He scored running from scrimmage, on passes, on punt and kickoff returns. When Sayers wound up for a return and skirted the first wave of defenders and out-ran the second, it was breathtaking to inhale his shiftiness and watch him elude the entirety of the other team.

Sayers scored six touchdowns in a game, equaling the longstanding league record. George Halas was so thrilled by Sayers's achievements that he compared him to Red Grange. In his second season, Sayers won the league rushing title with 1,231 yards, returned kicks at a rate of 31.2 yards a crack, and set an all-purpose yards record.

Even after Sayers injured his right knee, he tortured himself in rehab and returned to rush for more than 1,000 yards again to win the NFL's Comeback Player of the Year Award. Something had definitely been lost, however. When Sayers also tore up his left knee, the path was paved to retirement because he could no longer cut as effectively and his speed was affected.

"I had a career that was very short, but it had a lot of thrills," Sayers said.

In later years, Sayers worked in sports administration and private business. In early 2017, it was announced that Sayers, then seventy-three, was suffering from dementia and was slowing down in another way.

"I don't care to be remembered as a man who scored six touchdowns in a game," Sayers said. "I want to be remembered as a winner in life."

Before Sayers was handed No. 40, a handful of other players wore it. Al Campana (1950–52) debuted the number. He was also a running back. Frank Dempsey (1950–53) switched positions often on offense and defense, and then had a more successful career playing in Canada. Stan Wallace (1954–58) was a first-round pick out of Illinois and intercepted 10 passes for the Bears. Don Mullins (1961–62) predated Sayers in No. 40 and played 13 games as a defensive back.

Sayers had his turn with the number, but there was some lag time in the front office in deciding to retire No. 40 to honor him. The number was not used, but in 1987 defensive back Steve Trimble was handed the number for his one season with the Bears. That was it. No. 40 went out of business for Sayers's sake.

NO. 41: THE BRIAN PICCOLO STORY

All Time No. 41	
Player	Years
John Schiechi	(1945–46)
Jack Matheson	(1947)
Alf Bauman	(1948–50)
Babe Dimancheff	(1952)
Harland Carl	(1956)
Brian Piccolo**	(1965–69)

Retired for Piccolo

In one of the most unusual cases of a number being retired by a professional sports franchise in the United States, the Chicago Bears retired No. 41 in honor of Brian Piccolo, a fullback of the 1960s who did not set records or make all-star teams, but whose death affected so many others.

A cheerful man who was a hard-nosed football player, Piccolo was born in 1943 in Pittsfield, Massachusetts, and was a 6-foot, 205-pound running back at Wake Forest. Wake was only one of two schools to offer Piccolo a scholarship. Piccolo was a fine college player, being named a second-team All-American in 1964.

Although he wanted to keep playing football, Piccolo was not drafted by any NFL team when he graduated. A tryout with the Bears got Piccolo signed as a free agent, but assigned to the taxi squad his first year. He kept fighting, earned the right to wear No. 41 regularly, and became a well-liked player.

Piccolo and star running back Gale Sayers became particularly close. During this era of pro football, players still shared hotel rooms on the road. Sayers and Piccolo became roommates simply because they both played in the backfield. This mix was a departure from the time's general practice, as Sayers was black and Piccolo was white. Eventually, this arrangement— at the height of the Civil Rights movement in the United States—gained national attention, although it never fazed the two men.

Piccolo became a regular by 1967, although it was Sayers who still ran the ball most of the time. Slightly more than halfway through the 1969 season, Piccolo began having difficulties breathing. It came as a shock to coaches and teammates when he asked to be taken out of a game. That was the beginning of the end, leading to a cancer diagnosis that took his life in 1970.

A time of great turmoil followed the doctors' first reading of the situation as Piccolo showed signs of recovery and then relapsed. By then, Sayers had suffered his first major knee injury. But he rebuilt it to the point that in 1969 he rushed for more than 1,000 yards. He was awarded the George S. Halas Award for Most Courageous Player. When Sayers stepped to the microphone for an acceptance speech, what he said silenced the room. He explained about his friend and teammate Brian Piccolo lying in a hospital room and told the listeners that it was Piccolo, not him, who deserved this award. In one of the most moving and memorable speeches by an athlete, Sayers said, "I love Brian Piccolo, and I'd like all of you to love him, too. Tonight, when you hit your knees to pray, please ask God to love him, too."

Piccolo died a month later at age twenty-six.

In 1971, the made-for-television movie *Brian's Song* aired. It was partially based on Sayers's autobiography, *I Am Third*. The story of Sayers's and Piccolo's friendship and Piccolo's noble battle for life was a sensation. Across the nation, grown men cried. *Brian's Song* is one of the most revered sports films of all time.

By the time Brian Piccolo had been handed No. 41, it had been worn by other Bears. John Schiechl (1945–46) was the first. He was a center out of Santa Clara. End Jack Matheson (1947) played in three games with one catch. Defensive tackle Alf Bauman (1948–50) grew up in Chicago and played for Northwestern. The given name of Babe Dimancheff (1952) was Boris. After retiring, he moved into coaching and about fifteen years later became a Bears assistant coach. Harland Carl (1956) was the last player to wear No. 41 before Piccolo. He was rarely used and then the number went into hibernation for a decade.

Piccolo's name isn't on many all-time lists, but the story of his life made him unforgettable.

NO. 42: SID LUCKMAN

All Time No. 42	
Player	Years
Sid Luckman**	(1939–50)

"Hall of Fame, Retired for Luckman

Sid Luckman came out of Columbia University and became the Chicago Bears' greatest quarterback. He held down No. 42 from 1939 to 1950. Intriguingly, he was the first and last Bears player to wear that number.

After Luckman's tenture leading the Bears to three NFL titles in the 1940s, George Halas made the decision to retire Luckman's number. His instincts were correct. Neither he nor the Bears ever really had a player like Luckman again. There have been Bears quarterbacks that had better individual seasons for more yards and for more touchdowns, but there is no doubt Luckman had the finest quarterback career for the team.

The 6-foot, 197-pound Luckman was a five-time first-team All-Pro and also a one-time second-team All-Pro in the 1940s. His main competition for that honor was the Washington Redskins' Sammy Baugh. Luckman led the league in passing three times and won the Most Valuable Player Award in 1943. The Bears won four championships, in 1940, 1941, 1943, and 1946 with Luckman as signal-caller

On November 14, 1943, Luckman became the first NFL quarterback to throw for seven touchdowns in one game. He also threw for 433 yards. That day the Bears beat the New York Giants, 56–7. New York was actually honoring Luckman that day as a native of the city. His greatest day on the field turned into a better present than anyone anticipated.

"It was one of those days when the good Lord just embraces you," Luckman said. "That's the only way I can explain it."

The seven TDs in a single game is still a record, but it has been tied by seven others over the last seventy-four years. George Blanda, Y. A. Tittle, Peyton Manning, and Drew Brees are among the other quarterbacks who tied the mark.

Ironically, at first Luckman did not want to play pro football. George Halas wooed him hard and talked him into signing. The two men developed close ties and Halas later said Luckman was like a son to him. After his playing days were over, Luckman briefly coached full time in Chicago, but over time was always on call if Halas needed some help.

"You know how George is," Luckman said. "He won't take no for an answer. I am glad I went with the Bears. Those thirty-two years I spent with Halas, twelve as a player and twenty as a coach, were very rewarding."

Quarterbacks did not throw the pass nearly as often during Luckman's playing days, but he did throw for as many as 28 touchdowns in one season and lead the NFL in passing yards three times. His career high in yards was 2,712 in 1947.

Luckman is enshrined in both the College Football Hall of Fame and the Pro Football Hall of Fame.

NO. 43: JIM DOOLEY, PLAYER AND COACH

A solid player as an end for the Bears between 1952 and 1961 when he wore No. 43, Jim Dooley moved almost immediately onto George Halas's coaching staff after his playing days were over. Halas was aging and, although he had coached the Bears more or less non-stop since the inception of the franchise in 1920, there was always speculation about when he would retire to the front office for good and who would replace him. Dooley was on hand and on staff.

Dooley was a 6-foot-4, 198-pound receiver out of the University of Miami, a first-round draft pick in 1952. Much later, Elaine Dooley, Jim's wife, recounted the story of his signing with the team. She said Jim Dooley asked Halas about his signing bonus. Halas, notoriously cheap when it came to player salary demands, replied, "Your bonus is that you're drafted for the Chicago Bears!"

Mostly an offensive end during his career, Dooley played more on defense as a rookie and intercepted five passes. He made the switch to the other side of the ball in 1953, and emerged as one of Chicago's top threats in the ensuing years.

A steady receiver who caught 35 or so passes per season, Dooley did miss time with the Bears in the mid-1950s when he was in the Air Force. He returned to the team as the 1956 season was winding down to play in a few games. That gave him the opportunity to compete in the NFL title game that season, one the Bears lost dismally to the New York Giants.

Dooley caught 211 passes in his pro career and was barely away from the field before signing on as an assistant coach to Halas. At first Dooley was the receivers coach, which was an obvious match. But he quickly became the team's defensive coordinator, a job with much more responsibility. He came up with the defensive scheme that enabled the Bears to better defend against the pass in obvious throwing circumstances. His creation was later called "the nickel" defense because of its use of five defensive backs.

It may well be that Halas appreciated that innovative thinking, as it led to his anointing Dooley as the Bears head coach to succeed him. Dooley was just thirty-eight when he took command and led the Bears though the 1971 season. However, he did not fare nearly as well as his old boss. Chicago went 20–36 with him at the helm before he was fired.

Later, after incurring some financial problems, he went to work for Sid Luckman's business. At various times over the years Dooley returned to football as an assistant coach for various teams. Mike Ditka hired Dooley as a film scout and he played a part in the Bears' winning the 1986 Super Bowl. He died in 2008 at age seventy-seven.

"The Chicago Bears was his life until he died," Dooley's wife Elaine said of her husband's passion for the team.

Dooley was actually the first Bear to wear No. 43, which he did from 1952 to 1954 and again when he came out of the air force in 1956 until retirement in 1962.

Larry Glueck (1963–65) was next in 43. He was a defensive back who later was head coach at Fordham University and worked as an assistant at various other schools. Bob Jones (1967–68) was a receiver out of San Diego State who caught three passes for Chicago. George Farmer (1970–75) put some time in at 43. He caught 119 passes in the NFL after being a member of the 1969 UCLA NCAA basketball champions under John Wooden.

Earl Douthitt (1975) came out of Iowa and got into nine games. Craig Clemons (1972–77) wore No. 43 for a while. Clemons was a first-team All-American for Iowa and intercepted nine passes with the Bears. Mike Ulmer (1980) was a three-game defensive back. Emery Moorehead (1981–88) wore more than one number, but he played hard in all his uniforms as a tough tight end. Moorehead caught 224 passes in 12 seasons and was a member of the 1986 Super Bowl champs. His son Aaron also won a Super Bowl with the Indianapolis Colts, the first father-son duo to do so.

Cornerback Walt Williams (1982–83) played the last seasons of his career with the Bears, mostly as a backup. Lorenzo Lynch (1987–90) was a cornerback who played 11 seasons in the NFL and made 583 tackles. He is also the uncle of well-known running back Marshawn Lynch. Trevor Cobb (1994) won the Doak Walker Award as the finest running back in college while at Rice. He gained nearly 5,000 yards on the ground, but only got into one game with the Bears. Running back Dennis Lundy (1995) played just part of one season with the Bears after starring at nearby Northwestern. However, he got into trouble for dealing with gamblers while with the Wildcats.

Defensive back Mike Green (2000–05) was one of those infamous last-draft-choices in the NFL draft who forevermore are labeled "Mr. Irrelevant." He was the 254th player taken, the Bears' seventh-round draft pick, out of Northwestern State. Mike Green's career in Chicago overlapped several years with Mike Brown's, who was chosen in the same draft. Green fooled the experts and had a nine-year NFL career with 426 tackles.

Josh Gattis (2007–08) took over No. 43 after Green, but not for long. He now coaches at Penn State. The 5-foot-11, 242-pound Jason Davis (2008) came out of Illinois as a fullback, and scrambled to get a long-term foothold in the NFL, but could not. However, he was very active in charitable causes, especially those aimed at youths. Troy Nolan (2012) was a safety. Tony Fiammetta (2013–14) was a 6-foot, 250-pound fullback whose Bears stay was shortened by hamstring injuries. Thomas Gafford (2015) is a long snapper, and that specialty has taken him on a tour of NFL teams.

Linebacker Danny Mason (2016) had a revolving door relationship with the Bears, signed and released, assigned to the practice squad, cut and re-signed. In between, Joique Bell (2016) got a sniff of wearing No. 43, but he was off to the Detroit Lions at the end of the year.

NO. 44: TERRY SCHMIDT'S DIVERSE LIFE

Life began for Terry Schmidt in Columbus, Indiana. He was an All-American cornerback in college for Ball State, located in Muncie, Indiana. After that, it is unclear if he ever spent time as a Hoosier again.

Schmidt went into the NFL in 1974 and played two years with the New Orleans Saints before joining the Bears in 1976. No. 44 spent the rest of his NFL career with Chicago, retiring in 1984.

The 6-foot, 177-pounder grabbed 26 interceptions in 143 games in the pros, three of them run back for touchdowns.

After leaving football behind, Schmidt enrolled in dental school in Chicago and after graduation went to work for Veterans Administration hospitals, which has taken him to spots around the United States. Schmidt said he always wanted to be a dentist, and planned for his second career long before giving up football.

A retired commander in the U.S. Naval Reserve, through his faith Schmidt and his wife Nancy took on tasks around the world, devoted to helping the less fortunate with their dental problems. He has made numerous trips to visit those in Africa and South America as part of his evangelical missions. The trips involve free dental care and spreading the word of God.

In 2012, Schmidt joined the lawsuit of former NFL players brought against the league because of concussions. At the time he said he was reluctant to do so, although he had had some short-term memory loss, but was motivated by things that happened to former teammates, including Dave Duerson, who committed suicide and then donated his brain to science.

"What bothers me is when guys get to the desperation point where they take their own life," Schmidt said.

The first No. 44 for the Bears was Paul Goebel in 1925, which was an unusually high number in those days. An All-American at Michigan, Goebel was an All-Pro end for the Columbus Tigers before joining the Bears. Later a politician, Goebel was a three-term mayor of Grand Rapids, Michigan, and even advised a young man named Gerald Ford to run for Congress. That worked out for the future president of the United States.

Lineman Earl Evans (1926–29) kept the early No. 44 streak going after he came out of Harvard. The 6-foot-1, 230-pound Ray Richards (1933–36) came out of the University of Nebraska as an offensive lineman. In the 1950s, he made several assistant coaching stops in the NFL, with the Los Angeles Rams, Baltimore Colts, Chicago Cardinals, and Green Bay Packers. Bob Margarita (1944–46) probably took some ribbing about his name— especially in bars. A Boston guy, Margarita was an All-American running back at Brown University in Providence, Rhode Island, and spent his NFL career with the Bears, including in 1945 when he rushed for a team-high 497 yards. He later coached Georgetown University before the school shelved intercollegiate football.

Frank Minini (1947–49) was a running back out of San Jose State. Frank Szymanski (1949) took over 44 from Minini. A center out of Notre Dame, Szymanski once testified under oath that he was the greatest player at that position the Fighting Irish ever had. The anecdote was contained in collections of humor. W.D. "Dub" Garrett (1950) played both ways on the line.

Garry Lyle (1968–74) predated Terry Schmidt wearing No. 44. Lyle intercepted 12 passes and made four fumble recoveries as a safety. His son Keith also played in the NFL, collecting 31 interceptions and winning a Super Bowl with the St. Louis Rams. Mike Stoops (1987) is from the well-known college coaching family, and briefly passed through Chicago as a player. Todd Krumm (1988) was a free-agent defensive back signee.

Fullback Bob Christian (1992–94) out of Northwestern spent 11 seasons in the NFL and caught 230 passes. He later became a flight instructor. Running back Michael Hicks (1996–97) got into seven games for the Bears. Curtis Enis (1998–2000) also wore No. 39. Brock Forsey (2003) was a former Boise State star whose best day for the Bears was a 134-yard rushing game filling in for the ill Anthony Thomas.

Cameron Worrell (2003–06) also wore No. 24. Defensive back Kevin Payne (2007–09) made 88 tackles for the Bears in 2008, but was injured in both seasons sandwiching that fine season. Tyler Clutts (2011) played pro ball in eight cities, but performed admirably for Chicago as a long snapper during his one season with the Bears.

Jeremy Cain (2004–05, 2013–14), a long snapper and a linebacker, left more autographs on contracts in the Bears' front office than anyone who did not spend a virtual lifetime with the team, often being cut and re-signed. Antoine Smith (2015) is a former Florida State running back who has had close-call short terms with eight different pro rosters. Linebacker Nick Kwiatkoski (2016) made 44 tackles in his first year with the Bears.

NO. 45: GARY FENCIK

Certainly one of the finest and most important defensive backs in Chicago Bears history, Gary Fencik came out of the Ivy League when few players did so. He did not major in football at Yale, but later put his degree to use in the financial world.

From 1976 to 1987, Fencik was a key member of perhaps the greatest defense of all time. He was a starting safety on the Bears' Super Bowl champs of 1985 and also one of the fun-loving players who participated in the making of the Super Bowl Shuffle record and video. He and defensive backfield partner Doug Plank were known as "The Hit Men."

The 6-foot-1, 194-pound Fencik, who was born in Chicago, definitely did an enormous amount of hitting on the gridiron. He contributed to 1,102 tackles during his 12 seasons with the Bears, collected 38 interceptions, and was chosen for the Pro Bowl in 1980 and 1981.

After football, Fencik earned a masters degree and, while spending most of his time in the financial world, also invested some time as a pro football television commentator.

"I still have fun," Fencik once said, comparing the business world to football. "But nothing will ever replace the excitement of football."

In 2016, Fencik announced that, upon his death, he planned to donate his brain to science, to the Boston University research program that studies the effects of concussions on football players. He said it wouldn't make any difference to him since he plans on cremation.

Most assuredly, Fencik was known as a feared hitter when he played. He also notes that the game was different compared to the present day where so many rules have been installed that change the nature of tackling. No one told him to ease up or alter his style.

"You dive," he said. "What's first? Your head. If you lower your head, you'll break your neck. You're hurling your body and all you want to do is get them down."

The first Bear to wear No. 45 was Walt Stickel (1946–49), who was an offensive lineman. Gerald Weatherly (1950, 1952–54) was a linebacker who went by the nickname "Bones." Billy Stone (1951–54) came from Peoria, Illinois, and played for Bradley before gaining 907 yards rushing. African American Bobby Watkins (1955–57) was a running back at Ohio State, and Woody Hayes was criticized for recruiting him. Watkins helped lead the Buckeyes to a national title before turning pro.

Rocky Ryan (1958) was from the community of Tolono, Illinois, population 2,700, and played in a Rose Bowl with the University of Illinois before going pro. A fight between Ryan and an Iowa fan in 1952 that resulted in the fan's jaw being broken by a punch led to the suspension of Illinois-Iowa games for fifteen years.

Cornerback Don Bishop (1959) played just one game for the Bears, but made the Pro Bowl as a member of the Dallas Cowboys. Dick Gordon (1965–71) was only a seventh-round pick out of Michigan State, but led the NFL in catches in 1970 with 71 while gaining 1,026 yards and was selected to two Pro Bowls during his career, one of those for the Bears. In all, Gordon, who was 5-foot-11 and 190 pounds, caught 243 passes with 36 touchdowns.

Gary Fencik followed wearing No. 45 and he had to be good to in any way overshadow Gordon. Most of the career of Craig Heyward (1993) played out elsewhere. He was memorably nicknamed "Ironhead" in his youth, and was a monster of a fullback, topping 265 pounds. He made one Pro Bowl in 1995. Sadly, Heyward died at age thirty-nine after a second bout with cancer. His son Cameron currently plays for the Pittsburgh Steelers.

Cornerback Tony Stargell (1997) played eight seasons in the NFL, the last one with the Bears. Scott Dragos (2001–02) was a two-year backup fullback, weighing in excess of 250 pounds. No. 45 was just one of the numbers Cameron Worrell sampled. Long snapper Chris Massey (2011) played college ball at Marshall University. A native of Hawaii, Harvey Unga (2010–13) had a schizophrenic relationship with the Bears, asking for time off for personal reasons, being re-signed, re-released, and relegated to the practice squad. He's now a graduate assistant coach at Brigham Young, his alma mater.

Brock Vereen (2014–15) is a cousin of dancer-actor Ben Vereen, and Brock's brother Shane has played for the New England Patriots and New York Giants. One-time Oregon player Bralon Addison, a running back, was the most recent player to wear No. 45 for the Bears, but was waived in May of 2017.

NO. 46: DOUG PLANK AND THE "46" DEFENSE

All Time No. 46	
Player	Years
Al Babartsky	(1943–45)
Chuck Hunsinger	(1950–52)
William Anderson	(1953–54)
Don Bingham	(1956)
Jesse Whittenton	(1958)
Angelo Coia	(1960–63)
Curtiss Gentry	(1966–68)
Craig Baynham	(1970)
Matt Maslowski	(1972)
Pete Van Valkenburg	(1974)
Doug Plank	(1975–82)
Anthony Mosley	(1987)
Mickey Pruitt	(1988–92)
John Ivlow	(1993)
Marion Forbes	(1996–98)
Chris Harris	(2005–08, 2010–11)
Jeremy Jones	(2012)
Josh Shirley	(2016)

Doug Plank's Bears number was immortalized in team lore by defensive coordinator Buddy Ryan. Appreciating the way Plank flew to the ball and clobbered offensive players from his safety slot, Ryan named the team's defense the "46." That was the defense the 1985 Bears rode to their phenomenal season and their 1986 Super Bowl championship.

Plank is from Greensburg, Pennsylvania, and was a college player at Ohio State. The Bears did not take the 6-foot, 212-pound defender until the 12th round of the 1975 draft. Plank showed he was more than worthy, earning a starting spot as a rookie and remaining with the Bears through 1982, the entirety of his NFL career. Injuries and general wear-and-tear forced him to retire earlier than he would have liked. The Bears wielded their winning defense without him in it in 1985.

Along with Gary Fencik, Plank was referred to as one of "The Hit Men" during his playing days.

After retiring, Plank became a successful businessman, owning about fifteen Burger King franchises. Then he got the itch to get back into football and became a very successful Arena Football League coach with several teams, from the Philadelphia Soul to the Orlando Predators. He has since been an NFL assistant coach with the Atlanta Falcons and the New York Jets. Also part of Plank's busy schedule has been television football commentating for FOX Sports and several college programs.

At one point, ESPN ranked Plank as the fifth-toughest Bear of all time. He played in an anything-goes era for defensive hits, and he was known for launching his body hard at ball carriers. He paid the price with concussions, knee surgeries, and leg numbness.

"Chicago is where I perfected my head-first technique," Plank said, "which we know as spearing today. Some games, I couldn't tell you who I played against."

The player who defined No. 46 is older and wiser now, but enjoyed all of his playing time despite the physical toll.

In 1943, Al Babartsky pulled on 46, the first time it was shown off for the Bears, and wore it through 1945. Babartsky, a tackle, was one of the famed "Seven Blocks of Granite" at Fordham (along with Vince Lombardi), as the 1936 line was labeled.

Chuck Hunsinger (1950–52) was the Bears' No. 1 draft pick out of Florida in 1950. A running back, Hunsinger's most notable statistic was averaging 28.6 yards per play on kickoff returns in 1950. Billy Anderson (1953–54) was a running back out of Compton Community College in California. Don Bingham (1956), from Sul Ross State in Texas, carried the ball seven times for Chicago. Defensive back Jesse Whittenton (1958) never made it into a game for the Bears, transitioning from the Los Angeles Rams, but became a two-time Pro Bowl player for the Green Bay Packers. He also later played on the senior golf tour.

Angelo Coia (1960–63) was an end out of Southern Cal who got his pro start with the Bears, twice topping 20 catches while modeling No. 46. Defensive back Curt Gentry (1966–68) had six interceptions. He later dabbled in small-college coaching. Craig Baynham (1970) had his association with the Bears ruined by three major injuries after he was productive with the Dallas Cowboys. Wide receiver Matt Maslowski (1972) played one game for Chicago. Running back Peter Van Valkenburg (1974) made it into six games for the Bears.

Doug Plank, the most famous wearer of 46, came next. Anthony Mosley (1987) wore 46 after a decent interval and had a 4.4 yards per carry average on 80 yards in his only NFL season. Mickey Pruitt (1988–90) was a linebacker out of Colorado and recorded an interception in a playoff victory over Philadelphia as a rookie. John Ivlow (1993) played in two games for the Bears and later became a high school coach in the Chicago suburbs. A cornerback from Penn State, Marlon Forbes (1996–98) saw action in almost every single Bears game during his three years with the team.

Chris Harris (2005–08, 2010–11) was a good representative of No. 46. He started as a rookie, intercepted a pass in the Super Bowl against the Indianapolis Colts, and played well again when traded back to the Bears after three years in Carolina, intercepting five passes in 2010. Jeremy Jones (2012) was with the team, but did not play. Linebacker Josh Shirley (2016) got into one game for the Bears before being cut.

That left No. 46 up for grabs going into the 2017 season.

NO. 47: JOHNNY MORRIS

Wide receiver Johnny Morris was already working at his new career in Chicago while still catching passes for the Bears. A lot of passes. It would be a lie to say that the Bears expected so much from Morris when they selected him in the 12th round of the 1958 NFL draft out of Cal-State Santa Barbara.

It might be said that Morris shocked the football world in 1964 when he hauled in 93 passes for 1,200 yards and 10 touchdowns. That was in only 14 games, too. In those days, wide receivers did not catch nearly as many passes as they do today, although the new American Football League was beginning to change the thinking on that.

No. 47 spent his entire NFL career (1958–67) with the Bears and grabbed 356 passes for 5,059 yards and 31 touchdowns. At 5-foot-10 and 180 pounds, Morris was not particularly big. Nor was he a real burner. But he knew how to get open and had shifty moves that confused defensive backs who foolishly underrated him.

Interestingly, by 1964, Morris was already working as a Chicago sportscaster. He could play the game, go to the studio, and tell you about it. He remained in Windy City sports broadcasting until 1996, when he retired. He was more familiar to fans on the air than he was on the field, which is saying something in a Bears-crazy town.

Morris's wife Jeannie wrote a weekly sports column for a Chicago newspaper and then spent twenty-four years in Chicago sports television. She participated in the making of *Brian's Song*, the TV film about the relationship between the dying Brian Piccolo and running back Gale Sayers. She also wrote *Brian Piccolo: A Short Season*, adapted from tapes Piccolo made when he was ill.

Johnny Morris was a member of the 1963 Bears title team and was impressed by the people around him.

"We had a number of great players around that time," Morris said. He stuck around long enough to overlap with Hall of Famers Sayers and Dick Butkus, too. "As my career was drawing to a close, I had the opportunity to watch the beginning of two fantastic football careers."

Ted Rosequist (1934–36) wore No. 47, but also No. 23. Bill "Red" Conkright (1937–38) continued with several teams and then coached with others. Defensive back Rex Proctor (1953) got into three games for the Bears. Johnny Morris came next in No. 47.

Defensive back John "Butch" Davis (1970) from Missouri played 10 games. Ken Grandberry (1974) was an eighth-round draft pick who rushed for 475 yards as a rookie and never played another season in the NFL. Mike Spivey (1977–78) started his career as a defensive back with the Bears. After one season with the Bears, Jonathan Hoke (1980) began a long career as a college and pro coach, including returning to the Bears from 2009 to 2014 as their defensive backs coach.

Defensive back Egypt Allen (1987), he of the distinctive first name, got into six games for the Bears and got to wear No. 47. Anthony Blaylock (1993) was a cornerback who finished his six-year NFL career in Chicago. Cornerback Randy Hilliard (1998) played in nine games for the Bears at the end of his career. Chris Hudson (1999) won the Jim Thorpe Award as the best defensive back in the country while at Colorado. He had three interceptions for the Bears.

Cornerback Ray McElroy (2000) was another short-lived No. 47. Bryan Johnson (2004–05) was a fullback who caught fourteen passes his first year in Chicago, but was unable to play much his second season because of a hamstring injury and subsequently retired. Woodny Turenne (2009–10) was mostly a practice squad guy and wasn't around long enough for everyone to be sure of the odd spelling of his name. He won a Grey Cup championship in Canada, however. Chris Conte (2011–14) had some good moments and frustrating ones, especially with injuries, but did make 73 tackles, force two fumbles, and intercept three balls in 2013.

Paul Lasike (2015–16) is a 258-pound fullback of Tongan descent who went to high school in New Zealand. Linebacker Roy Robertson-Harris (2016) spent the year on injured reserve because of an illness. Both players were on the roster heading into the 2017 season, but Lasike was waived in May of 2017, and Robertson-Harris is presently listed as No. 74.

NO. 48: SHOOTING STAR BEATTIE FEATHERS

All Time No. 48	
Player	Years
Beattie Feathers	(1934–37)
Bob Swisher	(1938–41, 1945)
Charles O'Rourke	(1942)
Joe Vodicka	(1943–45)
Howie Livingston	(1953)
Harry Hugasian	(1955)
Vic Zucco	(1957–59)
Tommy Neck	(1962)
Andy Livingston	(1964–65)
Ron Smith	(1965, 1970–72)
Allen Ellis	(1973–80)
Reggie Phillips	(1985–87)
Clifton Abraham	(1996)
Van Hiles	(1997)
Gabe Reid	(2003–06)
J. D. Runnels	(2006–07)
Evan Rodriguez	(2012)
Patrick Scales	(2015–16)

After one season in the NFL, former University of Tennessee All-American Beattie Feathers (1934–37) seemed likely to become the greatest running back in pro football history. The first player to wear No. 48 for the Bears had a rookie season to top all rookie seasons. In 1934, Feathers became the first back to top 1,000 yards rushing when he finished with 1,004.

Feathers was 5-foot-10 and weighed 180 pounds, and startled the football world with his 1934 accomplishment. Pro football was not really a wide-open offensive game when Feathers turned pro. The NFL had just loosened up some passing rules. That would lead to Sid Luckman and other great early quarterbacks beginning to define the modern-era quarterback with their performances. However, the running game was still king.

In some ways, Feathers's achievements of 1934 were inexplicable. The Bears had seen the likes of such runners as Red Grange and Bronko Nagurski, but neither of those stalwarts produced the way Feathers did.

It was a 12-game season and Feathers was only healthy for 11 of them. More than simply becoming the first to rush for 1,000 yards from scrimmage in one season, Feathers reached his mark on just 119 attempts. To this day, his 8.4 yards gained per carry is the best ever recorded by a back with at least 100 carries in a season.

This was an outlier of an achievement, especially since Feathers ended up more as the answer to a trivia question than an all-time great. He remained in the league through 1940 with diminished playing time in each new club he joined. He concluded his seven-year NFL stay with 1,980 yards, the majority of those gained in his first season. Feathers never gained more than 350 yards in a season again. Still, his lifetime average remained an impressive 5.2.

After retiring from the field, Feathers spent decades as a college football and baseball coach at different schools.

Feathers's main explanation for his Bears success was to credit Bronko Nagurski's blocking. "Whatever way Nagurski knocked them, I cut into the opening," Feathers said.

To show how far ahead of his time Feathers was with his single-season rushing total, the next 1,000-yard season in NFL play was not recorded until 1947 when the Philadelphia Eagles' Steve Van Buren topped the mark.

Bob Swisher (1938–41, 1945) was the next No. 48, and was also a running back. Charles O'Rourke (1942) had his greatest football fame as a quarterback for Boston College, where he led the Eagles to an upset victory over Tennessee in the Sugar Bowl. His stay with the Bears was interrupted by World War II, and when he returned to football it was in the new All-America Football Conference. Running back Joe Vodicka (1943–45) took over No. 48 when O'Rourke left for the service, and was on the 1943 Bears NFL title-winner.

Running back Howie Livingston (1953) appeared in two games for the Bears during the last season of his pro career. His brother Cliff was around the NFL much longer. Harry Hugasian (1955) was an offensive lineman who made it into four Bears games. Vic Zucco (1957–59) intercepted eight passes during his four seasons with the Bears. Defensive back Tommy Neck (1962) chose the Bears over the Boston Patriots when the American Football League was competing for talent.

Running back Andy Livingston (1964–65) was just nineteen when he joined the Bears. He scored his first touchdown at age twenty, and is still the youngest player to score an NFL TD. In his best year with Chicago (1965), he gained 363 yards on the ground and caught 12 passes. Ron Smith (1965, 1970–72) was a defensive back, but a Pro Bowl kick returner in 1972. Allan Ellis (1973–80) was a 1977 Pro Bowl cornerback for the Bears and had 22 interceptions in his career.

Reggie Phillips wore No. 48, but he also wore No. 21. Clifton Abraham (1996) was a 5-foot-9 All-American defensive back out of Florida State who played two games for Chicago. Van Hiles (1997) only played one full professional season. Gabe Reid (2003–06) was born in Pago Pago, American Samoa, and showed promise as a tight end, but the promise went unfulfilled. Reid caught just seven passes for the Bears.

J. D. Runnels (2006–07) was a fullback out of Oklahoma who could never move to No. 1 on the depth chart. Evan Rodriguez (2012) was a tight end as well, but made just four catches in 12 games. The most recent No. 48 was Patrick Scales (2015–16), a long snapper out of Utah State.

NO. 49: BEARS STILL LOOKING FOR STAR AT 49

Charlie Bivins (1960–65) was a running back who stuck around to put a stamp on No. 49, but the alum of Morris Brown College in Atlanta was not used enough by the Bears to cause identification with the number—except by longevity. The 6-foot-1, 212-pound Bivins never rushed for more than 188 yards in a season despite being part of the Bears for six years.

To be truthful, No. 49 pretty much has been an orphan numeral for the Bears throughout their history.

The first Bear to wear No. 49 was James Lesane (1952–53), who played on both sides of the ball, in both backfields. He appeared in 10 games in '52 and three games in '53, and ran back some punts. Henry Mosley (1955) played one game for the Bears and carried the ball three times. Jack Johnson (1957–58) was not the heavyweight champion of the same name. Johnson played at 6-foot-3 and 198 pounds, and picked off four passes in 1957. Bivins came next in No. 49.

Major Hazelton (1968–69) came out of Florida A&M and played two years for the Bears, mostly on special teams. Injuries wrecked the career of Joe Moore (1971, 1973) a first-round choice out of Missouri. Defensive back Dave Becker (1980) played 11 games for the Bears. Donald Jordan (1984) was a running back from Hawaii. Safety David Tate (1988–92) out of Colorado had a pretty good career with a few teams, compiling 455 tackles and 11 interceptions for his NFL resume.

Tremayne Allen (1997) played two games as a tight end and caught one pass. Ty Hallock (1998–99) wore No. 49 as a fullback. Marq Cerqua (2002) was a linebacker who played in two games. Marc Edwards (2005) played his last five NFL games for the Bears. Winston Venable (2011) is a 5-foot-11 linebacker whose stay in Chicago was short, but who had a successful career in Canada. Winston is pretty much the odd man out in his family, since his father was Major League outfielder Max Venable and his brother Will Venable also chose baseball and reached the majors.

Anthony Walters (2014) also wore No. 37. Going into the 2017 season, linebacker Sam Acho (2015–16) still had a chance to make No. 49 his own.

NO. 50: MIKE SINGLETARY

On a different team, the No. 50 would probably have been retired by now for Mike Singletary. But the Bears have so many retired numbers they have to be particularly wary of boxing up any more. Singletary likely deserves the honor as much as other famous Bears of the past, but the team can't run around assigning players No. 101.

Singletary was a star linebacker for Chicago between 1981 and 1992, which included major contributions to the 1986 Super Bowl championship team. Singletary was elected to the Pro Football Hall of Fame in 1998, and has been a head coach in the NFL, too. Singletary was the boss of the San Francisco 49ers and most recently was an assistant coach with the Los Angeles Rams.

The 5-foot-11, 230-pound Singletary was a two-time All-American at Baylor. He was a good fit at the religious school and has been public about his faith as a player and coach. Singletary's father was a street preacher and the boy grew up next to a church. In college, Singletary averaged 15 tackles a game, the kind of production that might be a once-in-a-career showing for another player. In a single game, Singletary was somehow connected to 35 tackles, a figure so stunning as to be almost impossible to digest.

Before the on-the-short-size Singletary made his hard-hitting ability and attitude known, perhaps he was slightly underrated.

"The fact that I was a believer, a Christian, everybody immediately thought this guy's a minister, he's too nice, and, oh by the way, he can play a little bit," Singletary said. "The other thing for me is being undersized. What a great story. What an overachiever, kind of like Rudy."

Well, maybe things never went that far. But even after college some people felt Singletary was not a slam dunk for the NFL. He was not taken until the second round. Singletary wiped out that perspective quickly. A two-time defensive player of the year, Singletary was selected to 10 Pro Bowls. During his career with the Bears, he was involved in 1,488 tackles, 855 of them solo. He missed just two games in his entire career, and was either first or second on the squad in tackles each year. Singletary may have been surrounded by other great talents on the Bears' defense, but he was very much the focal point.

Sometimes it seemed foes were scared to venture into his territory—but his territory became the entire field. Singletary's nickname was "Samurai Mike." He could chop your head off it he wanted to do so.

A thoughtful speaker when questioned, Singletary has also put thoughts to paper, co-authoring four books about football and faith.

In the waning days of his life, as he was succumbing to cancer, Buddy Ryan, the architect of the great Bears defense of the mid-1980s, had regular visits from Singletary.

"I love Buddy Ryan," Singletary said, "and I've told him that many, many times. I think all of us know of someone in our life, whether it's a grandparent, an uncle, a big brother, who meant so much to you. And you can never say how much you appreciate (them)."

Gerald Weatherly, who also wore No. 45, was the first Bear given No. 50. John Damore (1957–58) was a two-season offensive lineman. Mike Pyle (1961–69) was the center of the Bears' 1963 title team and a rock of the offensive line. Pyle made the Pro Bowl that season, and was a long-time team captain. In retirement, Pyle was visible in Chicago through his sports broadcasting. He died in 2015 after a lengthy battle with dementia.

The Bears were only a small part of the NFL career of Bob Hyland (1970), who spent 11 years in the league as an offensive lineman. Gene Hamlin (1971) was a center. Waymond Bryant (1974–78) was a Bears No. 1 draft choice and played linebacker. Linebacker Chris Devlin (1978) played in six games. Mark Merrill (1979) was a linebacker who spent half a season with the Bears after coming over from the New York Jets.

Mike Singletary became the signature player wearing No. 50 as the next man up. More than twenty years passed before the Bears handed out No. 50 again, meaning it was quasi-retired, even if not officially. Either that, or the ticket to retrieve it from the dry cleaner's was lost for a very long time.

James Anderson (2013) was also a linebacker and a veteran joining the team from Carolina. His one Bears season was superb, being in on 129.5 tackles. That was his last top-shelf season in the league.

Shea McClellin (2012–15) was drafted by the Bears out of Boise State. After Anderson departed, he assumed the No. 50 numeral for 2014. In 2015, McClellin was involved in 81 tackles, but the Bears did not pick up his contract option and he left for the New England Patriots, where he won a Super Bowl title in 2016.

NO. 51: DICK BUTKUS

Sometimes it seemed the Chicago Bears took out a patent on the middle-linebacker position. They have had so many great ones that the rest of the league has to be jealous. Indeed, the team did pretty much invent the position, so it is proper that one great after another inhabited the role in Chicago.

Dick Butkus came out of the University of Illinois and was given No. 51 to wear. Inhabiting the jersey, his shoulders seemed wider than the Sears Tower. Although his career was short-circuited by repeated knee problems, Butkus was around long enough to demonstrate his singular ferociousness and fantastic ability to hunt down the ball wherever it might lead him.

In an ESPN Classic piece, the narrator called Butkus "the most dominant defensive player the game has ever known." His style was called "violent simplicity." Butkus said he intended to deliver messages that when he hit someone "it was not going to be just a plain old tackle."

Butkus played from 1965 to 1973 and deserved to compete much longer, but his desire outlasted the strength in his legs. The Bears did eventually retire 51 for Butkus, but several players wore the number after he retired. That is because Butkus's departure from the team was a messy one, with lawsuits and claims of poor medical treatment. So the player and the club were not buddy-buddy for some time.

At 6-foot-3 and 245 pounds, Butkus retained remarkable mobility for his size. He was also such a hard hitter that one poll taken decades after his retirement named him the most feared tackler of all time. An eight-time Pro Bowl selection, Butkus intercepted 23 passes and forced 27 fumbles. A two-time NFL defensive player of the year, Butkus had the distinction of being named to the NFL's Teams of the Decade for the 1960s *and* 1970s.

In a remarkable confluence of lucky events, the Bears were able to choose both Butkus and fellow Hall of Famer Gale Sayers with first-round picks in the same 1965 draft.

After football, Butkus appeared in numerous movie roles, including the acclaimed made-for-TV film *Brian's Song*. He played himself in that production. Butkus was probably better known for his roles in television commercials as part of the humorous series of Miller Lite beer advertisements featuring former athletes.

Butkus handled some sports broadcasting and has been a generous contributor to many charitable causes over the decades. Both his son Matthew and nephew Luke played college football, and the latter has been an NFL assistant coach, including with the Bears.

The first Bear to wear No. 51 was no slouch himself. Ken Kavanaugh (1940–41, 1945–50) was a terrific end, a two-time Pro Bowl choice, and a member of three Bears NFL championship clubs. Kavanaugh averaged 22.4 yards per catch on his 162 grabs. At 6-foot-3 and 207 pounds, he was bigger than many receivers of the day. At Louisiana State, Kavanugh was an All-American. After his playing days, Kavanaugh worked as an assistant football coach and eventually served the New York Giants as a scout for more than a quarter century.

Clinton Wager (1942–43) was a 6-foot-6 end and punter who once, somehow, kicked himself in the head and fractured his own skull. He also played professional basketball with teams in the forerunner leagues of the NBA, as well as in the NBA with the Fort Wayne Pistons. Rudy Smeja (1944–45) caught eight passes in two seasons, but his only TD grab gave the Bears a 21–0 victory over Philadelphia.

Wayne Hansen (1950–58) was a three-time All-Pro offensive lineman who switched to linebacker. Somewhat unheralded after playing collegiately for Texas at El Paso, Hansen made the most of his opportunities despite being only a sixth-round draft pick. He had a first-rate career, although at times he was slowed by injuries.

No. 51 took a rest after that until Dick Butkus wore it. Mel Rogers (1977) was the next Bear up using the number, playing five games at linebacker. Linebacker Doug Becker (1978) was drafted by the Pittsburgh Steelers and cut, signed by the Bears, played one game and was cut, and then went to the Buffalo Bills for eight games—all in one season.

Linebacker Bruce Herron (1978–82) saw considerable action during his Chicago stay, including special teams. Kelvin Atkins (1983) appeared in 13 games. Center Mark Rodenhauser (1987, 1992) had two stints with the

Bears wrapped around allegiances to other teams. Jim Morrissey (1985–93) was a solid contributor at linebacker for years and was a member of the Super Bowl–winning team of 1985, as well as being part of the Super Bowl Shuffle shenanigans.

Post-Morrissey, in 1994, the Bears retired No. 51 for Butkus.

NO. 52: BRYAN COX

It wasn't as if the best years of Bryan Cox's life were the two he spent in Chicago, but he did OK for the Bears and those years were just part of an adventurous NFL stay for the 6-foot-4, 250-pound linebacker who was never favored to become a big-time player.

Cox's career pretty much represents achievement despite being nearly overlooked coming out of a small school. Cox was kind of from Bears territory. He grew up in East St. Louis, Illinois, and attended Western Illinois. When it came to draft day in 1991, no team was jumping up and down with eagerness to grab him despite his All-American status. Eventually, the Miami Dolphins chose Cox in the fifth round.

He swiftly proved himself, and Cox was definitely a known commodity by the time the Bears acquired him for the 1996 and 1997 seasons, giving him No. 52. He was a three-time All-Pro for Miami. Cox was in on 59 tackles, including three sacks during his first season with the Bears. The next year he was in on 101 tackles with five sacks. After leaving the Bears, Cox won a Super Bowl with the New England Patriots.

After his playing days ended, Cox did some radio and television work and then went into coaching for the Dolphins, Tampa Bay Buccaneers, and Atlanta Falcons. One year Cox traveled to Iraq and watched a Super Bowl with U.S. troops deployed overseas.

No one wore No. 52 for the Bears until Rich Coady (1970–74), who also wore No. 37. John Babinecz (1975) was a backup linebacker. Offensive lineman Dan Neal (1975–84) spent 11 years in the NFL and then coached for 15 more. Cliff Thrift (1985) was a linebacker bridging his days between the San Diego Chargers and Los Angeles Rams. Center Larry Rubens (1986) played 16 games. Center Len Seward (1987) was a strike player. Mark Rodenhauser also wore No. 51.

Linebacker Mickey Pruitt (1988–91) intercepted a pass in The Fog Bowl playoff game versus the Philadelphia Eagles and won the team's Brian Piccolo Award for his spirit and dedication. Linebacker Darwin Ireland (1994–95) played in three Bears games total. Robert Bass (1995) played in two Bears games. Bryan Cox came next at No. 52.

Linebacker Andre Collins (1998) played just one of his 10 NFL seasons for Chicago. Linebacker Keith Burns (1999) was in on 192 tackles one year in junior college. He spent just one season with the Bears, but won two Super Bowl rings with the Denver Broncos and then became an assistant coach for the Broncos and Washington Redskins.

Former Notre Dame linebacker Bobbie Howard (2000–03) spent his entire NFL career with the Bears, making 63 tackles in 2002 while starting nine games. Marcus Reese (2004–05) got into 11 games in 2004. Jamar Williams (2006–09) had some good moments as a Bears linebacker before being traded to Carolina for defensive back Chris Harris. Williams finished his football career in Canada. Brian Iwuh (2010–11) was a linebacker out of Colorado. Another linebacker, Jabara Williams (2011), played five games. Blake Costanzao (2012–13) had nine tackles a year for the Bears.

Linebacker Khaseem Greene (2013–14) was a fourth-round draft selection out of Rutgers. He originally wore No. 59, but switched to 52 as a way to honor former Rutgers player Eric LeGrand, a former teammate who was paralyzed in a game.

Although Jonathan Bostic (2013–15) moved on without playing a game in 2015, he did record 57 tackles in 2013 and 84 in 2014. LaRoy Reynolds (2015) took over No. 52 from Bostic. He made 15 tackles in 13 games and then moved on to Atlanta.

Christian Jones (2014–16) is a second-generation defensive star out of Florida State, and is the incumbent with No. 52 for the Bears heading into the 2017 season. He recorded 86 tackles in 2015.

NO. 53: BILL WIGHTKIN

The 6-foot-3, 235-pound Bill Wightkin was an excellent end during his four seasons at Notre Dame, but was shifted into an offensive-line blocking role with the Bears (1950–57). At Notre Dame, Wightkin was part of a national championship team. With the Bears, he was a member of the 1956 club that advanced to the NFL title game.

Wightkin's reward for moving to the line was an All-Pro selection in 1955.

Wightkin, who died in 1997, did as well as anyone else who ever wore No. 53 for Chicago. Collectively, these players suffered from a paucity of great achievements and great moments. This was pretty much a revolving-door number one year at a time with few of the players sticking with the team long enough to make great memories or have their own names remembered.

The first wearer of No. 53 for Chicago was offensive lineman Pat Preston (1946–49). Bill Wightkin followed Preston. Billy Autrey (1953) was a center who played seven games. Ken Kirk (1960–61) was a linebacker out of the University of Mississippi. James Purnell (1964–68) had more staying power than most 53s. He was a 229-pound linebacker out of Wisconsin. Linebacker Dave Martin (1969) came out of Notre Dame and played eight games for the Bears.

Larry Rowden (1971–72) was another linebacker out of the University of Houston. Gail Clark (1973) was an 11-game linebacker. Dan Peiffer (1975–77) was a center. Tommy Hart (1978–79) was a defensive end whose best days were with the San Francisco 49ers. Paul Tabor (1980) was a center who played every game off the bench. Dan Rains (1982–86) was a linebacker and part of the Super Bowl group of 1985. Larry Rubens also wore No. 52.

Dante Jones (1998–94) was a linebacker out of Oklahoma whose best year was 1993, when he intercepted four passes for the Bears. Michael Lowery (1996–97) saw action in every game in each of his two seasons with the team. Lemanski Hall (1998) was a player whose name sounds more like a college dormitory. He was a nine-year NFL linebacker who made 18 special-teams tackles for the Bears in his only season in Chicago.

Warrick Holdman (1999–2003) had 75 tackles as a linebacker and special teams guy as a rookie, and upped that to 87 the following season. After a knee injury, Holdman returned to make 79 tackles. Corey Jenkins (2004) got into four games. Leon Joe (2004–06) played linebacker for six NFL teams and three Canadian teams.

Nick Roach (2007–12) was a reliable linebacking presence for the Bears during his stay. Although his best season was in Oakland, Roach played the bulk of his career in Chicago. Jerry Franklin (2012–13) was with four teams in 2012 alone, including the Bears. Darryl Sharpton (2014) got a Bears look-see for five games. The University of Washington's John Timu (2015–16) is on the current Bears roster.

NO. 54: BRIAN URLACHER

ALL TIME NO. 54	
Player	Years
Joe Savoldi	(1930)
Jesse Hibbs	(1950–57)
Dick Klawitter	(1956)
Chuck Howley	(1958–59)
Roger LeClerc	(1960–66)
Bill McKinney	(1972)
Adrian Young	(1973)
Larry Ely	(1975)
Tom Hicks	(1976–80)
Brian Cabral	(1981–86)
Doug Rothschild	(1987)
John Adickes	(1987–88)
LaSalle Harper	(1989)
Ron Cox	(1990–95, 1997)
Greg Briggs	(1996)
Ricardo McDonald	(1998–99)
Brian Urlacher	(2000–12)

At this point, Brian Urlacher is just waiting around until he is eligible for the Pro Football Hall of Fame—and that time is coming soon. Even if the Bears have sworn off retiring numbers, it is difficult to argue Urlacher does not deserve that honor.

Urlacher was definitely one of the greats in team history, as well as in the history of the sport. He was a gifted tackler and pursuit man, a defender with an attitude. He was a human wall who resented trespassing by players on the other team carrying the ball into any area of the field where he could reach them.

Coming out of New Mexico, Urlacher took over at linebacker and held his position for the Bears from 2000 to 2012 as a 6-foot-4, 258-pound guardian of the end zone. Foes did not relish seeing the human missile coming their way. Urlacher was selected to eight Pro Bowls, was the league's Defensive Rookie of the Year, and was the Defensive Player of the Year in 2005.

With his shaved head, Urlacher could look intimidating—although for some reason he felt others did not think so.

"People don't think I'm big enough to be mean," he said. "I don't look big enough, but I am."

At New Mexico, Urlacher won All-American honors and was a No. 1 draft selection for the Bears. He ran the 40-yard dash in 4.57 seconds during the NFL combine, an impressive clocking for a big man. It took a few weeks for Urlacher to gain his rhythm as a rookie, but by the end of the season he had compiled 124 tackles, including eight quarterback sacks. Except for some periodic injuries, nothing else ever held him back.

Over the course of his career, Urlacher collected eye-popping statistics that support his effectiveness as a defensive force. Anyone who watched Urlacher at his best walked away from the game admiring his speed and tackling prowess. In all during his career he totaled 1,353 tackles, 41.5 quarterback sacks, 22 interceptions, 16 fumble recoveries, and 12 forced fumbles. At times it seemed Urlacher got his hands on the ball as frequently as members of the opposing offense. In 2002, he was in on 153 tackles.

At one point opposition fans indicated they thought Urlacher was over-rated. His response was simple: "Just look at the film." Indeed, that should have been sufficient evidence.

At the tail end of his career, when his contract was up, Urlacher kept ne-gotiating with the Bears for a renewal. He was extremely disappointed by what he perceived was a lack of effort by then-general manager Phil Emery to re-sign him. The player became a free agent and it briefly appeared that he would suit up for another team, a horrifying image for Bears fans. At the last minute Urlacher chose to instead retire, although he retained bitterness toward Emery.

Urlacher retired in May of 2013, and said one factor is that he wanted to be remembered as a player who competed for just one team.

Brian's brother Casey had a brief fling with the Bears, but mostly played Arena ball. In retirement, Brian Urlacher did some TV football commentary for a short time, but quickly gave it up.

The No. 54 made its debut in 1930 for Joe Savoldi. Savoldi was a fullback who beyond his brief foray into pro football had a fascinating life after be-ing born in Italy. He moved to Michigan at twelve years of age. In college, Savoldi played football at Notre Dame and supposedly heard Knute Rockne deliver his famous "Win One for the Gipper" speech. He was a member of an undefeated team and shared All-American honors with all other mem-bers of the Fighting Irish backfield. His nickname was "Jumping Joe."

In somewhat of a crazy situation, Savoldi, who had been secretly married, was forced to quit school when he went through a divorce. After one year of pro football with the Bears he became a professional wrestler and stayed in that sport until 1950, known for his flying dropkick. However, Savoldi's sports participation was interrupted by World War II when he worked for the Office of Strategic Services (OSS), the American spy agency that was the forerunner of the CIA. He was an undercover spy in Italy, where he knew the country and the language.

Jesse Hibbs (1931) was a tackle from Southern Cal whose career diverged to the film and TV world. Among other things, Hibbs directed numerous episodes of *Gunsmoke* and *Perry Mason* for the small screen. Center Dick Klawitter (1956) played five games. Linebacker Chuck Howley (1958–59) had great success with the Dallas Cowboys post-Bears. Over 15 NFL years he was a six-time Pro Bowl player after recovering from a knee injury, which the Bears believed would hobble him. Howley was a Super Bowl MVP, won a Super Bowl ring, and intercepted 25 passes in his career.

Roger LeClerc (1960–66) was a Bears kicker who scored 377 points in eight seasons. Bill McKinney (1972) got into eight games. Born in Dublin, Ireland, Adrian Young (1973) was an All-American linebacker for Southern Cal, passed through Chicago, and also played for the Hawaiians of the World Football League. Larry Ely (1975) appeared in 12 games for the Bears.

Tom Hicks (1976–80) was a University of Illinois alum who intercepted three passes in 1979. Brian Cabral (1981–86) was captain of the Bears special teams for the Super Bowl club of the mid-1980s, representing No. 54 quite well. After nine years in the NFL he became a college coach, most recently at Indiana State. Doug Rothschild (1987) played three games. John Adickes (1987–88) was a 6-foot-3, 264-pound center. LaSalle Harper (1989) played three games for the Bears. Greg Briggs (1996) made a short stop as a linebacker in Chicago after winning two Super Bowls in Dallas. Ron Cox (1990–95, 1997) collected three sacks as a rookie. He left Chicago for one year and won a Super Bowl with Green Bay before returning to the Bears.

Ricardo McDonald (1998–99) handed No. 54 and a linebacking job off to Brian Urlacher. Although the Bears have not retired 54, they haven't given it to another player since Urlacher retired.

NO. 55: DOUG BUFFONE AND LANCE BRIGGS

One reason there have not been very many Bears players to wear No. 55 is because two linebackers, Doug Buffone and Lance Briggs, monopolized its use for years at a time.

Buffone played from 1966 to 1979, and Briggs played from 2003 to 2015. They both made their marks on D for a club that has always prized its prowess on that side of the ball. The Bears like being referred to as the "Monsters of the Midway." These guys were linebackers of different eras with the franchise.

While Buffone grew up in Yatesboro, Pennsylvania, once he was drafted in the fourth round by the Bears in 1966 he never left town. He played his entire NFL career in Chicago and made the community his home in retirement. The 6-foot-3, 230-pound Buffone was a dominant player at Louisville, leading his college team in tackles for three straight years while amassing 479 of those hits.

A lifetime Bears player and supporter, the unfortunate thing for Buffone was that he played for the franchise during some of its down days. Although he was a teammate of such stars as fellow linebacker Dick Butkus and running back Gale Sayers, the Bears had only recently come off their last title in 1963 and would not win another championship for a generation.

Buffone made 1,257 tackles in his career and intercepted 24 passes. He also unofficially recorded 18 sacks in one season (as sacks weren't an official stat at that time) and as many as 158 tackles in a single year. He was the Bears' defensive captain for eight seasons. Buffone was the last member of the Bears to retire who had played for George Halas as coach. Halas's last on-field year was 1967, when he was seventy-two years old.

After his playing days, Buffone moved smoothly into broadcasting, for years hosting his own sports show on television and working on radio shows related to Bears play. He was also a businessman and it may surprise Chicago residents to learn he was one of the founders of the famed local eatery "Gibson's Steak House."

Once doing radio commentary after the Bears dropped an overtime game to the Buffalo Bills, Buffone famously observed, "I'd rather spend a weekend in jail than watch this game again."

Not straying far from his roots, Buffone played a role in founding Arena football and the Chicago Bruisers, and similarly helped start the Chicago Blitz of the United States Football League. Five months after Buffone passed away at age seventy in 2015, his autobiography *Monster of the Midway: My 50 Years with the Chicago Bears* was published.

Lance Briggs was a seven-time Pro Bowl selection who also spent his whole career as a linebacker for the Bears. The 6-foot-1, 254-pound Briggs was a hard man to out-run and a hard man to escape once he got his hands on you.

A third-round selection out of Arizona in the 2003 draft, Briggs made it clear that if you roamed into his area code you were in trouble. Like so many great Bears linebackers, Briggs was a superior player who ranks among their best. Briggs totaled 1,173 tackles with 16 interceptions, 19 forced fumbles, and 15 sacks for his career.

Only once, in 2007, did Briggs come close to leaving the Bears. They had acrimonious contract negotiations and when fans had just about given up on retaining Briggs, a breakthrough kept him in town for the season and the remainder of his career. He had nearly been swapped to the Washington Redskins.

"It was pretty close to happening," Briggs said. "My deal was I wanted to be with the Bears long-term."

It did work out that way.

In early 2017, a year and a half into retirement, Briggs discussed the dangers of CTE and how the brain disease concerns him as he looks to his future.

"You get worried. I get concerned for myself," Briggs said. "Even though I've never had any suicidal thoughts or anything like that, for it to happen to some great men and great football players, I know I can't separate myself from that crowd. I get concerned for myself."

The first Bears No. 55 was Bob Fenimore (1947), a two-time All-American running back from Oklahoma A&M (now Oklahoma State). Fred Venturelli (1948) was a kicker who saw very limited action. J. R. Boone (1948–51) was a Bears 22nd-round draft pick out of the University of Tulsa, who managed over 80 percent of his 497 career rushing yards with Chicago. Robert Moser (1951–53) was a center who played his entire 30-game NFL career in Chicago. Larry Strickland (1954–59) played only for the Bears and was selected to one Pro Bowl as a center.

Doug Buffone was the next 55, and another darned good player replaced him. Otis Wilson (1980–87) was on the Super Bowl champion Bears team. A two-time All-Pro, Wilson was an All-American at Louisville and is the father of former Cincinnati Bengals running back Quincy. Wilson, who was in on the Super Bowl Shuffle entertainment, totaled 36 sacks in his career. He played a season with the Los Angeles Raiders after leaving Chicago.

Linebacker John Roper (1989–92) was a second-round pick of the Bears. In 1991, he had 90 tackles with eight sacks. Vinson Smith (1993–96) spent 12 years in the NFL as a linebacker, four of them starting for the Bears. He also won a Super Bowl ring playing for the Dallas Cowboys. Sean Harris (1997) was a third-round pick out of Arizona and was primarily a backup who intercepted two passes and made two sacks. Greg Jones (2001) was a linebacker who spent most of his career elsewhere in the NFL. Currently an assistant coach for the New York Jets, Mike Caldwell (2002) played for six NFL teams, but did well in his lone year in Chicago, making 61 tackles with three sacks.

Lance Briggs took over No. 55 after that, keeping the uniform for some time. Hroniss Grasu, a 303-pound center out of Oregon, got it later in 2015. He missed the 2016 season on injured reserve.

NO. 56: BILL HEWITT

The one-and-only. That would be a fair description of No. 56 for the Chicago Bears. In 1932, end Bill Hewitt was handed a uniform jersey with the No. 56 emblazoned on it, and played for the Bears through the 1936 season.

After that, the club never gave the uniform to anyone else. It was retired for Hewitt because of his magnificent play. No. 56 joins No. 42, which belonged to quarterback Sid Luckman, as the only numbers in Bear history that were used by just one player before being retired.

Hewitt was born in Bay City, Michigan, in 1909, and attended the University of Michigan. Typical of the era, Hewitt was not a very large man. He stood 5-foot-9 and played the game at 190 pounds. This was a time period in the NFL when players went both ways, playing offense and defense.

The NFL draft had not yet been instituted when Hewitt was coming out of college. Teams scouted players on their own and relied on word-of-mouth to obtain tips about players. Hewitt was a member of the Bears' championship teams in 1932 and 1933. Coach George Halas called him fearless, as he played much bigger than his size.

A major distinguishing factor of Hewitt's career was his refusal to wear a helmet. In those days the state-of-the-art was leather helmets, which offered at best limited protection, but Hewitt did not try a helmet until 1939 when the league asked that all players don them.

At one point during his playing days, Hewitt, a two-way player who averaged 50 minutes a game, was labeled "The Offside Kid" by fan detractors who thought he had to be jumping off-side before the snap of the ball because he was so quick to reach the ball carrier.

Hewitt played for the Philadelphia Eagles for a few years at the end of the decade, and was a six-time all-star in the 1930s. He came back briefly in 1943 when the NFL had a manpower shortage and the economy was so challenged that the Eagles and Pittsburgh Steelers combined their fortunes into the "Steagles."

"Now is the time to quit," Hewitt said of his retirement even though he was still young. "I want them to remember me as a good end. I've heard those boos from the grandstand before and believe me, it's a lot more fun to quit with cheers instead ringing in your ears."

Hewitt was only thirty-seven when he died in a car crash. He was inducted into the Pro Football Hall of Fame in 1971, twenty-four years after his death.

NO. 57: OLIN KREUTZ, A QUIET BIG MAN IN THE MIDDLE

For thirteen years, Olin Kreutz occupied the middle of the Bears' offensive line, the center that started all of the plays when the quarterback demanded the ball. A 6-foot-2, 292-pound hard hitter, Kreutz was a key blocker after the snap and was so good at the dual tasks he was voted to the Pro Bowl six times.

Kreutz was born in Honolulu, Hawaii, and attended the University of Washington where he received All-American recognition. The Bears made him a third-round pick in 1998 and he stayed with them through 2010 before playing a final season with the New Orleans Saints. By then it was difficult to imagine Chicago's No. 57 playing anywhere else. Apparently neither could he, as he retired six games into the 2011 season.

Centers do not run up statistics measuring yards gained the way some other members of the offense do, so it takes more to be noticed. Kreutz was chosen as a member of the NFL's All-Decade Team of the 2000s, covering the first part of the new century—a good way to get noticed.

The one controversy of his career was an altercation with Fred Miller, another offensive lineman. They both were fined $50,000 for their fight.

Kreutz was always available at his locker, but he wasn't a flashy quote man. He was more earnest. Yet, after retiring, Kreutz went into sports radio replacing the late Doug Buffone on a football talk show.

"I have the easy job now," Kreutz said compared to playing, though he was aware he might have to criticize players. "Being the critic is the easiest thing to be, but when you decide to do something you have to do it the best you can."

The first No. 57 for the Bears was halfback Billy Patterson (1939), who got into eight games. Ray McLean (1940–47) played for the club throughout the Bears' marvelous success of the 1940s. A four-time NFL champ, McLean didn't run the ball much, but he played regularly. J. R. Boone also wore

No. 55. Dick Leeuwenburg (1965) took on No. 57 after it had a long rest, but played in just nine games.

Dan Pride (1968–69) was a linebacker who appeared in three games each season. Don Rives (1973–78) was a six-year linebacker with six fumble recoveries. Lee Kunz (1979–81) played three seasons at linebacker for the Bears. Al Chesley (1982) played part of just one season in Chicago. Bruce Huther (1982) played part of the same season, though he spent most of his career elsewhere, including with the Pittsburgh Maulers of the USFL. The 13 games David Simmons (1983) played with the Bears capped his four-year career as an NFL linebacker.

Tom Thayer (1985–92) was a Notre Dame lineman who was an integral piece on the offensive line for the 1986 Super Bowl–winners. After his career, Thayer remained in Chicago and has been a fixture on the air doing Bears commentary for years. Eldridge Milton (1987) briefly held No. 57. Sean Harris also wore No. 55. Linebacker Tony Peterson (1997) spent most of his career with San Francisco.

Olin Kreutz took over No. 57 after that. Dom DeCicco tried on the jersey in 2012, was a contributor on special teams, and filled in at linebacker when Brian Urlacher was injured. Jonathan Bostic also wore No. 52. Lamin Barrow (2015) was mostly on the practice squad and injured reserve and, the next thing you knew, he was a Miami Dolphin.

NO. 58: WILBER MARSHALL

Playing on a team with such a history at linebacker as the Bears have makes it difficult to stand out at that positon. Although he was not a Hall of Fame player, Wilber Marshall was a member of probably the greatest defense of all time, the 1985 Bears who won the 1986 Super Bowl.

The Bears made Marshall a No. 1 pick in the 1984 draft, and he manned a key slot for them wearing No. 58 between that year and 1987, although he did also have success with other teams—winning a Super Bowl ring with the Washington Redskins in 1991.

Marshall is a native of Florida and played college ball for the University of Florida where he was a two-time All-American. He is from Titusville, the epicenter of the space program—which is why his school was named Astronaut High.

Often a spectacular player in the NFL, the 6-foot-1, 231-pound Marshall accounted for 1,043 tackles in his 12-season career. The hard-to-stop linebacker totaled 45 quarterback sacks and made 23 interceptions. Many believe Marshall should be in the Pro Football Hall of Fame. He is enshrined in the College Football Hall of Fame.

Although he only turned fifty-five in 2017, Marshall has experienced considerable pain and fallout from the beating his body took playing football with spinal, knee, and shoulder injuries resulting in his receiving disability payments from the NFL retirement plan. In addition, although he made many millions of dollars, Marshall declared bankruptcy in 2002.

"According to the doctors, I need both knees replaced and (a) shoulder," he said. "I have spine problems from all the hits, crushing blows from the neck to the tailbone. Carpel tunnel on the arms from the turf. You name it."

Marshall is also disappointed he hasn't had more support for the Hall of Fame and believes he compares very favorably with others who have had more consideration and even been chosen.

"Hate to say it, but I do believe I should be there," Marshall said.

Defensive tackle Ed Neal, in 1951, was the first Bear to model No. 58. It was his last season after spending most of his career in Green Bay. Running back John Kreamcheck (1953–55) was a two-time All-American at William & Mary, and all three of his NFL seasons were with the Bears. Bob Konovsky (1960) was a guard who never played in a Bears game. Frank McRae (1967) played in six games, but was a much more successful actor, appearing in *Rocky II*, *Paradise Alley*, and *Norma Rae*, among other films.

Jim Ferguson (1969) was a center who got into four games for the Bears. A linebacker out of UCLA, Bob Pifferini (1972–75) played regularly over four seasons. Linebacker Jerry Muckensturm (1976–82) spent his entire NFL career with Chicago. Wilber Marshall took over No. 58 next.

Steve Hyche (1989) borrowed No. 58 after Marshall fled to Washington and played in six games. Michael Stonebreaker (1991) had a linebacker kind of name. He played all 16 games, but also played for the Frankfurt Galaxy in NFL Europe, where he was part of a World Bowl championship. Jay Leeuwenburg (1992–95) was an offensive lineman and the son of Dick, who played for the Bears in 1965. When Jay shifted to the Redskins, he shifted his number to 57 in honor of his father.

Chris Villarrial (1996–2003) started 148 games, mostly at right guard, before moving on to Buffalo. Jeremy Cain (2004–05) also wore No. 44. Darrell McClover (2006–09) was an excellent special teams tackler. Tim Shaw (2009) one-upped McClover with 30 tackles in one season on special teams. Rod Wilson (2010) was another special teams guy. Although his Bears tenure ended with a broken arm, he became a special teams coach for the Kansas City Chiefs. Dom DeCicco (2011) pulled on No. 58, but also wore 57.

Geno Hayes (2012) played one season for the Bears, sandwiched between longer tenures with the Jacksonville Jaguars and Tampa Bay Buccaneers. Linebacker D. J. Williams (2013–14) had some huge years with Denver, including a 141-tackle season, but battled injuries with the Bears before making contributions. Jonathan Anderson (2015–16) has been back and forth between the active roster and practice squad recently.

NO. 59: RON RIVERA

All Time No. 59	
Player	Years
Rudy Kuechenberg	(1967–69)
Carl Gersbach	(1975)
Gary Campbell	(1977–83)
Ron Rivera	(1982–92)
Joe Cain	(1993–96)
Jim Schwantz	(1992–93, 1998)
Daryl Carter	(1997)
Rosevelt Colvin	(1999–02)
Joe Odom	(2003–05)
Rod Wilson	(2005–08, 2010)
Gilbert Gardner	(2008)
Cato June	(2009)
Pisa Tinoisamoa	(2009–10)
Patrick Trahan	(2011–13)
Jerry Franklin	(2012–13)
Khaseem Greene	(2013–14)
Christian Jones	(2014–16)
Danny Trevathan	(2016)

The head coach of the Carolina Panthers helped earn his stripes for becoming a head coach through his time with the Bears. Ron Rivera was a member of the Super Bowl 1986 defense and became defensive coordinator of the Bears in 2004.

"We have some characters that would most certainly equal up to what we had (with the Bears)," Rivera said of his Panthers.

No. 59 played his entire career with the Bears between 1984 and 1992, and knew his stuff as a linebacker, starting at Cal where he was an All-American. The 6-foot-3, 235-pound Rivera went right from the playing field to the TV booth where he became a Bears game analyst and college football commentator.

It didn't take long for Rivera to make the jump into coaching from there. In 1997, he returned to the Bears for a two-year stint as defensive quality control coach. He then became linebackers coach in Philadelphia and, in 2004, returned to Chicago for a three-year stint as defensive coordinator.

Rivera coached in San Diego in 2007–10, and obtained the head coaching position for the Panthers in 2011, where he has worked since. A two-time NFL coach of the year, Rivera led Carolina to the 2016 Super Bowl after a 15–1 regular season in the fall of 2015. His Panthers, however, lost to the Denver Broncos.

"He does an amazing job of growing men," said former Bear Charles Tillman, who moved to the Panthers in 2015. "And when I say that, I mean growing leaders."

No one wore No. 59 for the Bears before linebacker Rudy Kuechenberg (1967–69). Rudy's brother Bob was an All-Pro lineman with Miami. Carl Gersbach (1975) played for several teams, including the Bears briefly. Gary Campbell (1977–83) kept control of No. 59 for a while. Campbell was a seven-season linebacker, all in Chicago. Ron Rivera was next on the No. 59 list.

The whole career of Joe Cain (1993–96) was Bears and Seattle Seahawks, and he amassed 415 tackles during that time. Daryl Carter (1997) played in just one game. Jim Schwantz (1992–93, 1998) was from the Chicago suburbs and got little chance to play for the Bears. He is currently the mayor of Palatine, Illinois, not far outside of Chicago.

Linebacker Rosevelt Colvin (1999–2002) recorded 10.5 sacks in both 2001 and 2002, and later won two Super Bowl crowns with the New England Patriots. Linebacker Joe Odom (2003–05) was a sixth-round draft selection out of Purdue who had some good moments. Rod Wilson also wore No. 58. Gilbert Gardner (2008) won a Super Bowl ring with Indianapolis when the Colts beat the Bears, and played his last NFL down in a one-game cameo with Chicago.

Cato June (2009) had a nice career with several teams, but appeared in just one game for Chicago at the end of the line, making his occupation of No. 59 short. Pisa Tinoisamoa (2009–10) had his best days with the St. Louis Rams and ended his time in Chicago injured and yielding No. 59. Patrick Trahan (2011–13) had trouble sticking on the active roster, getting waived, brought back, and released again. Jerry Franklin also wore No. 53.

Khaseem Greene also wore No. 52. Christian Jones currently has No. 52.

This number is a prime example how quickly players can come and go. How about the poor jersey? It has probably spent most of the 2000s in the spin cycle in the washer being tidied up with Tide for the next guy.

Linebacker Danny Trevathon (2016) was trying to stick with the Bears (and No. 59) in 2017.

NO. 60: WALLY CHAMBERS

The Bears have had so many excellent defensive players that the line for recognition stretches deep. Naturally, the best-remembered defensive players have reached the Hall of Fame. After that, the best-remembered defensive players in team history were around for team titles.

Wally Chambers fits neither category. He was, however, a first-rate player for the Bears in the 1970s, just about equidistant from the 1963 NFL crown and the 1986 Super Bowl victory. The Bears were not winning very much when Chambers suited up in No. 60 as a defensive tackle between 1973 and 1977. In fact, the team had a 27–43 record during his time in Chicago.

Chambers was a 6-foot-6, 250-pound lineman out of Eastern Kentucky—where a scholarship is named in his honor. Chicago made Chambers a No. 1 draft pick, and he was worth the investment. Three times Chambers was chosen for the Pro Bowl, and was the NFL's Defensive Rookie of the Year.

Most of Chambers's NFL career and all of his major honors were on Bears time, although he also played two seasons for Tampa Bay. Later, he worked as an assistant coach for the New York Jets. Unfortunately, in more recent years, Chambers has been paying the price for his hard-nose play. Residual problems in his knees and back have cropped up, and Chambers mostly uses a wheelchair to get around.

The No. 60 was not in use for the Bears until 1957, when Dan Healy broke it in and kept it through 1959. The 6-foot-3, 259-pound offensive lineman from the University of Maryland was a backup who also played elsewhere. Another offensive lineman, Roger Davis, followed Healy in No. 60. Taken out of Syracuse in 1960, Davis (1960–63) is one of only two guards to be drafted in the first round by the Bears. The other is Kyle Long in 2013.

Brian Schweda (1966) was a defensive end out of Kansas. Doug Kriewald (1967–68) was a guard from West Texas A&M. Lee Roy Caffrey (1970), a 6-foot-3, 247-pound linebacker, was an excellent rookie for the Philadelphia Eagles in 1963, and was then part of three Green Bay Packer championship teams prior to his cameo with the Bears. He joined the Dallas Cowboys and San Diego Chargers after his single season in Chicago. Caffrey passed away of cancer in 1994 at the age of fifty-two.

Wally Chambers was next wearing No. 60. Lynn Boden (1979), an offensive lineman who was a first-round pick by the Detroit Lions, played his last NFL season in Chicago. Tom Andrews (1984–85) was a backup lineman on the 1985 Super Bowl team. Stan Thomas (1991–92) was a lineman. He was shot in the head in an incident in San Diego in 1992, but the wound turned out to be minor. Gene McGuire (1993) was a one-hit wonder who appeared in nine games.

Darwin Ireland (1994–95) also wore No. 52. Casey Wiegmann (1997–2000) was a center who spent 16 seasons in the NFL, appeared in 227 games, and made one Pro Bowl (with the Broncos in 2008). Guard Terrence Metcalf (2002–08) stood 6-foot-4 and weighed 310 pounds. He was a third-round draft pick by the Bears out of the University of Mississippi, and was a regular for seven years. His father Terry also played in the NFL as a runner and return man, as did his brother Eric. Terrence is twice his father's size at 325 pounds.

Lance Louis (2009–12) had a good hold on 60 for a while. The Bears brought Louis to the NFL as a seventh-round pick to play guard. Taylor Boggs (2013–14) played one game for the Bears as a rookie and four the next year before moving on and leaving Chicago's No. 60 vacant.

NO. 61: BILL GEORGE

All Time No. 61	
Player	Years
Richard Barwegen	(1950–52)
Bill George**	(1952–65)
Don Croftcheck	(1967)
Glen Holloway	(1970–73)

**Hall of Fame, Retired for George*

A very sturdy linebacker out of Wake Forest, Bill George not only got No. 61 retired for him with the Chicago Bears, but is credited with inventing the middle linebacker position with a spontaneous mid-game shift.

George stood 6-foot-2 and weighed in at 237 pounds, playing for Chicago between 1952 and 1965. When George passed through your offense, a scattered trail of flattened bodies was left behind. George was a eight-time Pro Bowl selection and his flat-top haircut made him appear meaner than he was. That was saying something, because George was a mean, tough guy on the field.

During a game, after watching the way the quarterback was throwing, it dawned on George that if he dropped into the middle of the field after the snap instead of rushing the passer, he would be interfering with the other team's plans.

"Hell, I could break up those passes if I didn't have to hit that offensive center first," George said to fellow linebacker George Connor.

George was chosen for the Pro Football Hall of Fame in 1974. No. 61 was retired by the Bears in his honor, but there was a delayed-reaction decision getting it done.

"Bill George was the first great middle linebacker," one-time Bears head coach Abe Gibron said at the time of George's Hall election.

The first Bear to wear No. 61 was Richard Barwegen, who also wore No. 26. George was next. Then the Bears lent No. 61 to Don Croftcheck (1967) and Glen Holloway (1970–73) before taking it out of circulation. Croftcheck was an offensive lineman who made it into nine games. Holloway played four of his five NFL seasons with Chicago. Those were the only other guys who got use out of 61.

Bill George was killed in an automobile crash in 1982, at age fifty-two.

NO. 62: DAN JIGGETTS

Not too many modern-era pro football players come out of the Ivy League. But at one time, the Ivy League represented the top tier of college football, though those days passed long ago—either because they are too smart to toss a pigskin around for a career or the Ivy League doesn't get the best players. It takes serious sleuthing for NFL scouts to turn up a gem from that conference.

Dan Jiggetts came out of Harvard to join the Bears in 1976 as a sixth-round pick. The 6-foot-4, 274-pound tackle had the size and the Bears gave him No. 62 as a wardrobe addition. He stuck around through the 1982 season and appeared in 98 games.

The erudite Jiggetts was the Bears' player representative, although his timing found him vice-president of the NFL Players Association during the 1982 strike, which was probably no fun at all.

Jiggetts was about as good a track weight man as he was a football player, and was a high school champion in the shot put and discus.

There is little doubt Jiggetts is the most popular Chicago player to wear 62. After retiring from on-field action, Jiggetts became even better known in the city off the field. He went into sportscasting and his face has graced local television sets ever since.

Even before Jiggetts gave off good vibes to teammates and the public, the late Walter Payton simply called him "a good, good man." One newspaper story labeled Jiggetts "the Jolly Bear Giant."

The number 62 made its debut for the Bears in 1950 on the back of Frank Dempsey, who also wore No. 40. Kline Gilbert (1953–57) was a five-year tackle out of the University of Mississippi. Linebacker Mike Reilly (1964–68) was a fourth-round choice out of Iowa. Glen Holloway also wore No. 61 after Bill George and before the Bears retired that number. Tom Forrest (1974) was a guard who played in eight games.

Dan Jiggetts came next. Mark Bortz (1983–93) took over No. 62 from Jiggetts and wore it during the 1985 Super Bowl championship season. He picked the right time to come around, since the Bears were perennial play-off entrants during his stay. Bortz was a two-time Pro Bowl guard who played 171 games for the franchise.

Offensive lineman Chris Gray (1997) had a 208-game NFL career, but most of it was for the Miami Dolphins and Seattle Seahawks. Defensive tackle Robert Newkirk (2000–01) tried on 62 and gave the Bears a little help over 15 games. Lennie Friedman (2005) played college ball for Duke and for four NFL teams, plus for the Barcelona Dragons in NFL Europe.

Johan Asiata (2009–10) was a 300-pound lineman who saw the world through football. Born in New Zealand, he played college football at UNLV, hung out on the Bears' practice squad, played in Saskatchewan and British Columbia, and then with the Los Angeles Kiss in Arena football. He got into two games for the Bears.

Chilo Rachal (2012) was a 323-pound guard who mixed in a single season with the Bears and played more elsewhere. Eben Britton (2013–14) was another big tackle. A one-time Pac-10 star for Arizona, he tipped the scales (or maybe dented them) at 308 pounds. He was mostly a fill-in for the Bears, but also missed time due to appendix surgery.

Tackle Vladimir Ducasse (2015) was born in Haiti and played college ball at the University of Massachusetts where his 329-pound bulk helped earn him all-conference honors. During his year in Chicago, Ducasse played all 16 games and started 11.

Ted Larsen (2016) replaced Vlad in No. 62 and played every game at guard, but then departed for the Dolphins.

NO. 63: JAY HILGENBERG

All Time No. 63

Player	Years
M. L. Brackett	(1956–57)
Bob Wetoska	(1960–69)
Jon Neidert	(1970)
Steve Kinney	(1973–74)
Mark Nordquist	(1975–76)
Fred Dean	(1977)
Jon Morris	(1978)
Tony Ardizzone	(1979)
Jay Hilgenberg	(1981–91)
Todd Burger	(1993–97)
Ryan Benjamin	(2001)
Jody Littleton	(2002)
Corbin Lacina	(2003)
Roberto Garza	(2005–14)

Football was the game in the Hilgenberg family. Given his roots and genes, it made perfect sense that Jay Hilgenberg grew up to be an all-star center. And Hilgenberg did excel at snapping the ball and blocking.

Hilgenberg owned No. 63 for the Bears for a decade (1981–91), played on the Super Bowl champs shuffling along in the mid-1980s, and was a seven-time Pro Bowl selection. The 6-foot-3, 250-pound Iowa grad also tossed in a couple of extra seasons with the Cleveland Browns and New Orleans Saints, but built his reputation in Chicago.

Not that anybody in the family was surprised. His father, Jerry, was an All-American center, also at Iowa. His uncle Wally was a well-known linebacker for the Minnesota Vikings. And Jay's brother Joel was a center for the Saints.

Hilgenberg was the rock-solid center of the offensive line for the Bears—the guy you could rely on. And like so many Bears players of the era, he now works in Chicago's sports broadcast media. Hilgenberg has been a Pro Football Hall of Fame nominee, and hopes his 188 games in the league will suffice to gain him admission. Once he worked his way into the lineup, Hilgenberg did not miss many games over the years.

The gravitation to the center position was no accident. Dad had a hand in the boys' development. He taught Jay and Joel everything he knew, and what he knew was sufficient for them to break into the best football league in the world.

Just as the father of Phil and Joe Niekro taught them the knuckleball in their backyard when they were growing up, Joel recalled unusual back-and-forth at the Hilgenberg home while other kids were going long for passes or some such.

"My brother Jay says we never played catch facing each other," Joel said.

There was a lot you could read into a Jay comment about the differences between quarterbacks, and he may been a little bit of a wise-ass when reporters once asked him if he had a preference between three Bears contenders for the QB job.

"All quarterbacks feel the same to me," Jay said.

Pause. Laugh.

No. 63 for the Bears made its debut in 1956 with M. L. Brackett, who also played in Chicago in 1957 after attending college at Auburn. Bob Wetoska (1960–69) was one of the best at the position for the Bears. He came out of Notre Dame and started every game for years. John Neidert (1970) won a Super Bowl with the New York Jets before joining the Bears for his final season in the NFL.

Steve Kinney (1973–74) took his crack at keeping No. 64 for a while, but as a tackle. Mark Nordquist (1975–76) was a guard who played 14 games one season and only one game the following year. Fred Dean (1977) was only a member of the Bears' practice squad before winning a Super Bowl with the Redskins. Jon Morris (1978) was at the end of a terrific 15-year career as a center when he paused in Chicago. Morris is pretty much the all-time best center for the Boston/New England Patriots, a six-time all-star in the American Football League who also played for Detroit. He retired after his 10-game Bears season.

Tony Ardizzone (1979) was a center, but not like the few Bears owners of the position who were line anchors for years. Jay Hilgenberg was next, showing how things should be done and making No. 63 proud. Todd Burger (1993–97) was a guard from Penn State who weighed in at 303 pounds and later got into trouble with the law. Ryan Benjamin (2001) was a long snapper who played one game in Chicago, but won a Super Bowl with Tampa Bay.

Jody Littleton (2002) gave No. 63 a try, but didn't last long. Another long snapper, Littleton's championship was earned in NFL Europe. Guard Corbin Lacina (2003) was a 302-pound karate expert who got one start in eight games for the Bears.

Roberto Garza (2005–14) was a different matter. Following in the large footsteps of Bob Wetoska and Jay Hilgenberg, he could be termed the third personal dynasty player wearing No. 63. That trio made up for the one-and-dones, with each playing about a decade while wearing this number. Garza, who played center and guard, was another behemoth at 310 pounds. He played in 206 NFL games (including his time in Atlanta) and was a member of the Bears squad that advanced to the Super Bowl vs. the Colts. Always proud of his Mexican heritage, Garza is fluent in Spanish.

NO. 64: TED ALBRECHT

As if being a professional football player is not enough of a fascinating career for most people, Ted Albecht dreamed up interesting ways to keep busy for the rest of his life. Injuries and bad publicity about the long-term effects of concussions aside, probably most American males would love to live the life of a professional football player.

The smartest athletes are aware the life-span of an NFL player is limited and, the 2017 big-money contracts aside, they should be preparing for the rest of their time on earth even while playing. Albrecht is Exhibit A. He wore No. 64, but he didn't want to be nowhere when he turned sixty-four.

Born in the Chicago suburb of Harvey in 1954, essentially in the shadow of Midway Airport, Albrecht grew up to be a 6-foot-4, 253-pound offensive tackle. He then attended the University of California at Berkeley, where he was a good enough football player to attract the attention of the Bears in 1977 when they made him a No. 1 draft pick.

Albrecht spent his whole NFL career in Chicago, starting 75 of 77 games. Since he was still a young man, less than thirty years old, and his body was aching most of the time, he realized he was not long for the hard-knocks football world. His overall health was not helped along by ruptured discs. Albrecht pretty much knew football had its limits, and he would have to work at something else.

The one-time tackle tackled a new business. He started a travel business in a Chicago suburb, gained more than eighty corporate clients, became a color commentator for Northwestern University football, delved into charity work, and became a public speaker.

Albrecht said he had to learn a lot about the business world and he sensed that not everyone felt an athlete, a jock, could handle more sophisticated work.

"I had a lot of stereotypes to overcome," he said.

Terrell "Ted" Daffer wore 64 first for the Bears in 1954. He was an All-American guard for Tennessee, but after his sole year in Chicago went into the service. Daffer later played ball in Canada. Mike Rabold (1964–66) was an Indiana University star lineman who died at age thirty-three in a car crash a few years after finishing up with the Bears. Defensive end Larry Horton (1972) played 10 games for Chicago. Guard Ernie Janet (1972–74) saw playing time over three seasons.

Ted Albrecht came next at 64. Except for his three-game Bears cameo, the football career of John Roehlk (1987) over nearly a decade took him to the Washington Commandos, Detroit Drive, the Miami Hooters, and the Iowa Barnstormers. Although it is not clear how many people know there is one, Roehlk is in the Arena Football Hall of Fame, so the two-way lineman was doing something right. Offensive lineman Dave Zawatson (1989) played one season each with four NFL teams. Linebacker Glenell Sanders (1990) also played one season each with four NFL teams, getting into two games for the Bears.

Mirko Jurkovic (1992) gave No. 64 a try, but the Notre Dame All-American guard could not bust the lineup. Andy Heck (1994–98) gave the NFL a heck of an effort as a 12-year tackle out of Notre Dame. Born on New Year's Day, 1967, in North Dakota, Heck competed in 185 NFL games. He was a five-year starter for Chicago. Rex Tucker (1999–2004) moved right in at No. 64, though at guard. His brother Ryan was also an NFL lineman.

A guard out of Nebraska, Ricky Henry (2011) made his first NFL stop in Chicago, but kept right on going to other teams as he sought playing time. Andre Gurode (2012) made a next-to-last pro stop in Chicago for less than a month at the tail end of a solid 11-year career that included selection to five Pro Bowls. Christian Tupou (2013) kept the quick looks at No. 64 going strong. The Bears gave the 303-pound Tupou a chance as a defensive end free agent out of Southern Cal. He played five games and has since tried out with other teams.

Center Brian de la Puente (2014) has been part of seven NFL organizations, two of them twice, and played eight games for the Bears. Will Montgomery (2015), another center, tried on No. 64, but it didn't fit too well. He was gone from Chicago after four games. Still another center, Eric Kush wore the shirt for eight games in 2016 and was trying to keep it for 2017.

NO. 65: PATRICK MANNELLY

All Time No. 65	
Player	Years
Herman Clark	(1952, 1954–57)
Johnny Hatley	(1953)
Stan Fanning	(1960–62)
Tom Bettis	(1963)
Randy Jackson	(1967–74)
Noah Jackson	(1975–83)
Eugene Rowell	(1987)
Tony Woods	(1989)
Terry Price	(1990)
Jim Schwantz	(1992–93, 1998)
Tory Epps	(1993–94)
Evan Pilgrim	(1995–97)
Patrick Mannelly	(1998–2013)
Patrick Omameh	(2015)
Cody Whitehair	(2016)

Who could have predicted when Patrick Mannelly showed up as a sixth-round draft pick out of Duke in 1998 that he would have a stranglehold on No. 65 for sixteen years? It is surprising the long snapper-center ever gave it back.

Considering his relatively anonymous role, Mannelly was pretty much loved by Bears fans and definitely respected by teammates. He was a special teams captain for seven years. That's one of the highest honors a guy at his position can aspire to since long snappers do not get elected into the Hall of Fame.

Unlike many specialists, like placekickers, Mannelly looked like a football player at 6-foot-5 and 265 pounds. That may have enhanced his image even when he was entrusted simply with hiking the ball long distances. Mannelly, who did make 81 tackles on special teams, played longer with the Bears than any other player, appearing in 245 games. That is more games than any other Bears player either.

Proving there are statistics for just about anything and everything in pro sports, Mannelly set a record for most consecutive snaps without a punt being blocked—920. In all, he hiked the ball 2,282 times for Bears kickers.

Unlike so many other players who wore No. 65, or many other numbers for the Bears, Mannelly was not forced to depart through waivers, lack of a contract, or lack of interest. The Bears were willing to take him back for another season, but he chose his retirement moment.

"My body's tapping me on the back and saying, 'That's it, bud. I think you're done,'" Mannelly said. "So it has been an awesome sixteen years, and I am fortunate to be able to walk away."

Mannelly promptly signed on with a Chicago radio station to handle their on-air sports, but found he wasn't passionate enough about other sports, though he stayed on as a football analyst.

Herman Clark (1952, 1954–57) wore No. 65 first for the Bears. A guard who was born in Hawaii, Clark was a regular during his stay in Chicago.

Guard Johnny Hatley wore 65 in 1953 before Clark wore it again. Tackle Stan Fanning (1960–62) was also a regular for most of his time with the Bears. Tom Bettis (1963) was a linebacker who put in nine NFL seasons, the last of them with Chicago. However, he coached for more than twenty years afterward, much of that time with the Kansas City Chiefs.

Tackle Randy Jackson (1967–74) spent his entire NFL career in Chicago, appearing in 105 games. Guard Noah Jackson (1975–83) was next and the Jacksons just handed off No. 65. Defensive tackle Eugene Rowell (1987) played in just one game. Tony Woods (1989), another defensive tackle, got one sack in his 15 games. Defensive end Terry Price (1990) made it into two games. Jim Schwantz also wore No. 59. Tory Epps (1993–94) was a 280-pound defensive tackle who died of a blood clot at age thirty-eight in 2005. He played eight games in two years for Chicago.

Guard Evan Pilgrim (1995–97) started his NFL career as a Bears third-round draft choice and saw the bulk of his pro action in Chicago. He also appeared in the 2005 remake of the film *The Longest Yard*. Patrick Mannelly took what was seemingly permanent possession of No. 65 after that.

Guard Patrick Omameh (2015) put the numeral back in circulation when he played one year for the Bears. Cody Whitehair (2016) became the Bears' starting center as a rookie, and was holding onto that job in 2017 . . . and no, he does not have white hair.

NO. 66: CLYDE "BULLDOG" TURNER

Many players have gone both ways on offense and defense in the history of the NFL—especially in the early decades of the league. Things began changing to more specialization in the 1950s and have continued to move in that direction.

One must wonder if Clyde "Bulldog" Turner would recognize today's game. Turner was such a ferocious blocker at center and tackler at linebacker that it's possible he would have ended up in the Hall of Fame if he'd only concentrated on one position. Instead, he was about equally as scary playing on both sides of the line.

Turner came out of poverty, living a hardscrabble existence in dry, rural Texas and coming of age during the Depression. He was from the same area and went to the same high school in Sweetwater as the great quarterback Sammy Baugh, although they did not play together.

Anxious to play college football and build a better life than he experienced as a youth, Turner was dismayed to be overlooked by college recruiters. He had to sell himself to a school and finally convinced Hardin-Simmons to accept him. Turner had less success in the classroom than he did on the football field, sometimes getting in trouble with school officials.

But by the time he departed college it was obvious to such talent seekers as George Halas that Turner could be a difference-maker in the pro game. An eight-time All-Pro, Turner made his mark wearing No. 66 between 1940 and 1952. At 6-foot-1 and 237 pounds, he was a powerhouse whose strength was legendary. Once, in college, Turner hefted a 350-pound calf on a dare and posed for a Hardin-Simmons photo.

Turner was a tough tackler, got his share of interceptions, and led the interference for the men coming out of the backfield. The Bears won four NFL titles with Turner in the lineup, and Halas considered Turner one of the greatest football players he had ever seen.

"I out-ran every man on the team except two backs," Turner said. "Speed was my biggest asset as a pro."

After retiring from the field, Turner joined Halas on the sidelines as an assistant coach for the Bears between 1953 and 1958. In 1962, Turner became head coach of the old New York Titans in the American Football League before the club changed its name to Jets.

Turner is a member of the Pro Football Hall of Fame and, after an interval, the Bears retired No. 66 for him.

There is probably no one alive who knows exactly what was going on with No. 66 during this time period. The Bears media guide says Phil Martinovich also wore No. 66 in 1940, although it seems Turner never wore another number. The same publication suggests John Schiechl, who also wore No. 41, wore No. 66 at a time when Turner was with the team as well.

However, even if Martinovich and Schiechl tried on No. 66 in the locker room when Turner wasn't looking, everyone knows that was the Bulldog's number, the one Turner is identified with.

NO. 67: ABE GIBRON

Big Abe weighed just 243 pounds when he played guard for the Bears at the end of his career in 1958 and 1959. But he was much bigger when he coached the Bears between 1972 and 1974, after working as an assistant coach starting in 1965.

Abe Gibron loved food and didn't keep it a secret. He had to stay relatively trim on the field, but later let his preferences run wild. Sometimes it seemed Gibron enjoyed discussing mouthwatering eats more than X's and O's. Sometimes the food wasn't necessarily mouthwatering, either.

Charlie Hannah, a lineman on one of the teams where Gibron coached, once said, "He was eating things we wouldn't even go swimming with in Alabama."

Before he pulled on No. 67, Gibron grew up in Michigan City, Indiana, one of the seashore resorts favored by Chicagoans. He played college ball at both Valparaiso and Purdue, two Indiana schools, and was in the All-America Football Conference and the NFL as a player from 1949 on before wrapping things up with the Bears.

Big Abe was a good player. He was on three NFL title teams during his association with the Cleveland Browns and made four Pro Bowls.

Yet he always made time for his hobby. Browns teammate Dante Lavelli said, "He used to eat until two o'clock in the morning."

Gibron brought a glass of whiskey to press conferences and announced that until he raised the glass to his lips and sipped, everything he said was on the record, but once he drank everything else was off the record.

His coaching apprenticeship was with the Washington Redskins. When Jim Dooley was fired as George Halas's first successor, Gibron got the head Bears job. It did not work out.

The Bears represented Gibron's only head coaching gig and he went 11–30–1, which did not ensure job security. Following that episode, he spent seven years working as an assistant for the Tampa Bay Buccaneers and then as a scout for the Seattle Seahawks—although for a couple of months between his NFL coaching assignments Gibron coached the Chicago Winds of the World Football League. Neither the team, nor the league, made it to the end of that season.

Gibron's waistline continued to expand over the years and as a coach it was suggested he might have weighed over 400 pounds. Gibron was considered a sharp judge of football talent and quality cuisine and combined the two into a personally enjoyable lifestyle, though he couldn't mesh the talent into winners.

When Gibron died at seventy-two years of age in 1997, part of the *New York Times* headline on his obituary included the comment, "Wit and Lover of Good Food."

Ed Bradley (1950, 1952) was member of the Bears for a few years and also played minor league baseball in the Boston Red Sox system. Tom Roggeman (1956–57) was a guard out of Purdue who played two full seasons in Chicago. Abe Gibron came next.

Ted Karras (1960–64) was another well-known No. 67 guard and the older brother of star defensive tackle-actor Alex Karras. Ted was a member of the 1963 Bears championship team and another brother, Lou, also played in the NFL. His grandson, also named Ted, plays for the New England Patriots and appeared in Super Bowl LI. George Seals (1965–71) played on both sides of the line. Bill Line (1972) not only played the line (defensive tackle), but he was named after it. Guard Mike Hoban (1974) played one game. Defensive tackle Don Hultz (1974) played in eight games for Chicago. As a rookie in 1963 with Minnesota, he recovered nine fumbles.

Tackle Phil McKinnely (1982) was in the NFL for seven years, played a couple more with the USFL, and then returned to the NFL as an official. His number with the Bears was 67; as an official 110. Tackle Tim Norman (1983) played in just one game. John Arp (1987) played two games at tackle. Jerry Fontenot (1989–96) was a center who had a long NFL career and then a long assistant coaching career with the Green Bay Packers.

Bill Schultz (1997) was a guard whose NFL career concluded with eight games in Chicago. Greg Huntington (1997–99) was a 300-pound center. After 12 games for the Bears in No. 67, Josh Warner (2003–04) moved on to the Berlin Thunder in NFL Europe. A first-team All-American out of Boston College, Josh Beekman (2007–09) went into college coaching after his NFL days.

Guard Herman Johnson (2010) stood 6-foot-7 and weighed in at 386 pounds, but never got into a Bears game. His playbook may have been Abe

Gibron's menu. Center Chris Spencer (2011–12) squeezed in two seasons for the Bears in the middle of stops in Seattle and with Tennessee. In his first Bears season, Jordan Mills (2013–14) became a starting tackle after being a fifth-round pick out of Louisiana Tech. Then after being injured while seeing considerable action his second year, he was cut.

NO. 68: JIM FLANIGAN JR.

Between 1994 and 2000, Jim Flanigan Jr. was a Bears defensive anchor, although he only wore No. 68 for his first season. He was a popular player with the fans because of his obviously good attitude. Also, for another good reason. Once in a while a Bears coach would grab Flanigan off the bench, push him into the offensive lineup as a tight end—and he would make a touchdown catch. The oddball nature of the success appealed to Bears fans.

Flanigan stood 6-foot-2 and weighed 290 pounds. He starred in college at Notre Dame and had good genes. His father, Jim Sr., was also an NFL defensive lineman, mostly with the Green Bay Packers up the road. That explains why Jim Jr. was born in Green Bay.

The younger Flanigan flourished in Chicago, although he played a few last seasons elsewhere, including one year in Green Bay. In all, he amassed 46 sacks—most of those for the Bears.

His greatest off-field honor was being named co-winner of the Walter Payton Man of the Year Award in 2000 for his community and charitable work. The James Flanigan Foundation focuses on child literacy, partially through the Great American Book Drive which gives hundreds of thousands of books to underprivileged children.

"My life is rich," Flanigan said, "but it would not be nearly as rich without the words I have known and the things I have learned through reading."

Presumably, Flanigan learned how to tackle people from his father, but he probably owes another coach for his catching prowess. In his fill-in role, Flanigan caught four touchdown passes.

The first time No. 68 was worn for the Bears was 1951 when guard Gerald Stautberg got the shirt for his only season. Guard John Badaczewski (1953) was in his last season when he paused in Chicago. Offensive lineman George Burman (1964) came out of Northwestern and played several years after his one-year stop with the Bears. The 6-foot-2, 254-pound Howard Mudd (1969–70) was a three-time Pro Bowl selection with San Francisco before joining the Bears and a long-time coach after leaving them.

Jim Osborne (1972–84) wore No. 68 for a long time in Chicago. A seventh-round pick out of Southern University, Osborne spent 13 seasons with the Bears—many of them lean ones, but he started 154 of his 186 games. Paul Blair (1986–87) saw two years of action coming out of Oklahoma State. Sean McInerney (1987) was a defensive end out of Frostburg State who played in three games wearing No. 68.

A 305-pound tackle from Washington State, Chris Dyko (1989) played in eight games. Jim Flanigan Jr. followed. The whole NFL career of Carl Reeves (1996–98) was spent on the Bears' defensive line. Bryan Anderson (2003–04) did not get to wear No. 68 for too long. A guard drafted in the seventh-round out of Pittsburgh, Anderson got into four games. Anthony Oakley (2007) played three games at guard. Frank Omiyale (2009–11), the big dude (315 pounds) out of Tennessee Tech, had his moments. Matt Slauson (2013–15), a bigger dude at 320 pounds, looked larger than Jupiter. He was a scrappy, hungry player who gave the Bears good service.

Matt McCants was with the Bears for part of the 2016 season modeling No. 68. He played in two games.

NO. 69: FRED MILLER

The funniest part about Fred Miller's broken jaw was the way the Bears tried to spin it. Not that there is much humor in a broken jaw. The usual requirement which follows is sipping your meals through a straw for a while.

Miller's employment wearing No. 69 with the Bears came at the end of his career, between 2005 and 2008, after he had played tackle for the St. Louis Rams and the Tennessee Titans, winning a Super Bowl with the former. A gargantuan man at 6-foot-7 and 320 pounds, Miller attended Baylor University and had a good, solid career.

In 2005, Miller showed up for work one day with a broken jaw. When Miller's training camp injury was announced to the media this was the crux of the phrasing: "Fred Miller broke his jaw while getting out of bed in the middle of the night." Good one.

That was the cover-up fairy tale. Actually, Miller's jaw was broken by a punch delivered by the fist belonging to center Olin Kreutz, another 300-pound offensive lineman. Witnesses probably thought they were watching a rumble between two dinosaurs.

Although both men were fined, coach Lovie Smith was extremely unhappy with the way the truth gradually came out instead of hearing it right away. The big guys fessed up to reporters.

"We're still going to go out there and play and we're going to work together," said Miller, who was talking with a steel plate in his jaw at the time. "We're still going to go out on our regular nights and have dinner together as an offensive line and as a unit."

Miller played in 192 NFL games.

Guard Ralph Jecha (1955) was the first Bear to wear No. 69. Bill Roehnelt (1958–59) gave the Bears two seasons at linebacker. Ted Wheeler (1970) was a guard for six games. Revie Sorey (1975–82) kept No. 69 longer than any other Bear. A guard from the University of Illinois, Sorey was a fifth-round draft pick. Later in life he experienced a series of tragedies when his wife died of cancer, an adult son drowned in a pool, and he had a stroke.

A guard out of Florida A&M, Vernice Smith (1993) got into six games with Chicago. Tom Myslinksi (1993–94) was a guard who played for many teams, including five games with the Bears, and has also coached for several others. Octus Polk (1995–96) was heralded as a good free agent signing, but never got into a Bears game. Tackle Mike Gandy (2001–04) put in four seasons after being drafted out of Notre Dame, and then played elsewhere.

Fred Miller was next wearing No. 69. Tackle Kirk Barton (2008) came out of Ohio State. Defensive end Henry Melton (2009–13) was a fourth-round draft pick chosen for the Pro Bowl with the Bears before playing for other teams. Melton had seven sacks in 2011 and six sacks in 2012 for Chicago. A star with the Kansas City Chiefs and Minnesota Vikings (five Pro Bowls combined), Jared Allen took over No. 69 for the Bears in 2014 and played two seasons in Chicago.

Defensive end C. J. Wilson, who won a Super Bowl before joining the Bears, was the incumbent with No. 69 going into the 2017 season.

NO. 70: HENRY WAECHTER SCORES IN NINTH INNING

All Time No. 70	
Player	Years
Alvin Cutler	(1932)
Art "Buddy" Davis	(1953–54)
Herman Lee	(1958–66)
Bob Pickens	(1967–68)
Kenneth Kortas	(1969)
Jeff Curchin	(1970–71)
Andy Rice	(1972–73)
Dennis Lick	(1976–81)
Henry Waechter	(1982, 1984–86)
Jim Altoff	(1987–88)
Troy Auzenne	(1992–95)
Ken Anderson	(1999)
Alfonso Boone	(2001–06)
Babatunde Oshinowo	(2007)
Edwin Williams	(2010–12)
Michael Ola	(2014)
D'Anthony Smith	(2015)
Bobby Massie	(2016)

Defensive linemen do not score points very often in NFL games, so it is a special treat for them when it happens. They are paid to tackle, not to pile up points. In fact, many, many defensive tackles and defensive ends complete their entire careers without putting a single point on the scoreboard. In the normal course of events they get more excited by sacks. They keep closer track of those achievements.

Henry Waechter was not the biggest contributor to the Chicago Bears' great 1985 season, but he played regularly. The 6-foot-5, 270-pound defensive tackle out of Nebraska showed up in 13 games that season and recorded 2.5 sacks—so he earned his Super Bowl ring.

On the field near the end of the 1986 Super Bowl victory over the New England Patriots, Waechter rushed the quarterback and sacked Steve Grogan in the end zone. Not only did No. 70 obtain a sack, but the play scored the Bears two points.

"I'm still really proud of that fact," Waechter said years later of his safety.

That was a high point of Waechter's stay with the Bears—call it two stays. He was with the team in 1982, played a couple of seasons for the Colts, and then was back with the Bears from 1984 through 1986.

Interestingly, during an era when most players wore low numbers, not going higher than the 20s, Alvin Culver was the first Bear to show off No. 70 in 1932. Culver was a tackle who got into three Bears games. No. 70 was forgotten about for a long time after that, until Buddy Davis (1953–54) got into three games. Herman Lee (1958–66) was a long-time regular lineman out of Florida A&M.

Tackle Bob Pickens (1967–68) assumed No. 70 post-Lee for three seasons. Pickens was also a US Olympic heavyweight wrestler in 1964 and played for the Edmonton Eskimos of the CFL. A six-year player, Kenneth Kortas (1969) played the last three games of his NFL career with the Bears. Jeff Curchin

(1970–71) put in a couple of years at tackle. Andy Rice (1972–73) was a defensive tackle who spent most of his pro years in the American Football League.

Dennis Lick (1976–81) took good care of No. 70 for a while. Lick was a six-year tackle out of the University of Wisconsin. Henry Waechter came next in No. 70. Jim Althoff (1987–88) had 3.5 sacks in four games for Chicago. An All-American out of Cal, Troy Auzenne (1992–95) was a solid tackle for the Bears before leaving for Indianapolis and seeing his career end due to a knee injury. Defensive tackle Ken Anderson (1999) played in two games, but also appeared in the World League and XFL. He died of a heart attack at age thirty-three.

Alfonso Boone (2001–06) was one of the most distinguished wearers of No. 70. Although he also played for other teams, the 320-pound Boone, out of Mt. San Antonio Junior College, experienced most of his best seasons in Chicago. Babatunde Oshinowo (2007) was one of those guys whose length of last name made it difficult to find room to put a 70 on the back of the uniform, too. While some people may have wished Babatunde could have stayed around longer than just the 2007 season to give them time to learn how to pronounce his last name, he spent more time with other teams. He was a speaker of the West African language of Yoruba.

Edwin Williams (2010–12) was a guard and center from Maryland who, much like the proud Waechter, scored a touchdown on a fumble recovery. Michael Ola (2014) made nine team stops in five years as a tackle, including with the Canadian Football League and the Arena league, plus practice squads. He was an important fill-in for the Bears. D'Anthony Smith (2015) got to try on No. 70. Born in Berlin, Germany, Smith became a free agent after his two games with the Bears. Tackle Bobby Massie (2016) is holding down No. 70 for the Bears now.

NO. 71: GEORGE CONNOR

A Hall of Famer was the first player to wear No. 71 for the Bears, but it was never retired. George Connor (1948–55) was a great for Chicago as a linebacker and tackle, although he did not don No. 71 until 1952.

Connor was born in Chicago in 1925, went to high school in Chicago and, after splitting his college days between Holy Cross and Notre Dame, played his entire NFL career in Chicago. He was good enough in college to win the Outland Trophy as the best lineman, and was named to three All-American teams. With the Bears he was a five-time All-Pro and a member of the NFL's 1940s All-Decade Team.

At 6-foot-3 and 240 pounds, Connor was a hard hitter who was on the large size for a linebacker of his era. Connor was in on seven interceptions and 10 fumble recoveries in his 90 pro games. Connor was regarded as equally good on offense, although there were no numbers to quantify it. He was elected to the College Football Hall of Fame in 1963 and Pro Football Hall of Fame in 1975.

Connor would have kept playing longer if he had not been injured as often. When he died, his wife said he had undergone thirty-two surgeries. None of that dented his attitude toward football.

"I'd do it again," Connor said. "I loved the game. I loved the practices. I loved my teammates. We had pride. We had fun. We had loyalty."

Another very solid football player, Earl Leggett (1957–66) took over No. 71 after Connor. A first-round draft pick out of Louisiana State, the defensive lineman was a member of the Bears' 1963 title team. After his Chicago stint, Leggett played a few more seasons elsewhere, totaling 11 in the NFL. Then he became a defensive line coach for six teams, including the Raiders in more than one location, for more than twenty years. Leggett picked up two Super Bowl rings along the way.

Rufus Mayes (1969) was a first-round draft choice at tackle out of Ohio State whom the Bears traded away prematurely. He had much better luck in Cincinnati. Defensive end Tony McGee (1971–73) had an episodic career.

In college at Wyoming, he was one of more than a dozen African Americans thrown off the team because they wanted to protest the Mormon church's policies against accepting black men as priests before a game against Brigham Young. He was a Bears' third-round pick and began to establish his reputation as a quarterback sacker supreme, expanded upon elsewhere. McGee won a Super Bowl with the Washington Redskins and has hosted a football radio show in DC for three decades. He was in on 106 sacks (unofficially) during his career that also included many years playing for the Patriots.

Defensive lineman Roger Stillwell (1975–77) played in 31 games for Chicago during his only pro action. Rocco Moore (1980) was a less well-remembered No. 71. The guard who was originally affiliated with the Phila-delphia Eagles, died at age fifty-two of a heart attack. Guard Perry Hartnett (1982–83) was a fifth-round draft selection out of Southern Methodist. Tackle Andy Frederick (1983–85) did his time in No. 71 and won two Super Bowls during his career, including one with the 1985 Bears, for whom he was a backup tight end.

Jack Oliver (1987) was a three-game tackle out of Memphis. Caesar Rentie (1988) was a five-game tackle the following season. James Williams (1991–2002) played at 6-foot-7 and 330 pounds. The popular tackle was known as "Big Cat" for his size and quickness. Competing for the Bears for his entire 12-season, 166-game career, Williams was voted to one Pro Bowl and was a Pro Bowl alternate another time. He had a talent for blocking field goals, getting a hand on eight opponent tries.

Israel Idonije (2004–12) was a worthy wearer of No. 71. Another big fel-low at 6-foot-6 and 275 pounds, Idonije was born in Nigeria and played college ball in Manitoba where his family migrated. The Cleveland Browns took a chance on the free agent, but cut him. The Bears obtained him for the practice squad, and he worked his way onto the roster—first as a special teams star. He played an extra season or two with other teams, but demon-strated his versatility off the field by creating a comic book series, doing some acting, and starting a charitable foundation.

Nick Becton (2015–16) has scrambled for a permanent spot with the Bears and other teams, but after five games with the Bears he was last seen on injured reserve.

NO. 72: WILLIAM "THE REFRIGERATOR" PERRY

All Time No. 72	
Player	Years
Bill Wightkin	(1950–57)
Bill George	(1952–65)
Ed Nickla	(1959)
Jim Cadile	(1962–72)
Gary Hrivnak	(1973–76)
Brad Shearer	(1978–80)
Jerry Doerger	(1982)
John Janata	(1983)
Andy Frederick	(1983–85)
William Perry	(1985–93)
Scott Adams	(1995)
Jon Clark	(1996–97)
Chris Maumalanga	(1997)
Carl Powell	(2001)
Ernest Grant	(2002)
Qasim Mitchell	(2003–06)
Jimmy Kennedy	(2007)
Dan Buenning	(2008)
James Marten	(2009)
Gabe Carimi	(2011–12)
Tracy Robertson	(2013)
Charles Leno Jr.	(2014–16)

When it comes to appliances, William Perry is probably the most famous of them all. The Fridge was also one of the great characters in Chicago Bears history, a genial man with unusual talents who arrived on the scene just as the Bears were about to be appreciated as perhaps the greatest defensive squad of all time.

While No. 72 is not going to be retired to honor Perry, it will always be identified with him. An All-American defensive tackle at Clemson, the Bears made Perry a No. 1 draft pick in 1985. Clemson won a national title while he was on the team. He remained with the Bears into 1993 before playing out his last NFL days with the Philadelphia Eagles. Still, Perry will always be a Bear in most minds.

Weight was always a subject brought up in connection with Perry, going back to his youth in South Carolina. He topped 200 pounds as an eleven-year-old, and during his days with the Bears Perry reached 350. His height was 6-foot-2, so he wasn't tightly proportioned. At times coaches forced him to lose pounds, though for a big man he was incredibly agile. Perry had the type of speed many high schoolers envy in the 100-meter dash. He could not only dunk a basketball, but do 360s.

"Even when I was little, I was big," Perry famously said.

Perry acquired the nickname "The Refrigerator" legitimately, as in being compared to the size of one. A member of the 1985 Super Bowl champs, Perry occasionally carried the ball as a fullback in goal-line offenses, an idea of coach Mike Ditka. It was assumed no team could bring Perry down if he set his mind on the end zone from a yard out. While some considered that play a gimmick, it was also effective. Many defensive players cringed when they saw No. 72 coming at them. It was like trying to tackle a mountain.

For the same reason, Perry was also the lead blocker near the end zone. The first time Perry played that role he steamrolled the Green Bay Packer assigned to crash into the backfield.

"It was like a Mack Truck smashing a Volkswagen," Perry said.

That's how a witty sportswriter might have put it, but Perry beat the scribes to it.

Obtaining that offensive role was a quirk in-house. Defensive coordinator Buddy Ryan sneered at Perry, calling him a wasted draft pick and he refused to use him much on D. Ditka countered with his own use for Perry, showcasing his agility on offense. Perry, who featured a gap-toothed smile, one he flashed constantly, could get away with messing with Ditka's hair when no one else would dare.

In all, Perry scored three offensive touchdowns and collected 29.5 sacks on defense while appearing in 138 games in 10 NFL seasons.

Perry had a much better sense of humor than Ryan. He was personable, quotable, and knew how to have fun. He participated in a Wrestlemania, was part of the Super Bowl Shuffle operation, recorded rap tunes, and appeared on a mix of television shows. While still playing, The Fridge was invited to endorse numerous products in exchange for quite respectable fees.

He appeared on the cover of *Time* magazine with the great Walter Payton, and the story referred to Perry, not Payton, as "the most famous football player in the world."

Well into retirement, however, Perry began suffering from a laundry list of physical ailments that sometimes required him to travel in a wheelchair. At the beginning of 2017 he was only fifty-four, but was hobbled much like an older man. He was said to have problems with alcohol, had ballooned up to 425 pounds, and coped with the effects of Guillain-Barre Syndrome, a disease which attacks the peripheral nervous system. Also, Perry required medication for diabetes and high blood pressure.

Somewhere along the way Perry replaced his missing tooth and walked around with a million-dollar-smile, not merely an appealing one. Ditka, always a fan, repeatedly tried to aid Perry on his health matters, but The Fridge did not always cooperate. Perry has admitted he is an alcoholic and at times refused to take his necessary medication saying he doesn't need it. Overall, he has not taken good care of himself despite the pleas of family members who love him the most.

The sad perspective is that the man who once brought so much joy to so many does not seem to be having much fun anymore.

The first Bear to wear No. 72 was Bill Wightkin, who also wore No. 53. Bill George also wore No. 61. Ed Nickla (1959) played one year on defense before spending the rest of his pro football career in Canada. A fourth-round pick, guard Jim Cadile (1962–72) played 11 seasons for the Bears. Gary Hrivnak (1973–76) was a defensive end. Defensive end Brad Shearer (1978–80) was an All-American at Texas and a third-round draft pick.

Jerry Doerger (1982) took over No. 72. The center was an eighth-round pick out of Wisconsin. John Janata (1983) played one season at tackle. Andy Frederick also wore No. 71. William Perry came next and pretty much immortalized No. 72.

Post-Fridge the Bears had a series of players wearing No. 72 who drank the proverbial cup of coffee with the team, so many they could have formed their own line at Starbucks. Scott Adams (1995) was a guard who moved around to other teams, dying of a heart attack at only forty-six. Jon Clark (1996–97) was a tackle who played one game in each season for the Bears. Defensive tackle Chris Maumalanga (1997) was on three NFL teams in this season. Defensive tackle Carl Powell (2001) had just one season in Chicago, but played all over the map.

Ernest Grant (2002), who was drafted by the Dolphins in 2000 out of the small school of Ark-Pine Bluff, played in 11 games for Chicago in his final NFL season, recording 9 tackles. Qasim Mitchell (2003–06) was an undrafted left tackle out of North Carolina A&T in 2002, and was signed by the Browns. He would not appear in a game until joining the Bears, where in three years he would appear in 21 games (with 14 starts in 2004). After leaving Chicago he would go on to play for the Frankfurt Galaxy, Panthers, Cardinals, and 49ers, but never appeared in a regular-season game. A former first-round pick, defensive tackle Jimmy Kennedy (2007) spent 9 years in the NFL. In his lone season with Chicago, he only appeared in 3 games. Jim Buenning (2008) was a left guard who appeared in 10 games with the Bears. James Marten was claimed off waivers by the Bears, and was on the active roster but never made it into a game. He was on the practice squad as well before being released. The Bears drafted offensive lineman Gabe Carimi (2011–12) with the 29th overall pick in the 2011 NFL Draft. While he started 14 games in 2012, Chicago traded him to the Buccaneers for a sixth-round pick in 2013. Tracy Robertson (2013) was undrafted out of Baylor in 2012, and went on to play for the Texans, Lions, Patriots, and Dolphins before joining the Bears. He would appear in one game (the only of his career), and in 2014 signed with the CFL's Toronto Argonauts. Charles Leno Jr. (2014–16) is the current player wearing No. 72. A tackle out of Boise State, Leno started all 16 games at left tackle in 2016.

NO. 73: BILL BISHOP, DREAMING OF A BIGGER CAR

All Time No. 73	
Player	Years
Bill Bishop	(1952–60)
Steve Barnett	(1963)
Frank Cornish	(1966–69)
Steve Wright	(1971)
Rich Buzin	(1972)
Mike Hartenstine	(1975–86)
John Wojciechowski	(1987–93)
Marcus Keyes	(1996–97)
Kevin Dogins	(2001–02)
Tron LaFavor	(2003)
J'Marcus Webb	(2010–12)
Austen Lane	(2014)
Tayo Fabuluje	(2015)

An eighth-round draft pick out of North Texas State by the Bears (from a pick via the Pittsburgh Steelers), defensive tackle Bill Bishop was immediately traded to Chicago and went to work for the Bears. He began his tenure with the Bears in 1952 and stayed through the 1960 season. He was so excited to be making big money as a rookie (to him at the time) that he took one look at his salary of $5,200 and invested in an Oldsmobile.

Coach George Halas took one look at the Oldsmobile, dismissed Bishop as a wasteful spender, and made him return the car for something smaller and cheaper. This could only happen in the paternalistic old days of the NFL and with the Bears having nit-picking, never-mind-his-own-business Halas in charge.

When Bishop died in 1998, his wife recounted the car story and told reporters Halas's reasoning was, "You can't afford it."

Bishop was the first Bears played to wear No. 73, and he made one Pro Bowl with Chicago. The Bears let him go to the Minnesota Vikings in the expansion draft in 1961, and he retired after that season. He was one of Minnesota's first captains.

Bishop broke in No. 73 with a long ownership. Steve Barnett (1963) was a tackle with good timing, being drafted out of Oregon in time to play for the championship Bears and then moving on. Frank Cornish (1966–69) was a 300-pound product of Grambling when coach Eddie Robinson was churning out top-caliber players. Cornish spent the rest of his career with American Football Conference teams right after the AFL merged with the NFL.

Before he retired and bridged his Packers days with writing a book, Steve Wright played the 1971 season with Chicago wearing No. 73.

Tackle Rich Buzin (1972) ended his career with two games for the Bears. Defensive end Mike Hartenstine (1975–86) was a full-time Bear for a long time after coming out of Penn State, where he was an All-American. In 1983, Hartenstine amassed 12 sacks. Tackle John Wojciechowski (1987–93) is a Michigan State guy who was a solid, long-term performer for Chicago.

A two-year Bear, Marcus Keyes (1996–97) was on three NCAA Division II title teams at North Alabama. Chicago made him a seventh-round draft pick to play offensive line, but he got into just two games. Kevin Doggins (2001–02) was a center who played five years in the NFL. Defensive tackle Tron LaFavor (2003) played four games for Chicago and then went on to other NFL teams.

Tackle J'Marcus Webb (2010–12) was a Bears seventh-round draft pick and got to wear No. 73 in Chicago. He has played for other teams since. Defensive end Austen Lane (2014) came out of Murray State and played elsewhere before retiring from the Bears without getting into a game. The 342-pound tackle Tayo Fabuluje (2015) was born in Nigeria.

NO. 74: JUMBO JIM

Given how many extra-large linemen populate the NFL, a player must be pretty special to earn the nickname Jumbo. That's because every one of them could be labeled Jumbo. "Jimbo" Jim Covert was an All-American for the University of Pittsburgh and a multiple All-Pro for the Chicago Bears while wearing No. 74 between 1983 and 1991.

Actually, at 6-foot-4 and 271 pounds, Covert wasn't even really jumbo-sized compared to the tackles that followed him into the game. It seems the linemen just keep getting bigger and bigger. But Covert knew how to block and excelled immediately after being a No. 1 draft pick.

The 1985 Bears that won the Super Bowl after that season were famed for their defense, but the team finished 18–1 so the offense did its share as well. If it seemed like the Bears had stars at every position, that was mostly true.

Covert played his entire pro career with Chicago, appearing in 111 games, and was later named to the NFL's 1980s All-Decade Team. He has been nominated for the Pro Football Hall of Fame, but has yet to be selected. His old school, Pitt, however, retired his number a couple of years ago. For the Panthers, Covert wore No. 75.

"Everything I was able to accomplish as a player, and most importantly as a person, is a credit to my parents and the people who taught and coached me at the University of Pittsburgh," Covert said.

The No. 74 first appeared on the field for the Bears worn by Herman Clark who also wore 65. Paul Lipscomb (1954) was a four-time Pro Bowl selection with the Washington Redskins before he played his last NFL season in Chicago. Bob Kilcullen (1957–66) was a defensive end who was part of the 1963 title team. Tackle Dan James (1967) spent most of his career, and most of the 1960s, with the Steelers and played his final pro year with the Bears. Tackle Wayne Mass (1968–70) was a fourth-round pick out of Clemson who played a few more years post-Bears.

Bob Asher (1972–75) was a tackle out of Vanderbilt who won a Super Bowl with Dallas before playing for the Bears. Jerry Meyers (1976–79) was a star for Northern Illinois before becoming a 15th-round Chicago draft pick as a defensive lineman. He died young at age fifty-three. Guard Jeff Williams (1982) ended his career as No. 74 in Chicago.

Jim Covert was the most distinguished No. 74. He was followed by guard Garland Hawkins (1994–95), who was affiliated with the Bears for two seasons, but played in just one game. Tackle Jimmy Herndon (1997–2001) had possession of 74 longer and also played a couple more seasons elsewhere. Bernard Robertson (2001–02) was a fifth-round pick out of Tulane who played every game in 2002 after not appearing in a game the year before. Scott Sanderson (2003) played one game for the Bears at the end of his six-year NFL career that was spent mostly with the Tennessee Titans.

A nine-time Pro Bowl pick, Ruben Brown (2004–07) was an exceptional guard whose reputation was well established before he played his final seasons for the Bears wearing No. 74. A 300-pounder who played for Pitt, Brown appeared in 181 NFL games. Guard Chris Williams (2008–12) was a No. 1 draft pick out of Vanderbilt, but struggled with some injuries before going elsewhere. Guard Jermon Bushrod (2013–15) fared better in New Orleans, where he was twice All-Pro prior to signing with Chicago. Defensive end Jonathan Bullard (2016) was still trying to prove he belonged.

NO. 75: FRED WILLIAMS

Fred Williams was not only the first Bear to wear No. 75 representing the team, but he might have been the best.

A native of Little Rock, it was natural for Williams to attend the University of Arkansas. A fifth-round draft pick, Williams settled into Chicago and the Bears' lineup as a defensive tackle from 1952 to 1963. A member of the Bears' 1963 title team, Williams was a four-time Pro Bowl selection—all in the 1950s. He played another couple of seasons for the Washington Redskins, retiring in 1964 for 14 total seasons in the NFL.

In an era when linemen were a little bit lighter, Williams stood 6-foot-4 but weighed 250 pounds. He was even called "Fat Freddy" at times, though one wonders if anyone did so to his face. Williams appeared in 168 NFL games.

Williams and his pal Doug Atkins, the famed defensive end, once committed to a martini-drinking contest. Neither man wilted. They tied at twenty-one drinks ingested apiece. And Williams was supposed to be the designated driver. It was said that George Halas assigned Williams to take care of Atkins off the field because Atkins was known to engage in adventures. Rather Williams, it seemed, occasionally got caught up in them.

Riley Mattson (1965) followed Williams in No. 75, but not for long after previously playing for Washington. Defensive tackle Dave Hale (1969–71) was busy on-field for two of his Chicago years. But he was very much a long-shot to make it at all after not playing high school football and only playing small-college ball at Ottawa University in Kansas.

Tackle Jeff Sevy (1975–78) inherited No. 75. He was another long-shot as a 12th-round draft pick out of Cal. Henry Waechter also wore No. 70. Guard Stefan Humphries (1984–86) out of Michigan also played for the Denver Broncos, but was part of the Super Bowl champion Bears squad and the Super Bowl Shuffle video. Tackle Chuck Harris (1987) got into three games for Chicago and spent plenty of time in Arena ball. Defensive end John Shannon (1988–89) appeared in 25 games. Tackle Ron Mattes (1991) played most of his NFL career elsewhere.

Todd Perry (1993–2000) put some longevity into No. 75, starting for most of his affiliation with the Bears and playing in 165 NFL games altogether. Marc Colombo (2002–05) was a highly touted No. 1 draft choice for the Bears, whose tenure in Chicago was ruined by injuries. He bounced back with other teams later and is currently an assistant coach for the Dallas Cowboys.

Matt Toeaina (2007–12) was born in San Francisco, but the 308-pound defensive tackle grew up in American Samoa. He had some good moments for the Bears, but also had some injury problems. Former Oregon star Kyle Long (2013–15) is the son of Hall of Famer Howie Long and brother of Chris Long, also in the NFL. Kyle was the Bears' first No. 1 draft selection of a guard since Roger Davis in 1960 and the 320-pounder was a three-time Pro Bowl pick by 2015. His 2016 season was cut short by injury.

NO. 76: STEVE MCMICHAEL

Many players have worn No. 76 for the Chicago Bears, but it is doubtful any of the others are as memorable as defensive tackle Steve McMichael. He was one of the leading actors in the Bears' run to the 1986 Super Bowl championship, outspoken, fun-loving, entertaining, and a killer on the field. He also had the nickname of "Mongo." What more could anyone ask for?

You have to go to the wayback machine to first note any notoriety for the 6-foot-2, 270-pound McMichael. He was an All-American for the University of Texas and his first NFL action was with the New England Patriots in 1980. But he found his home with the Bears in 1981, staying through 1993. He tacked on a season with the Green Bay Packers, but nobody in Chicago likes to talk about that treasonous period as all McMichael wanted to do was extend his NFL time a little bit longer.

McMichael was selected to the Pro Bowl in 1986 and 1987, so he was more than just a funny guy. He collected 838 tackles during his career. Among those hits were 95 sacks, which means many more quarterbacks got to meet McMichael up close than wanted to.

Long before the NFL and New Orleans Saints got embroiled in a scandal over whether coaches offered bounties to players to put opposing stars out of games, McMichael had his own take on the matter regarding Hall of Famer Joe Montana.

"When I played pro football, I never set out to hurt anyone deliberately," McMichael said, "unless it was, you know, important, like a league game or something."

Supposedly McMichael included this offer as an inducement to teammates to KO the San Francisco quarterback in a game: "Ten thousand bucks if ya knock him outta the game. I don't care if ya hit him with a whiskey bottle when he gets off the bus."

Coach Mike Ditka once called McMichael the toughest of all players he coached, which given the well-known alternatives, represented a noteworthy comment.

McMichael proved that in his own way, not only on the gridiron, but later in professional wrestling. He acted as a commentator, which was a good forum for someone who liked to say whatever popped into his head. Then McMichael went into training and competed between 1995 and 1999, taking part in some outrageous story lines revolving around jealousy and revenge. Of course that could sum up most WWF and WWE plots.

Once, in mid-match, McMichael started out in a grudge battle with Ric Flair, then part of The Four Horsemen, simultaneously defending his wife at ringside from insults. Before the evening was over he had accepted a payoff to turn on his partner Kevin Greene (another ex-NFL player) and smashed him in the head with a briefcase full of cash, initiating him into The Four Horsemen. That was the beginning of a long-running soap opera in the wrestling world.

Back in Chicago, McMichael became a popular sports radio commentator. He sang "Take Me Out To The Ballgame" as one of the pregame Chicago Cubs guests at Wrigley Field. He even ran for mayor in the Chicago suburb of Romeoville, although he lost.

Milford "Dub" Miller also wore No. 26. Center Charles Miller (1932–36) was nicknamed "Ookie." Lester McDonald (1937–39) was an end out of Nebraska. End Hampton Pool (1940–43) was a solid end on two Bears' title teams, and then had a lengthy coaching career in the NFL and Canada. Elmo Kelly (1944) got into three games. Bob Cross (1952–53) was a Bears draft pick at tackle and also played for several other teams. Defensive end Ed Meadows (1954, 1956–57) had a solid career. He was only forty-two when he died.

The number 76 got passed around frequently in the Bears locker room. Offensive lineman John Mellekas (1956–61) hung onto it a little bit longer than most. So did defensive tackle John Johnson (1963–68), a regular for six seasons. Defensive end Bill Staley (1970–71) should have had the advantage of having roughly the same last name as the original nickname of the team. Being from California and playing college football in Utah, however, it is unknown if he ever set foot in Decatur, Illinois.

Defensive tackle Dave Gallagher (1974) was a No. 1 draft pick out of Michigan who jump-started his NFL stay with a single season in Chicago. Ron Rydalch (1975–80) was a defensive tackle out of Utah. Steve McMichael took command of No. 76 next. The 320-pound tackle Marcus Spears (1995–96) played collegiately at Northwestern State. Defensive tackle Shawn Lee (1998) had a decade-long NFL career, the last season of which was with Chicago. Defensive end Brad Culpepper (2000) also ended his NFL days with a final season in Chicago.

Bobby Setzer (2002) was one of many defensive linemen who tried on No. 76 briefly, in his case for two games. Tackle John Tait (2004–08) had a good career, but injuries hastened his retirement. Orlando Pace (2009), a two-time All-American at Ohio State and a 2016 Pro Football Hall of Fame inductee, was one of the great tackles of his era, but his stay in Chicago didn't last long. Long snapper Joe Long signed with the Bears, but never appeared in a game. Cory Brandon (2012–13) was a tackle whose football career took him to different NFL cities, Canada, and the Arena League.

The Bears' portion of the defensive end career of Trevor Scott (2014) consisted of nine games. Defensive tackle Bruce Gaston (2015) played in seven games for the Bears, but also was a member of the Cardinals, Patriots, Dolphins, Packers, Vikings, Chargers, Eagles, and Panthers—nine NFL teams by 2016, coming so close to finding a steady job over and over again.

Mike Adams (2016) succeeded Gaston in Chicago and played 12 games, but a back injury put him on injured reserve.

NO. 77: HAROLD "RED" GRANGE

One of the many striking aspects of Red Grange's football career was that he wore No. 77 in the 1920s and 1930s. For the first stretch of Grange's career few players on the Bears wore numbers that stretched higher than the 20s. And if he had come along later, under NFL rules, as a running back, Grange would not have been permitted to wear 77.

Instead, Grange was a man for his times, a legend for all time, and he made 77 legendary. It was also retired by the Bears in his honor, with only Link Lyman, his contemporary in Chicago who became intimate with more numbers than a mathematician, also ever donning the jersey for the Bears.

Just about every part of Grange's football career is the stuff of legend. He was a superstar at the University of Illinois in the early 1920s before anyone used the word. The fans, however, knew what they were seeing. In those leather-helmet days long before the Internet or television, Grange became famous for his Big Ten football exploits. Nothing did more to put him on the map of public consciousness than his October 1924 game vs. Michigan.

The Wolverines were defending national champions when they came to Illinois for the opening of the Illini's new Memorial Stadium. Starting with returning the opening kickoff 95 yards, Grange scored six touchdowns and Illinois thumped Michigan, 39–14.

Seemingly untouchable coming out of the backfield, Grange was nicknamed "The Galloping Ghost," one of sports' greatest nicknames. He was also called "The Wheaton Iceman" because he was from Wheaton, Illinois, and worked an off-season job delivering ice blocks to homes without refrigeration. This supposedly gave him strength, although Grange, at 5-foot-11 and 175 pounds, was not one of football's giants.

Grange said he made his terrific moves by instinct and said he would not become a coach.

"No one ever taught me and I can't teach anyone," he said. "If you can't explain it, how can you take credit for it?"

Many people believe famed sportswriter Grantland Rice bestowed the Galloping Ghost name on Grange, but Grange told anyone who asked that it was Warren Brown, a Chicago sportswriter, who thought it up.

The 1920s was an unsettled time for the fledgling NFL. Teams folded constantly. Recognizing the box office appeal of Grange, both his agent C. C. Pyle and Bears owner George Halas concocted a scheme to make Grange and the Bears rich. Immediately after playing his final game for Illinois, Grange joined the Bears for a nationwide, 19-game barnstorming tour. The instincts of the promoters were correct. The tour was a smash hit, like bringing a Broadway play to the hinterlands.

Halas sought to sign Grange permanently, but he would not match the salary demands of Pyle and the player. Instead, Pyle created a competing football league from scratch to showcase Grange with a team called the New York Yankees. That venture fizzled after a short while and Grange did become a Bear for the rest of his pro career, ending in 1934. As did everyone at the time, Grange played offense and defense in the Bears' backfields. A serious knee injury robbed him of some of his speed and grandeur in the open field, but that did not stop him from being selected to the College Football Hall of Fame and the Pro Football Hall of Fame.

For quite some time the public was skeptical pro football was played at a higher level than college football, an opinion that drove Halas crazy. Grange made comments that supported Halas.

"A professional player is smarter than a college man," Grange said. "He uses his noodle. He knows what to do and when to do it."

Grange lived a long life, dying at age eighty-seven in 1991, after spending many years doing TV and radio commentary on Bears games and forever being recognized as one of the greatest figures in NFL history. There is a statue of Grange at the University of Illinois.

NO. 78: STAN JONES

All Time No. 78	
Player	Years
Art "Buddy" Davis	(1953–54)
Stan Jones*	(1954–65)
Harry Gunner	(1970)
Bob Newton	(1971–75)
John Ward	(1976)
Greg Johnson	(1977)
Keith Van Horne	(1981–92)
Pat Riley	(1995)
Blake Brockermeyer	(1999–2001)
Aaron Gibson	(2003–04)
John St. Clair	(2005–08)
Kevin Shafer	(2009–10)
James Brown	(2012–13)

Hall of Fame

Linemen hardly ever get much attention and rarely get the credit they deserve. Stan Jones was so good that he was hard to overlook—even when sports announcers rarely talked about the guys who played his positions.

Jones could play offensive and defensive tackle with equal facility, one of the last NFL stars who tried. In Jones's case, he moved where coach George Halas saw the need, which meant he played guard and (mostly) tackle on offense and defensive tackle on the other side of the ball. He was a superb player in any role so he drew attention to No. 78 in different positions.

A seven-time Pro Bowl fixture and a member of the Bears' 1963 championship team, the 6-foot-1, 250-pound Jones was drafted out of the University of Maryland. He was a Bears mainstay between 1954 and 1965, and then played one last season with the Washington Redskins. In the off seasons Jones was a teacher—the profession he planned to go into before ending up in football.

One distinctive aspect of Jones's career was being an early devotee of weight lifting. During his era professional athletes eschewed the weight room. Jones embraced it and said the strength he gained is what set him apart as a football player.

"There's no chance I'd be in the Hall if I hadn't lifted," Jones said. "Some of my teammates thought I was nuts. Some guys figured you became so narcissistic, all you did all day was look at yourself in the mirror. Other guys were afraid you'd get muscle-bound."

Jones made those comments in 1991, when he was inducted into the Pro Football Hall of Fame.

Perhaps surprising to some given his irascible nature and suspicion of anything that did not smack of tradition, Jones had the backing of Halas to weight lift.

"Mr. George Halas liked the idea of having the strongest man in football," Jones said.

He was probably smiling when he said that.

Teaching ended up in Jones's rearview mirror for good after he retired as a player. He spent the next twenty-five years as an assistant coach for several teams around the NFL and even threw in a final season on the sidelines working for the Scottish Claymores of NFL Europe in 1998.

Jones is a member of the College Football Hall of Fame, as well as the Pro Hall.

Buddy Davis was the only Bear to wear 78 before Jones, and also wore No. 70. After Jones came defensive end Harry Gunner (1970) and then Bob Newton (1971–75), who started his 11-year NFL career in Chicago. John Ward (1976) was a guard who got into 10 games. Defensive end Greg Johnson (1977) was a Florida State guy and got the uniform number, but did not get into a Bears game.

Keith Van Horne (1981–92) might have been the best No. 78 outside of Jones. Van Horne was an All-American tackle for Southern Cal, a member of the Super Bowl champs, and a player who spent all 13 seasons of his NFL career with Chicago.

Pat Riley (1995) was a defensive tackle who got into one game. Blake Brockermeyer (1999–2001) was an All-American from the University of Texas who was a tough, insightful player. His middle name was Weeks, but Bears fans wish he had been around years longer. An immense man at 6-foot-7, Aaron Gibson (2003–04) was the first player in NFL history to record an official weight of 400 pounds. Gibson mostly struggled to gain a secure foothold in the NFL as he moved between teams, but had one fine season in Chicago.

John St. Clair (2005–08) took over No. 78 and at 6-foot-6, 320 pounds, it wasn't as if he was Tinkerbell either. The All-American tackle from Virginia actually scored a Bears touchdown on a pass from Rex Grossman. He played in the Super Bowl for Chicago against Indianapolis. Defensive tackle Kevin Shaffer (2009–10) hooked up with the Bears at the end of his career.

James Brown (2012–13) got into five games in his first year with the Bears, but spent time on the practice squad later before being cut and going to the Browns. William Poehls out of Montana had No. 78 going into the 2017 season.

NO. 79: KURT BECKER

Although he was an All-American for the University of Michigan, Kurt Becker was not seen as an automatic NFL starter. A sixth-round draft pick, Becker was the 146th player taken in the 1982 draft. But he made it as a guard with the Bears (1982–88, 1990) and had a nine-year career in the league.

This No. 79 earned a Super Bowl ring with Chicago.

Becker was born in the Chicago suburb of Aurora and played high school ball there. His local ties made Becker a good get from Michigan, a popular signee. The 6-foot-5, 270-pound Becker was a regular, spent a season away from the team in Los Angeles, and then wrapped up his NFL career with a 10-game stint back in Chicago.

He played 94 games in the league, all but two with the Bears. Later, Becker returned to high school football coaching in Aurora. He cited famed coaches like Mike Ditka with the Bears and Bo Schembechler at Michigan as influences in his life.

"They instilled morals and values in me through the game of football that could be applied to life," Becker said.

A tackle out of Iowa, Dick Klein (1958–59) was the first No. 79 on the Bears. His nickname was "Sleepy." Art Anderson (1961–62) signed with the Bears for $750 and, after a short NFL career lasting one more year, embarked on a long Marine Corps career. Tackle Dick Evey (1964–69) was a first-round draft pick out of the University of Tennessee. John Hoffman, a defensive end, played one game for the Bears in 1971. Tackle Lionel Antoine (1972–76) came out of Southern Illinois and played his whole NFL career with Chicago.

Guard Emanuel Zanders (1981) spent most of his career with New Orleans before joining the Bears. Kurt Becker took over No. 79 after that. Post-Becker, Louis Age (1992) was briefly a tackle in Chicago. Marcus Spears also wore No. 76. Scotty Lewis (1995) was a defensive end who did not make it into a game for the Bears. Jerry Wisne (1999–2000) did, seven of them in fact, as a tackle.

Lineman Steve Edwards (2002–05) lined up for four NFL teams and four Arena league teams during his career—all but two of his 40 NFL games were for the Bears. Levi Horn (2011) tried on No. 79, but basically was a practice squad player. Tackle Jonathan Scott (2012–13) has been part of five NFL teams and seen as much action with the Bears as anyone else. Ryan Groy (2014) got into four games as a center with Chicago. Nose tackle Terry Williams (2015) was on the fringe for the Bears and was then waived.

NO. 80: CURTIS CONWAY

All Time No. 80	
Player	Years
Earl Britton	(1925)
Clement Neacy	(1927)
Ted Drews	(1928)
Tom Hearden	(1929)
John Helwig	(1953–56)
Ralph Anderson	(1958)
Ed Cooke	(1958)
Robert Jencks	(1963–64)
Jimmy Jones	(1965–67)
Jon Kilgore	(1968)
Jerry Simmons	(1969–70)
Craig Cotton	(1973)
Bo Rather	(1974–78)
Rickey Watts	(1979–83)
Tim Wrightman	(1985–86)
James Thornton	(1988–92)
Curtis Conway	(1993–99)
Dez White	(2000–03)
Bernard Berrian	(2004–07)
Brandon Lloyd	(2008)
Earl Bennett	(2009–13)
Marc Mariani	(2014–15)
MyCole Pruitt	(2006)

Curtis Conway was an athlete. He proved it in football in several ways. Conway had been a talented quarterback, but became a wide receiver at the University of Southern California and catching the ball is the role the Bears saw for him when they drafted Conway in 1993 with a first-round pick.

The 6-foot-1, 196-pound Conway spent 12 seasons in the NFL, the first seven of them with Chicago. Conway caught 594 passes in his career for 52 touchdowns. He was a dangerous runner after the grab, accumulating 8,230 yards on catches. Twice, in 1995 and 1996, Conway topped 1,000 yards receiving for the Bears.

Also in 1996, Conway collected a career-high 81 catches. It was also the first time in Bears history that a receiver had gone over 1,000 yards in a season two years in a row.

Harkening back to his early days in the sport, Conway threw two touchdown passes in the NFL on tricky plays.

In retirement, Conway went into radio and then became a TV analyst for Pac-12 football games.

Unusual for its time, Earl Britton pulled on the No. 80 jersey for the Bears in 1925 when most members of the team were wearing numbers that didn't go nearly that high. Perhaps he was inspired by Red Grange's use of 77. Britton was a fullback and a kicker but lasted just that one year for the Bears. However, over the next four seasons he suited up for the Frankford Yellow Jackets and the Dayton Triangles, among other NFL clubs.

Britton made wearing No. 80 a habit for the Bears. Clement Neacy (1927) put it on next, for two games. Ted Drews (1928) was briefly an end. Tom Hearden (1929) was an end out of Notre Dame who also played for Green Bay and then coached mostly high school for years in Wisconsin.

John Helwig (1953–56) was a four-year linebacker. After he died, family members got into trouble for continuing to collect his NFL pension. Ralph

Anderson (1958) also wore 39. Ed Cooke (1958) got into three games with the Bears and then went on to a decade-long career with other teams. Robert Jencks (1963–64) was a two-year kicker. Jimmy Jones (1965–67) caught 56 of his career total 69 passes with Chicago.

Jon Kilgore (1968) slipped into No. 80 long enough to punt for a bit. Wide receiver Jerry Simmons (1969–70) took up the jersey next as it hit a period where it mimicked family hand-me-downs in a big family. Tight end Craig Cotton (1973) caught 13 passes for Chicago. Bo Rather (1974–78) caught 91 passes for the Bears and won a Super Bowl ring with Miami.

Rickey Watts (1979–83) played all five of his NFL years with Chicago and caught 81 passes, the bulk of them in his first three seasons. Tim Wrightman (1985–86) was a well-liked backup tight end during the team's Super Bowl days. He caught 24 and 22 passes, respectively, during his two seasons and also played with the Chicago Blitz in the United States Football League. Wrightman now owns a hunting ranch in Idaho.

James Thornton got to wear No. 80 between 1988 and 1992. The tight end was nicknamed "Robocop" because he looked tough enough to out-arm wrestle the movie character. Curtis Conway came next. Dez White (2000–03) was a well-respected receiver who three times caught between 45 and 51 passes in a season for the Bears.

Bernard Berrian (2004–07) was an air force kid born in Barcelona, Spain, although he grew up in California. Berrian split his NFL career between the Bears, who drafted him in the third round, and the Minnesota Vikings. With Chicago Berrian caught as many as 71 passes in 2007. Although it seemed as if Berrian would spend a long time wearing No. 80, he left in free agency.

Brandon Lloyd (2008) caught 26 of his 399 balls in the NFL with the Bears, although he was injured for a chunk of his lone season in Chicago. The Bears liked the way Earl Bennett (2009–13) looked as a three-time Southeastern Conference selection for Vanderbilt, and made him a third-round draft pick. Bennett's best season was a 54-catch campaign in 2009.

Marc Mariani (2014–15) was a 2010 All-Pro elsewhere, but did a good job running back kicks for the Bears. MyCole Pruitt (2016) goes into the 2017 season as a tight end wearing No. 80, picked up from Minnesota's practice squad.

NO. 81: DOUG ATKINS

It was almost amazing that any team ever blocked Doug Atkins. When the defensive end charged in from the side, putting quarterbacks and running backs both in jeopardy, it tested the bravery of those assigned to keep their teammates alive. Atkins steamrolled some would-be blockers and sometimes even leapt right over others' heads.

The most prominent wearer of No. 81, Atkins was immensely strong and athletic. He stood 6-foot-8, so he towered over many offensive linemen of the day and he played at about 260 pounds, which was actually pretty svelte.

Atkins was a No. 1 draft pick out of the University of Tennessee in 1953 by the Cleveland Browns, who were foolish enough to send him to Chicago. Atkins wrote his own ticket out of Chicago eventually, to the expansion New Orleans Saints, because his irreverent ways often drove George Halas batty. In all, Atkins was an eight-time Pro Bowl selection who was inducted into the Pro Football Hall of Fame in 1982.

Fellow Hall of Famer Fran Tarkenton, the New York Giants and Minnesota Vikings quarterback, knew what it felt like to be decked by Atkins.

"He is the strongest man in football and also the biggest," Tarkenton said. "When he rushes the passer with those oak tree arms of his way up in the air, he's 12 feet tall. And if he gets to you, the whole world starts spinning."

Take that as an ouch.

As one of the cornerstones of the Bears defense, Atkins won a championship with Chicago in 1963, but he also had a title ring from his days with Cleveland. Atkins wore No. 91 at Tennessee and his alma mater retired that number. He stuck with No. 81 with the Saints, and New Orleans retired that number for him.

Players who never went head-to-head against Atkins wondered if the stories about his strength and skill at jumping over players could be true. Halfback Tommy Mason, another Viking, certainly had vivid memories of being victimized.

Once Atkins essentially flew over Mason's head and he was determined not to let that happen again. "Next time I kept my head up," Mason said, "and he grabbed me by the seat of the pants and scruff of the neck and tossed me aside like a bouncer throwing a drunk out of a beer joint."

People ever wondered if Atkins was going to retire, and he kept pressuring NFL ball carriers as long as he could into 1969, through 205 games. Atkins actually sacked a quarterback on the final play of his career. That was fitting since he led the football world in intimidation.

Atkins had a quirky sense of humor and did not always respond well to authority. He took great glee in tweaking Halas. Atkins could be casual about reporting to practice on time. Once he famously darted out of the locker room naked except for his helmet just as Halas was about to send a search party for him. As Halas and other Bears gaped, Atkins nonchalantly ran a lap around the field.

One of Atkins's most oft-quoted comments from his testy relationship with Halas was uttered when the coach, who was known to be cheap at the salary negotiating table, told the player he wasn't working hard enough in practice.

"You don't pay me enough to play *and* practice," Atkins said.

Atkins liked to have fun off the field and also undertake convenient challenges. When former teammate Richie Petitbon told a story about watching Atkins eat forty-five pieces of fried chicken, Atkins pooh-poohed it.

"I really was never much of a big eater," Atkins said. "Now, drinking was something else. I think Richie might be confusing chicken with martinis."

Atkins was eighty-five when he died at the end of 2015. The Bears should have retired 81 for Atkins, but they started running out of numbers so they have a moratorium on taking more out of circulation.

George Connor, who also wore 71, was the first Bear to wear No. 81. Larry Brink (1954) made two Pro Bowls as a defensive end, but they were with the Rams before coming to Chicago. Doug Atkins claimed 81 next.

Defensive end Marty Amsler (1967–68) had one interception and one fumble recovery in his first Bears season after trying to make NFL rosters elsewhere, but then got hurt. Mike Reppond (1973) was a wide receiver who got into two Bears games. Clint Haslerig (1974) played mostly on special teams as he began his NFL career in Chicago. Tight end Gary Butler (1975) had a cameo in Chicago. Tight end Bob Bruer (1976) did not make it into a Bears game. Chuck Bradley (1977) came at the end of a line of players who didn't have much time to sweat while wearing No. 81.

Robin Earl (1977–82) was a third-round draft pick out of the University of Washington who played tight end and fullback for the Bears over the course of his NFL career. He also wore No. 39. Primarily a blocking back, Earl averaged 4.1 yards per carry when Chicago gave him the ball. He also caught 47 passes. While Earl was switching positions, Harry Washington (1979) also got a glimpse of No. 81 and played in six games. Jay Saldi (1983–84) played his last two seasons with the Bears after spending several years with Dallas. Saldi was part of a Super Bowl champ with the Cowboys.

James Maness (1985) caught one pass in eight games, but was cut by Chicago after failing a drug test. Lew Barnes (1986) was a wide receiver out of Oregon. Tight end Don Kindt Jr. (1987) was the son of former Bears running back Don Kindt from the 1940s and 1950s. Anthony Morgan (1991–93) was a wide receiver who caught 27 passes in Chicago, played more in Green Bay, and then became a minister. Fred Banks (1993), like so many other wearers of 81, didn't keep it long, appearing in only eight games. Jeff Graham (1994–95) was an Ohio State product who caught 542 passes for 30 touchdowns in the NFL, his best season being '95 with Chicago when he grabbed 82 passes for 1,301 yards.

Bobby Engram (1996–2009) came out of Penn State to catch 650 passes in his 14-year NFL career, including an electrifying 88 with Chicago in 1999 while also returning kicks. Upon his retirement, Engram promptly jumped into pro coaching and is now working as an assistant with the Baltimore Ravens.

Ahmad Merritt (2001–03) struggled to stay with the Bears, but also spent time playing Arena football. Rashied Davis also wore No. 21 when he played defensive back; he had a 100-yard kickoff return, too (which came in the preseason). Sam Hurd (2011) went from being special teams captain to being arrested on drug charges. Cameron Meredith (2015–16) got No. 81 and aimed to keep it in 2017 after catching 66 passes the year before.

NO. 82: ALAN PAGE, KEN MARGERUM, AND JOHN DAVIS

All Time No. 82	
Player	Years
Del Bjork	(1937–38)
Ray Bray	(1939–42, 1946–51)
Anthony Ippolito	(1943)
Tom Roberts	(1943–44)
Jack Hoffman	(1949–56)
Dick Hensley	(1953)
Maury Youmans	(1960–63)
Rich Kreitling	(1964)
Emilio Vallez	(1968–69)
Earl Thomas	(1971–73)
Matt Maslowski	(1972)
Fred Pagac	(1974)
Royce Berry	(1976)
John Gilliam	(1977)
Alan Page	(1978–81)
Ken Margerum	(1981–86)
Brian Glasgow	(1987)
Wendell Davis	(1988–93)
Nate Lewis	(1994–95)
Fabien Bownes	(1995, 1997–98)
John Jackson	(1996)
Eddie Kennison	(2000)
John Davis	(2001–03)
Daryl Jones	(2003–04)
John Owens	(2004)
Gabe Reid	(2005–06)
Greg Olsen	(2007–10)
Chris Williams	(2013–14)
Khari Lee	(2015)
Logan Paulsen	(2016)

Many Bears have worn No. 82, some for a very short time. While they may not have had much in common besides being on the Chicago roster, the trio of Alan Page, Ken Margerum, and John Davis did wear this number.

Alan Page was more famous with his prior NFL team, the Minnesota Vikings, and more famous for his post-football career as a Minnesota Supreme Court Justice than he was during his 1978–81 time on the Bears roster at the tail-end of his playing days. However, the nine-time Pro Bowl selection was still a feared pass rusher.

The NFL's Most Valuable Player in 1971, Page was a two-time Defensive Player of the Year as well. He collected more than 40 sacks (unofficially) with Chicago, so the 6-foot-4, 245-pound defensive tackle was not washed up when he departed Minnesota. Compared to other defensive tackles, Page was light at 245 pounds and the Vikings did not appreciate his long-distance running routine training for a marathon, so they put him on waivers. Good news for the Bears.

Page did considerable charity work aimed at improving the lives of children in poverty and providing opportunities.

"I don't know when children stop dreaming," Page said. "But I do know when hope starts leaking away, because I've seen it happen."

Page, who attended law school, was elected to Minnesota's highest court in 1992 and kept being re-elected until he retired at age seventy in 2015.

Ken Margerum was a completely different type of No. 82, seemingly a fun-loving guy who liked to goof around with quarterback Jim McMahon. Margerum was a wide receiver who weighed 180 pounds when he came out of Stanford in 1981. He played on the Bears' Super Bowl championship squad as a third-down receiver and special teams participant.

He brought a reputation out of college as a guy who could be the life of the party, including breaking beer bottles over his own head and smashing his head through an oil painting or two.

A knee injury nearly derailed Margerum's pro career early on and he missed the entire 1984 season, but he refused to let the setback get him down, working so hard he impressed hard-to-impress coaches while retaining a sunny attitude.

"Why be down?" Margerum said. "I made the injury into a positive situation. I considered it as something that gave me a year off in which I could go to Hawaii, have a good time, and get to know my friends better."

After his Bears tenure (1981–86), Margerum played a couple of seasons for the San Francisco 49ers and then went into high school, college, and Arena ball coaching.

Tight end John Davis (2001–03) played college football at little Emporia State, so it was miracle enough he ever got noticed. Dallas picked him up in the draft and Davis made a lap around the league before the Bears signed him. He was more blocker than pass catcher during his few seasons in Chicago, though he caught 55 passes in his NFL career.

Del Bjork (1937–38) introduced No. 82 to the masses for the Bears. Bjork was a tackle out of the University of Oregon who made a Pro Bowl team before World War II. During the conflict he was awarded with the Purple Heart. Defensive lineman Ray Bray (1939–42, 1946–51) had a long career sandwiched around World War II, making four Pro Bowl teams and being part of the 1940 Bears championship squad.

Anthony Ippolito (1943) was a guard and NFL champ in his only season. Tom Roberts (1943–44) played parts of two seasons during the war. Jack Hoffman also wore No. 29. Dick Hensley (1953) was a two-way end out of Kentucky. Maury Youmans (1960–63) came out of Syracuse University and was on the '63 title team, but suffered injury and illness. Rich Kreitling (1964) was a more effective end with Cleveland before his last stop with the Bears. Emilio Vallez (1968–69) appeared in nine Bears games.

Earl Thomas (1971–73) continued the parade of No. 82 models and had two 20-plus-catch seasons in Chicago. Matt Maslowski (1972) only appeared in one game. Fred Pagac (1974) had a six-catch season for Chicago, but has had a lengthy college and pro coaching career, including twenty-two years at Ohio State and is currently with the Denver Broncos. Royce

Berry (1976) was mostly a Cincinnati Bengal, but played his last year with the Bears after a trade. A four-time Pro Bowl receiver and return man, John Gilliam (1977) caught 382 passes in his career which was spread across the country, but most notably with the Minnesota Vikings. Gilliam's first year was New Orleans' first year, and he returned the opening kickoff 94 yards for a touchdown in the franchise's debut.

Alan Page came next in No. 82, and Ken Margerum followed him. Brian Glasgow (1987) was a tight end out of Northern Illinois, who played in three games for the Bears. Wendell Davis (1988–93) brought some stability. A first-team All-American out of Louisiana State, Davis caught 207 passes for 3,000 yards for Chicago, but his career was ruined by devastating knee injuries. In recent years he has been coaching in the pros and in college.

Nate Lewis (1994–95) split his career between San Diego and Chicago, but the better years were with the Chargers. John Jackson (1996) was a wide receiver out of Southern Cal who now works as a radio football commentator and kept the revolving door going on the Bears' No. 82. Fabien Bownes (1995, 1997–98) caught 12 passes in '97. Eddie Kennison (2000) played for five teams, including the Rams twice, and caught 548 passes. He grabbed 55 balls for the Bears in his one year in Chicago. John Davis came next in No. 82.

Daryl Jones (2003–04) barely played as a receiver. John Owens (2004) played in two games. One hopes No. 82 was washed before it was transferred in 2004.

Tight end Gabe Reid (2005–06) was rarely used as a target. Greg Olsen (2007–10), another tight end, was a first-round pick in 2007 who caught 194 passes before moving on to Carolina, where he was selected for three Pro Bowls. Chris Williams (2013–14) also wore No. 74. Tight end Khari Lee (2015) caught one pass for Chicago before giving up No. 82 and moving on to the Detroit Lions.

Logan Paulsen (2016) caught three passes in his 16 games and after the season went to the San Francisco 49ers.

NO. 83: WILLIE GAULT

It used to be that track and field stars did not respect football speed. They believed the clockings they heard were fake times, recorded under less-than-strict conditions. Willie Gault was a different case. He was track and football fast.

Gault was born in Griffin, Georgia, in 1960, and at 6 feet tall and 178 pounds, he enjoyed a fascinating all-around athletic career. At the University of Tennessee he was a star football player and a track star in hurdles and sprints, the winner of Southeastern Conference and NCAA championships.

A member of the 1980 American Olympic track and field team that was part of the US boycott at the Summer Games in the Soviet Union, Gault was unable to participate. However, in 1983, at the track world championships in Helsinki, Finland, Gault was a member of the American team that set a world record in the 4×100-meter relay. He won gold in that event and took a bronze in the 110-meter hurdles.

Gault spent the first half of his NFL career with the Bears. He was a member of the Super Bowl championship squad and, as befits a future movie actor, he played a part in the Super Bowl Shuffle. Gault caught 333 passes in his pro career, which also included a long stint in Oakland with the Raiders, and was a superb return man. In all, he scored 45 touchdowns.

The speed that was so advantageous in track helped in football. Gault averaged 19.9 yards per catch and 24.2 yards per kickoff return. That's what can be produced when a runner can dash 10.10 in the 100 meters and 13.26 in the hurdles. Gault even switched sports completely for a while, qualifying for a Winter Olympic squad in the bobsled.

As he aged, it might be said Gault refused to admit he was slowing down. At the least he mastered masters running competitions. He set world records in the 100 and 200 in the 45–49 age group and then returned to set world records when he reached the 50–54 age group.

End Bill McColl (1952–59) was the first Bear to wear No. 83. He spent eight years in Chicago and caught 201 passes. He became a doctor after his football career was over. Two sons, Duncan and Milt, also played in the NFL. Roger LeClerc also wore No. 54. Mac Percival (1967–73) was discovered by the Dallas Cowboys at a free-agent tryout, but did not play for them at the time.

After his last season in Chicago, Percival went back to Dallas and got into three games. In between he scored 456 points for the Bears. That included a much-talked-about boot that won a game over Green Bay in 1968. In a 10–10 game, Bear return man Cecil Turner called a fair catch of a Packer punt at the Green Bay 43-yard line. Although most fans have never seen such a play, the NFL rulebook allows for a free kick from the spot of the ball. Percival took the kick, made it, and the Bears won.

Charles Wade (1974) came into possession of No. 83 next, catching 39 passes that season. Randy Burks (1976) caught one pass for 55 yards for the Bears. Steve Rivera (1977) played three games at wide receiver. Golden Richards (1978–79) had 27 catches in 1978. Kris Haines (1979–81) caught four passes for the Bears after coming out of Notre Dame.

Willie Gault was next in line wearing 83. A parade of other wide receivers followed wearing No. 83 for short periods. Lawrence White (1987) got into two games and caught one pass. Eric Wright (1991–92) caught five passes for the Bears. Terry Obee (1993–94) caught 26 passes his first year in Chicago and ran back nine kicks, but did not get into a game in 1994. Michael Timpson (1995–96) caught 300 passes in his career with a Bears high of 62 in '96. Eric Smith (1997) got into seven games and caught two passes.

Macey Brooks (1999–2000) caught 26 passes his last year in Chicago while appearing in every game. David Terrell (2001–04) arrived in Chicago with great fanfare after an All-American receiving career at the University of Michigan. Unfortunately, it just never truly worked out as expected for Terrell, although he caught as many as 43 and 42 balls in different seasons before being cut by the Bears. Comeback attempts with other teams did not pan out either.

The 6-foot-1, 206-pound Mike Hass (2007) had trouble getting noticed out of high school, but ended up recording three straight 1,000-yard receiving seasons for Oregon State and won the Biletnikoff Award as the best college receiver. However, he made it into just one game with Chicago and did not do much better in attempts to play for other teams. Max Komar (2011) got into two games for Chicago.

Martellus Bennett (2013–15) ranks as a first-rate tight end with 403 catches entering the 2017 season. He grabbed 65 passes for the Bears in 2013. He then brought honor to No. 83 by setting a team record for catches by a tight end with 90 in 2014, eclipsing an old Mike Ditka mark. He then became an increasingly unhappy camper, feuding with other players and management in 2015. Still, he landed on his feet, winning a Super Bowl with the New England Patriots. Bennett, who also writes children's books, even recorded a music album. He joined the Green Bay Packers for the 2017 season.

Daniel Braverman (2016) succeeded Bennett in Chicago wearing No. 83, but played in only three games.

NO. 84: JOHN FARRINGTON

All Time No. 84	
Player	Years
Gerald Weatherly	(1950, 1952–54)
John Farrington	(1960–63)
Ron Smith	(1965, 1970–72)
Austin Denney	(1967–69)
Jim Seymour	(1970–72)
Richard Harris	(1974–75)
Brian Baschnagel	(1976–84)
Sam Bowers	(1987)
Ron Morris	(1987–92)
Chris Gedney	(1993–96)
Kerry Cash	(1996)
John Allred	(1997–2002)
Fred Baxter	(2001–02)
Bobby Wade	(2003–05)
Brandon Rideau	(2006–08)
Blake Annen	(2014)
Ben Braunecker	(2016)

The terrible automobile crash at training camp in Indiana in August of 1964 demoralized the Bears for the upcoming season. Halfback Willie Galimore and end John Farrington were killed in the one-vehicle accident on the way back to their dorms after eating in the town of Rensselaer. It is likely that those in the know still acknowledge the tragedy when they drive past today on the interstate and see the sign for the community.

Galimore was more ingrained as a Bears fixture. Farrington, No. 84, was still fighting to become more of a focal point in the team's offense. There was probably more attention on Galimore because of his longer association with Chicago. But Farrington, whose nickname was "Bo," should be not forgotten either.

They were returning to their rooms at St. Joseph's College, site of preseason training for the defending 1963 champions. At the wheel, Galimore was apparently caught off guard by a tight turn in the dark and the car flipped over. Both players were killed at the scene.

The season before, the Bears won their first crown since 1946 and their last until 1985. The feat was accomplished with great satisfaction as the club edged out the Green Bay Packers at the height of their Vince Lombardi fame.

Farrington was a 6-foot-3, 217-pound receiver out of Prairie View A&M who had been with the Bears since the 1960 season and seemed poised to take on a bigger role. He caught 21 passes in 1963, following seasons of 13 and 21. In 1961, Farrington gathered in a Bill Wade pass and went all the way, running 98 yards for a touchdown. He was twenty-eight years old in the summer of 1964.

Crushed by the deaths of the young men, George Halas referred to the crash as "the saddest day" Chicago Bears history.

The first No. 84 for the Bears was Gerald Weatherly, who also wore No. 45. John Farrington came next. Ron Smith (1965, 1970–72) had the nickname of

"Trousers." He took over No. 84 a couple of years later, but didn't have it his whole time with Chicago, especially since he was mostly a defensive back. Austin Denney (1967–69) started at tight end for a bit, catching 23 passes in 1968 and 22 the following year.

Jim Seymour (1970–72) was a huge star at Notre Dame, a three-time All-American and a centerpiece of the 1977 national champions. He once totaled 276 yards on receptions in a single game, yet in his three seasons in Chicago Seymour caught just 21 passes. The explosive end who had appeared on the cover of *Time* magazine with quarterback Terry Hanratty died of cancer at age sixty-four.

Richard Harris (1974–75) was an All-American defensive end out of Grambling who later had a lengthy coaching career, much of it in the Canadian Football League. Another well-remembered 84 was Brian Baschnagel (1976–84), who had the bad luck to be on injured reserve for the entire Super Bowl season, although he stayed with the team and aided the coaches. Baschnagel's season-high for catches was 34 in 1981. Sam Bowers (1987) had one season with Chicago, his only one in the NFL, but also played for Toronto in the CFL and New Jersey in the USFL.

Ron Morris (1987–92) caught 121 passes for the Bears, grabbing between 20 and 31 over a four-year stretch. An operation for a knee injury resulted in the end of Morris's career and him winning a $5.2 million malpractice suit for poor treatment.

No. 84 mostly belonged to tight ends, one after the other. Tight end Chris Gedney (1993–96) split a six-year NFL career between Chicago and Arizona and later moved into sports administration at Syracuse University. Kerry Cash (1996) got into just three games in Chicago after much bigger production with the Indianapolis Colts. Tight end John Allred (1997–2002) spent five seasons in Chicago and in 1999 got into every game, catching 13 passes. In a 11-year career, the majority of it spent with the New York Jets, the best season Fred Baxter (2001–02) had with the Bears was 22 catches in 2001.

Wide receiver Bobby Wade (2003–05) came out of Arizona and began his career with the Bears. He caught 244 passes in his career with a season-best of 42 with Chicago. He had some success as a punt returner, too, but when Wade fumbled 10 times in 2005, the Bears cut him.

Brandon Rideau (2006–08) came and went on the practice squad, was cut and re-signed often, but saw his only game action—two games—in '08.

Blake Annen (2014) has been on and off the rosters of five NFL teams, but going into 2017 his only playing time was five games with the Bears in 2014. Ben Braunecker (2016) got into 13 games after joining the team out of Harvard and was on the 2017 roster hoping to hang onto No. 84 longer than many of his recent predecessors.

NO. 85: DENNIS MCKINNON

Listed as a wide receiver during his 1983 to 1989 stay with the Bears, Dennis McKinnon did play that position and that's why he wore No. 85, but that was an oversimplification. The former Florida State notable was much more versatile than that. The 6-foot-1, 185-pound McKinnon could hurt opposing teams in many ways.

McKinnon's time with the Bears included the Super Bowl championship victory in 1986, but he was an effective weapon to be deployed during his entire involvement with the team.

As a receiver, McKinnon hauled in 180 passes for Chicago. His best season was 1988, when he caught 45. Once in a while McKinnon was asked to carry the ball and he did score one rushing touchdown, but his other value was as a punt returner and he returned two punts for touchdowns in one season.

Except for a brief fling when McKinnon signed with the Miami Dolphins and Dallas Cowboys to prolong his career (didn't get into a game for the Dolphins, but played in 9 for the Cowboys), the majority of his time was spent with the Bears, who originally signed him as an undrafted free agent.

The 1985 regular-season Bears are considered one of the greatest teams of all time. After they easily swept through the 1985 playoffs to the title, everyone expected them to repeat—but they did not.

"We just couldn't score inside the 20 or capitalize on turnovers," McKinnon said of why another title did not follow.

The first Bear to wear No. 85 was Bob Carey in 1958. He was an end in his final season after playing for the Los Angeles Rams. Bill Martin also wore No. 22. Duane Allen (1966–67) caught three passes total for Chicago. Willie Holman (1968–73) came out of South Carolina State and gave the Bears good play at defensive end. Wayne Wheeler (1974) caught five passes in 12 games. Steve Schubert (1975–79) occupied 85 for a while and caught 23 passes for Chicago after part of a season in New England.

Bob Fisher (1980–81) was a tight end out of Southern Methodist who caught 12 passes in 1980. Dennis McKinnon inherited 85 next. Clemson product Keith Jennings (1991–97) got it after McKinnon. Jennings had double-figure catches in five seasons at tight end in Chicago. He also played in the XFL and the World League of American Football, as well as one year with the Dallas Cowboys prior to signing with the Bears. Alonzo Mayes (1998–2000) caught 33 passes in his three NFL seasons. all with Chicago.

Kaseem Sinceno (2000–01) caught 11 passes for the Bears and also played with three other teams in a lap around the NFL. John Gilmore (2002–07) slowed the turnover at tight end and in No. 85, though he caught just 55 passes during his 10 years in the league. Earl Bennett also wore No. 80. Tight end Matthew Mulligan (2014) appeared in two games for the Bears, but also was affiliated with seven other NFL teams. Daniel Brown (2016) came out of James Madison. He caught 16 passes in just six games for the Bears in his debut season and was on the roster as No. 85 going into 2017 training camp.

NO. 86: MARTY BOOKER

For at least a certain period of time, Marty Booker was the best receiver in Chicago Bears history. He may not be remembered so clearly on a team that has been flooded with Hall of Famers and all-time greats, but during his peak seasons the wide receiver out of Louisiana-Monroe was one of the best in the business.

At 6 feet tall and 205 pounds, No. 86 was not huge. And it did take a couple of seasons for the third-round draft pick in 1999 to make a breakthrough. But then, look out. Between 2000 and 2001, Booker went from 47 catches to 100. Any receiver at any time that makes 100 grabs in a season is doing something special. In Booker's case, that was a team record and couple the total catches with 1,071 yards and it was a season to remember.

Booker also pretty much duplicated that performance in 2002, grabbing 97 passes for 1,189 yards. If the Bears wanted to move the ball downfield, they got the ball to Booker. He was chosen for the Pro Bowl after that campaign.

Things tailed off for Booker a little bit after that. In 2003, an ankle injury sidelined him for three games, although he still caught 52 passes. In 2004, Booker took off for Miami, played several seasons there, and then returned to Chicago for one more year. So his involvement with No. 86 was interrupted.

In all, Booker caught 539 passes in his career, 37 touchdowns included among them.

During an era when the forward pass is dominating offenses, the Bears could definitely use another Marty Booker.

Bill Wightkin wore 86 for the Bears first, but also wore 72. Brad Rowland (1951) was around Chicago for one season. Ed Meadows (1954, 1956–57) also wore No. 76. Bob Jewett (1958) caught 15 passes in his only NFL season. Defensive back Pete Manning (1960–61) is not a long lost Manning brother, and spent most of his football-playing days in Canada. Gary Barnes (1964) played for four teams in five years and caught four passes for Chicago. A two-time All-American, Loyd Phillips (1967–69) won the Outland Trophy in college for Arkansas and was a defensive lineman for the Bears.

Tight end Jim Hester (1970) got into five games and caught seven passes in Chicago after a few years with the New Orleans Saints. Bob Parsons (1972–83) had a stranglehold on No. 86 for a while. Parsons was a punter and tight end out of Penn State. Even though Brad Anderson (1984–85) only caught four passes for Chicago, he was a Super Bowl champion. Clay Pickering (1986) got into four games. Cap Boso (1987–91) was a tight end out of Illinois, who brought some consistency to 86. Unfortunately, he had to retire because of knee problems.

The 6-foot-3, 213-pound Barry Wagner (1992) caught just one pass for Chicago and in his NFL career. However, he was voted the greatest Arena football player of all time and did spectacular things to deserve the recognition, including once scoring two touchdowns and two extra points, recovering an onside kick, and making a notable defensive play all within the last minute of a game.

Wagner made the Arena league's first all-star team eight times and won the Ironman award recognizing the best two-day player six times. He amassed some incredible numbers, including 991 catches for 265 touchdowns, plus 677 tackles. Wagner just killed it with such teams as the San Jose SabreCats, Daytona Beach Thunder, and others. There should be a statue of Wagner somewhere.

Willie Harris (1993) did not get into a Bears game. Marv Cook (1994) caught 21 passes for Chicago, but was a two-time Pro Bowl pick elsewhere. Chris Penn (1997–98) is not the actor, but the wide receiver out of Tulsa and he acted pretty well for Chicago. In his two seasons for the Bears he caught 47 and 31 passes. Marty Booker came next in No. 86.

Eddie Berlin (2005) caught two passes in Chicago after playing for Tennessee. Tight end Michael Gaines (2009) made six stops and got into one game for Chicago. Brandon Manumaleuna (2010) caught five passes for the Bears after playing most of his career in San Diego and St. Louis.

Kyle Adams (2011–13) played musical chairs in No. 86 for a while, going from the roster to the practice squad and back a few times. Adams caught four passes in 15 games in 2012. After several years with the Jacksonville Jaguars and Tampa Bay Buccaneers, Zach Miller (2014–16) has fought for a regular spot with the Bears.

NO. 87: HARLON HILL

All Time No. 87	
Player	Years
Harlon Hill	(1954–61)
Ed O'Bradovich	(1962–71)
Steve DeLong	(1972)
Tom Reynolds	(1973–74)
Billy Newsome	(1977)
Mike Cobb	(1978–81)
Emery Moorehead	(1981–88)
Tom Waddle	(1989–94)
Greg Primus	(1994–95)
Andre President	(1995)
Bobby Neely	(1996)
Ricky Proehl	(1997)
D'Wayne Bates	(1999–2001)
Vinny Sutherland	(2002)
Jamin Elliott	(2002, 2004–05)
Justin Gage	(2003–04)
Muhsin Muhammad	(2005–07)
Kellen Davis	(2008–12)
Steve Maneri	(2013)
Greg Scruggs	(2015–16)

You must be doing something right if they not only give you trophies, but start naming them after you. Harlon Hill was not only the first Bear in No. 87, but kept it from 1954 to 1961. Hill, who starred at North Alabama, represents the Heisman Trophy of NCAA Division II. The best player in that division each season receives the Harlon Hill Trophy. It is a nice way to be remembered—probably better than having a street named after you.

Hill was born in Killen, Alabama, in 1932. He had a tremendous nose for the ball and a terrific ability to gain yards after the catch. At the time Hill enrolled, the University of North Alabama was called Florence State Teachers College. In terms of the NFL, that was playing in obscurity despite his being named an NAIA All-American. It was one of the biggest surprises of Hill's life that he was drafted by the Chicago Bears, even if it was in the 15th round.

The NFL draft was more or less an in-house operation in the 1950s. ESPN itself lay a quarter of a century in the future, and networks were not televising football teams' draft choices. Hill was not even promptly notified he had been selected by Chicago. He made a very good first impression on the veteran Bears, though.

Star George Connor was one player who took note of Hill's skills. Connor said, "I came home from camp one weekend and told my brother, 'You should see this kid we got from Alabama. He can run all day and all night and never break a sweat, never drop a football.'"

Once he got the chance to shine, Hill did so. The 6-foot-3, 200-pound wide receiver made an immediate impact. Hill was the NFL's Rookie of the Year and the next season, 1955, he was the league MVP. Hill was a three-time Pro Bowl player who was targeted somewhat sparingly during an era where the Bears had no star at quarterback, but he always made his catches count.

They totaled 226 in number with the Bears, but Hill had such seasons with 12 and 11 touchdown grabs. In his prime, Hill caught 40-plus passes in 12-game seasons. More impressive was how Hill eluded capture after the catch. As a rookie, he averaged 25 yards per catch. He also had seasons when he averaged 24 and 23 yards per catch. His lifetime average was 20.2.

Hill had "an uncanny knack for pulling down impossible passes," coach George Halas said in his autobiography.

Hill probably would have had a much longer career if not for problems with injuries and with alcohol. It was not until he retired that he beat that addiction. Then Hill later became a high school teacher and coach and principal before passing away at age eighty in 2013.

The Bears hit it big with the next player to wear No. 87, too. Defensive end Ed O'Bradovich (1962–71) sampled pro football in Canada and then spent the rest of his career with the Bears. His stint included playing for the 1963 title team. Later, O'Bradovich had a long second career in Chicago sports radio.

Defensive lineman Steve DeLong (1972) won the Outland Trophy at Tennessee and chose to sign with the upstart American Football League out of college. One season DeLong had 17 sacks (unofficial) for the Chargers. DeLong's one year in Chicago was his last in the pros. Tom Reynolds (1973–74) was a wide receiver and caught seven passes for the Bears. Defensive end Billy Newsome (1977) out of Grambling won a Super Bowl with the Baltimore Colts, and Chicago was only a short stop for him.

After briefly playing in Cincinnati, Mike Cobb (1978–81) made all 11 of his NFL career catches with the Bears. However, he did have a couple of big seasons with the Michigan Panthers of the USFL. Emery Moorehead (1981–88) was a sterling tight end who was part of the Super Bowl run and who kept No. 87 out of circulation for a while. A tough blocker with good hands, Moorehead caught 224 passes in his career, most of those in Chicago. Moorehead's season high was 42 in 1983. His son Aaron was a wide receiver for the Indianapolis Colts and is now an assistant college coach.

Tom Waddle (1989–94) was a star receiver at Boston College, but was not drafted. The Bears picked him up as a free agent and he hustled his way into the lineup with hard work. At 6 feet tall and 185 pounds, Waddle was on the smaller side, but overcame that. He had seasons of 55, 46, and 44 catches, and developed a large fan following. Those fans followed him into a sports broadcast career in radio and TV in Chicago and beyond.

"You can never recreate the adrenaline rush you get from being on an NFL field," Waddle said, "but this is as close as I can get."

Greg Primus (1994–95) didn't hang on to No. 87 as long. He caught three passes over two seasons carrying medical books along with his play books and then became an orthopedic surgeon. Tight end Andre President (1995) got into two games. Bobby Neely (1996) caught nine passes during his one year in Chicago. Ricky Proehl (1997) was next man up, and only played one season of a 17-year career with the Bears. However, Proehl was part of the Rams' "Greatest Show on Turf," and helped them win a Super Bowl in 1999.

D'Wayne Bates (1999–2001) came out of Northwestern as a receiver, but was mostly a special teams player with the Bears. Vinny Sutherland (2002) was an explosive player in college, but not in the pros. He returned kicks for the Bears for one game and then had to turn in No. 87. Jamin Elliott (2002, 2004–05) got into two games in 2002, but was mostly on the practice squad. Justin Gage (2003–04) was never the No. 1 receiver in Chicago, but caught a high of 31 passes in 2005 before leaving for the Tennessee Titans in free agency.

A stand-up teammate out of Michigan State, Muhsin Muhammad (2005–07) was a two-time Pro Bowl selection with the Carolina Panthers and caught a startling 860 passes in his career. He grabbed 64, 60, and 40 balls in three seasons with Chicago. Muhammad had a distinctive touchdown dance and partially due to that, as well as alliteration with his name, was nicknamed Moose. Muhammad described Chicago's offense as the place where receivers "go to die." The comment was not a big hit with the Bears.

Kellen Davis (2008–12) took over 87. He was more of a backup than starter in Chicago, but became a starter his last two seasons with the Bears. Then he won a Super Bowl with Seattle. Tight end Steve Maneri (2013) was with five NFL teams and played four games for the Bears.

Greg Scruggs (2015–16) switched from defensive end to tight end during his four-game stay with Chicago.

NO. 88: GOOD CATCHES: MARCUS ROBINSON AND DESMOND CLARK

All Time No. 88	
Player	Years
Gene Schroeder	(1951–57)
Willard Dewveall	(1959–60)
Bobby Joe Green	(1962–73)
Jim Kelly	(1974)
Greg Latta	(1975–80)
Marcus Anderson	(1981)
Brooks Williams	(1981–82)
Ken Knapczyk	(1987)
Glen Kozlowski	(1987–92)
Danta Whitaker	(1993)
Greg McMurtry	(1994)
Fabien Bownes	(1995, 1997–98)
Jack Jackson	(1995–96)
Harper LeBel	(1997)
Marcus Robinson	(1997–2002)
Desmond Clark	(2003–10)
Brody Eldridge	(2012)
Dante Rosario	(2013–14)
Rob Housler	(2015)

Wide receiver Marcus Robinson wore No. 88 first, from 1997 to 2002. He was followed by wide receiver Desmond Clark, who wore it from 2003 to 2010. Both of them had some terrific moments for the Bears.

The Bears chose Robinson with a fourth-round pick out of South Carolina in 1997. The 6-foot-3, 215-pounder was just the right size for his position. Although Robinson had to contend with a series of injuries that slowed down his later production, his 1999 season was unforgettable. Robinson made 84 grabs and accumulated 1,400 yards receiving, still No. 3 on Chicago's all-time list.

During his career, Robinson caught 325 passes and scored 43 touchdowns through the air. Community-minded, he also began the Marcus Robinson Foundation, aimed at helping underprivileged children.

In appalling treatment, the Minnesota Vikings cut Robinson from the team on Christmas Eve of 2006. In 2008, Robinson re-signed with Chicago to retire as a Bear.

Desmond Clark played a few years for the Denver Broncos and Miami Dolphins before settling in as a fixture with the Bears. Lining up mostly at tight end, Clark also was sometimes called a fullback and even was on call as a long snapper. But he was mostly a pass catcher and, with 323 receptions, he ended up with almost exactly the same amount as Robinson.

At 6-foot-3 and 250 pounds, Clark drew attention at Wake Forest before the Broncos drafted him. Clark's single-season high for catches was 51 with Denver, but four times for the Bears he caught between 41 and 45 passes in a year. Like Robinson, Clark started an organization to help youths. For a time he and ex-defensive teammate Alex Brown co-hosted a Chicago sports radio show.

The No. 88 made its debut for the Bears with Gene Schroeder (1951–57). Schroeder was a No. 1 draft pick out of Virginia who caught 104 passes for the Bears, 39 of them in 1952. Schroeder remained a Bears supporter for life.

"I could sit here and talk to you for half an hour about what Coach Halas did for me," Schroeder said. "He was so good to me. I was well paid. I made more money than some of the guys who are in the Hall of Fame."

Willard Dewveall (1959–60) was another case altogether. Dewveall had played in Canada for a year before the Bears signed him. He had a good season for the Bears in 1960 with 43 catches while averaging 18.7 yards per reception. Only the American Football League had come into existence challenging the NFL and Dewveall realized he could cut a better deal for himself. So he became the first NFL player to jump to the AFL at the start of the decade-long war. Dewveall was very successful with the Houston Oilers, catching as many as 58 passes in a season. However, his name was a dirty word to George Halas forevermore.

Bobby Joe Green took over No. 88 in 1962, and for a while it seemed he might wear it forever. He did stay around through 1973. Those years included the 1963 title season. Although sometimes listed as a running back, Green was a punter first, foremost, and almost exclusively. Counting two years with the Pittsburgh Steelers before coming to Chicago, he played 14 NFL seasons. His career punting average was 42.6 and his career long kick was 74 yards. Green was only fifty-seven when he died of a heart attack.

Jim Kelly (1974) caught eight passes in his only NFL season. Tight end Greg Latta (1975–80) caught 90 passes for Chicago spread over six seasons, with a high of 26 in 1977. Wide receiver Marcus Anderson (1981) out of Tulane caught nine passes, two of them for touchdowns. Tight end Brooks Williams (1981–82) spent most of his career with the New Orleans Saints.

Ken Knapczyk (1987) has lived an adventure story. A wide receiver with a limited career partially due to a knee injury, he caught four passes in three games for the Bears. He then became a business owner, went bankrupt, became homeless with his family, and had to live in a tent, and then rebounded to become a high school football coach.

Born in Hawaii, Glen Kozlowski (1987–92) was a star at Brigham Young where his pass catching talents meshed well with a group of quarterbacks as good as those he would play with in the NFL—Jim McMahon, Steve Young, and Robbie Bosco. A stream of injuries messed with Kozlowski's Bears career, and he caught just 31 passes.

Kozlowski's brother Mike also played in the NFL. After retiring, Glen Kozlowski coached high school football in the Chicago area, but most prominently became a regular on Chicago sports radio.

Danta Whitaker (1993) was a tight end who caught six passes in five games for the Bears. Greg McMurtry (1994) took a turn in No. 88, but had most of his success with the New England Patriots, only appearing in nine games with eight catches for Chicago. Fabien Bownes also wore No. 82. Jack Jackson (1995–96) had his only NFL chance with the Bears and otherwise played in the Arena Football League. Tight end Harper LeBel (1997) played several seasons with four other teams.

Marcus Robinson and Desmond Clark came next in the No. 88 rotation. Brody Eldridge (2012) did not get into a Bears game after his time with Indianapolis. Dante Rosario (2013–14) caught 17 passes in Chicago and was part of six NFL organizations. Tight end Rob Housler (2015) caught three passes for Chicago.

NO. 89: MIKE DITKA

Skipping George "Papa Bear" Halas, owner and coach for decades, there has never been a Bear who was more of a Bear than Mike Ditka.

As a Hall of Fame player wearing No. 89 and coach of the Bears team that won its only Super Bowl title, Ditka's contributions have been immeasurable. Even since retiring from coaching, Ditka has remained the Alpha Bear in public eyes, the go-to man for commentary on the fortunes of the team; a symbol of better days for the organization.

Mike Ditka the player was a 6-foot-3, 230-pound block of granite—a tight end who helped revolutionize his position. Coming out of the University of Pittsburgh, the Western Pennsylvania product was the Bears' No. 1 draft pick in 1961 and went on to win Rookie of the Year honors.

Strong, tough, ferocious, Ditka's nickname "Iron Mike" was appropriate. He was the type of player opponents wanted to avoid on the field, never mind try to tackle. In 1964, he caught 75 passes. He was a five-time Pro Bowl pick and probably should have been a Bear for life except for his disputes with the equally iron-willed Halas. Famously, Ditka called Halas someone who threw "nickels around like manhole covers," an insult referencing his cheapskate nature in contract negotiations.

In 1967, Halas traded Ditka away to the Philadelphia Eagles. Ditka then moved on to the Dallas Cowboys where he began his coaching days after retiring. As a player, Ditka caught 427 passes. Up until then the tight end was viewed as more of a blocker than an offensive weapon, but Ditka brought excellence to both tasks.

By then Ditka owned a 1963 championship ring from the Bears' NFL title triumph and just as he was about to retire won a Super Bowl with the Cowboys, scoring a touchdown in the game.

In the early 1980s, the Bears were in the market for a new head coach and Ditka wrote Halas a conciliatory letter asking to be considered for the position. Halas, who was in failing health, was looking ahead to a team without his guidance for the first time in sixty-three years. He put his faith in Ditka and, although he passed away before Ditka drove the 1985 Bears to the championship in the 1986 Super Bowl, had his judgment proven correct.

"What I'll always remember and cherish are the players, the men who came together to get us to the top of the mountain," Ditka said thirty years after the victory over the New England Patriots. "You can talk about coaching all you want, but you can't win without great players. Now, they were as different as different can be, but they wanted to win—all of them."

A team of talented misfits came together to win a title and yet Ditka emerged as the biggest celebrity of them all. He operated a popular eatery in downtown Chicago, sponsored his own brand of wine, and spouted enough opinions that eventually someone suggested he run for the US Senate. He squeezed an unsuccessful second-time-around coaching tenure in with the New Orleans Saints, but remained the cigar-puffing savant for football commentary everyone loved to listen to and watch on TV.

Elected to the Pro Football Hall of Fame in 1988, Ditka has used his prominence and forums as a front man for the Gridiron Greats assistance fund to campaign for health payments and care for former NFL players who cannot afford to take care of situations on their own.

"There's a need to help these former players who have suffered injuries and racked up medical bills," Ditka said.

The first Bear to wear No. 89 was Jack Hoffman, who also wore No. 29 and 82. Defensive tackle Les Cowan (1951) played in nine games. John Aveni (1959–60) kicked 51 extra points for the Bears. Mike Ditka wore 89 next. The Bears eventually retired the number, but not for decades so others wore it into the 2000s.

Tight end Terry Stoepel (1967) caught one pass in six games post-Ditka. Bob Wallace (1968–72) out of Texas El Paso had a bit more success, catching 109 passes for the Bears over parts of five seasons with a high of 47 grabs in 1969. Mel Tom (1973–75) was a defensive end with three Bears seasons following seven with the Philadelphia Eagles. James Scott (1976–80, 1982–83) sandwiched his wide receiving days for Chicago around stints in the World Football League and Canada. He caught between 36 and 50 passes for the Bears three times.

Ken Margerum also wore No. 82. Tight end Mitch Krenk (1984–85) caught two passes in '84 and was on injured reserved for all of 1985, but got a Super Bowl ring. Wide receiver Keith Ortego (1985–88) was part of the Super Bowl Shuffle group and caught 23 passes in 1986. Will Johnson (1987) was a Bears linebacker for 11 games, but was a star defensive lineman in Canada afterward. Tight end Brent Novoselsky (1988) got into eight games.

Another tight end, James Coley (1990), caught one pass for Chicago. Kelly Blackwell (1992) was an All-American tight end, also from TCU, who played in 16 games and caught five passes. Tight end Ryan Wetnight (1993–99) came out of Stanford and played all but one of his NFL seasons with the Bears. He caught 46 passes in 1997 and 38 in 1999. Dustin Lyman (2000–04) spent his whole NFL career with the Bears and caught 37 passes for three touchdowns. Matt Spaeth (2011–12) earned the designation as college football's best tight end at Minnesota, and spent seven other years with the Steelers in the NFL.

When Spaeth left for Pittsburgh, the Bears decided that was it for No. 89. Neither cigars nor wine were mentioned as reasons, but the team finally retired the number to honor Mike Ditka.

Did He Really Play for the Bears?
Golden Richards

Golden Richards gained his National Football League fame with the Dallas Cowboys as a wide receiver in the early 1970s. At 6-foot-1 and 181 pounds, Richards was not extremely large, but was fleet of foot.

Certainly the segment of his career most fans remember was his time spent with the Cowboys. Time spent with the Bears? Not so much, although he wore No. 83—the same number he wore with Dallas.

During his heyday, Richards was a dangerous receiver in the long game. He did not catch very many balls per season, typically around 20, but he made the most of every grab, putting together seasons with some tremendous yards-per-catch averages.

In 1974 he averaged 18 yards a catch on 26 grabs. A year later his average was 21.5 on 21 catches. And in 1976, Richards caught 19 passes with a 21.8 yards-per-catch mark.

Those were some of the Tom Landry years in Dallas when the Cowboys were a hot commodity and almost always a playoff team.

It was in 1978 that Richards came to the Bears for all but one game that season. He caught 27 passes, but a season later he caught just five in five games for Chicago. After that season, at age twenty-nine, he was out of football.

Richards wore 83 for every game of his 86-game NFL career.

Ricky Proehl

Yes, Ricky Proehl played for the Bears and it wasn't just a sign, show up, and get sent on his way deal. Proehl had a first-rate long career and played one full, genuine season for the Bears in 1997 wearing No. 87.

While the 6-foot, 190-pound Proehl put up Hall-of-Fame-like numbers over the course of a 17-season career while winning Super Bowls with the St. Louis Rams and Indianapolis Colts, Proehl made an impression in Chicago.

During that single season for the Bears, Proehl made 58 catches and scored seven touchdowns. For him, it was a bridge season between a lengthy stay with the Seattle Seahawks and moving on to St. Louis.

As a wide receiver, Proehl caught 669 passes in his career and gained 8,878 yards through the air. His play accounted for 54 touchdowns. Proehl also spent four years as an assistant coach with the Carolina Panthers where he gained notoriety for his work with receivers.

NO. 90: ALONZO SPELLMAN AND JULIUS PEPPERS

Two guys who lived to kill the quarterback both wore No. 90 for the Bears in recent years. Both made large impacts and both made news elsewhere during their careers—and after.

Chicago drafted Alonzo Spellman out of Ohio State in the first round and turned him loose on the defensive line in 1992. At 6-foot-4 and 292 pounds, he wreaked havoc on many opponents during his Bears stay through 1997, collecting 32 sacks in Chicago. He later played for the Dallas Cowboys and Detroit Lions, completing his NFL career with 43 sacks and 207 tackles.

His 1994, 1995, and 1996 seasons in Chicago were noteworthy for the fear he threw into quarterback foes, as Spellman accumulated 7, 8.5, and 8 sacks in a row.

Spellman's problems with bipolar personality issues began when he was in Chicago. He sometimes did not take his medication and flew into rages and some incidents led to altercations with the law and legal cases. He piled up numerous warrants. Later, Spellman took up mixed martial arts as a competitor.

Julius Peppers may well end up in the Hall of Fame. The 6-foot-7, 290-pound defensive end out of North Carolina has been a nine-time Pro Bowl selection, won an NFL Defensive Player of the Year Award, and has excelled with the Carolina Panthers, the Bears (2010–13), the Green Bay Packers, and most recently back with Carolina. He brought 143.5 sacks into the 2017 season, and also had 73 pass defections and 47 forced fumbles on his resume.

A one-time college All-American who also dabbled in college basketball for the highly ranked Tar Heels basketball team, Peppers was as outstanding with the Bears as he was elsewhere. He had 11 sacks for Chicago in 2011, and 11.5 in 2012.

Peppers, who was thirty-seven entering the 2017 season, is closing in on the end of a magnificent career.

The first Bear to wear No. 90 was Henry Mosley (1955), who actually was a halfback and carried the ball three times for the Bears in one games (he also wore No. 49). Al Harris (1979–87) was a first-round draft choice out of Arizona State. Harris made the mistake of holding out for more money in 1985 and sat out the entire Super Bowl season.

In 2014, Harris reflected on his choice: "That is almost thirty years ago and I have gotten over that," he said. ". . . I was always happy for my team-mates. I have kind of forgiven the Bears and forgiven myself and I have moved on."

Harris also moved on to the Philadelphia Eagles and in the 2000s was an assistant coach with the San Francisco 49ers for a couple of years. Alonzo Spellman took over No. 90 after Harris.

Van Tuinei (1999–2001) was a defensive end who got his last 3.5 sacks with the Bears. Bryan Knight (2002–03) was a linebacker the Bears made a fifth-round draft pick out of Pitt. He only had two starts in 31 games, but was in on 50 tackles. Antonio Garay (2006–07) was affiliated with three other teams besides the Bears. His tenure in Chicago was cut short by injury, and he had eight tackles in 10 games as a non-starting nose tackle.

Joey LaRocque (2008) was a linebacker drafted out of Oregon State who made six tackles. Defensive end Jarron Gilbert (2009) got into four games and made one tackle. Julius Peppers came in and took No. 90 next.

Jeremiah Ratliff (2013–15) was a four-time Pro Bowl defensive lineman for Dallas before coming to Chicago. His 37 tackles included 6.5 sacks for the Bears in 2014. Ziggy Hood (2015) took over with Ratliff playing just two games in their overlapping year. Hood was a 305-pound nose tackle who also only played in two games that season. Greg Scruggs also wore No. 87. The Bears wanted Cornelius Washington (2013–16) as a defensive end and drafted him out of Georgia. He left for Detroit with three sacks.

NO. 91: TOMMIE HARRIS

For the most part, use of numbers in the 90s did not come into vogue until at least the 1950s and, in many cases, depending on the team, not until much later. After the NFL compartmentalized the distribution of numbers by position, the 90s became a more popular choice.

So the Bears, as is the case with most teams, do not have a long track record with stars wearing such high numbers. No old-time Hall of Famers ever wore such a high numeral. And also the list of players ever donning a jersey with a number in the 90s is shorter than it is for many other numbers.

One player who had some longevity wearing No. 91 was Tommie Harris. After being born in Germany and growing up in Texas, Harris became a two-time All-American defensive lineman at Oklahoma which led to his becoming a first-round pick of the Bears in 2004.

While the 6-foot-3, 295-pound Harris was fine with that recognition, he refused the offer to pose for the team picture for the *Playboy* All-American team because it was in a skin magazine. He said he did not want to embarrass his sisters and promote publisher Hugh Hefner's agenda.

Harris was also fine with hitting people on the field, something he did quite often playing for the Bears between 2004 and 2010, and then briefly in an affiliation with the Indianapolis Colts and San Diego Chargers in 2011.

Most of Harris's career 226 tackles and 31.5 sacks were amassed on behalf of the Bears, and he was chosen for three Pro Bowls representing Chicago.

No member of the Bears wore No. 91 until Pat Dunsmore (1983–84) pulled the jersey over his head. Dunsmore caught 17 passes for the Bears, but was on injured reserve for the whole Super Bowl season. This was the only season Jay Norvell (1987) had in the NFL, but he has been a college coach for twenty years and is currently head coach of the University of Nevada.

Defensive tackle Fred Washington (1990) was a second-round draft pick out of Texas Christian. Sadly, he died in an auto accident his rookie year. Linebacker Myron Baker (1993–95) spent more than half his career in

Chicago, but also suited up for the Carolina Panthers. Rob Davis (1996) was a long snapper for five teams, mostly with the Green Bay Packers. Defensive end John Thierry (1997–98) was a first-round Bears pick out of Alcorn State. He made 12.5 sacks for the Bears, but did better elsewhere. Khari Samuel (1999–2000) played mostly on Bears special teams. Tommie Harris came next in No. 91.

Defensive tackle Amobi Okoye (2011–12) lived in Nigeria until he was twelve. When he came to the US, he was so far ahead of the school levels that he graduated high school at fifteen and enrolled in Louisville. He was just sixteen playing for the Cardinals as a freshman and graduated in three and a half years with a degree in biology. The Houston Texans saw potential in the 6-foot-2, 310-pound lineman and, after a few seasons with that club, Okoye joined the Bears. He made contributions, including four sacks in 2011, but never became a starter.

Although generally a linebacker, David Bass (2013–14) intercepted a pass as a rookie while playing the line and ran it back 24 yards for a touchdown, the first time that had happened for the Bears in nine years. Linebacker DeDe Lattimore (2014–15) bounced back and forth to the practice squad, but made three tackles in 10 games. A hard-nosed nose tackle Eddie Goldman (2015–16) out of Florida State, had seven sacks in his first two Bears seasons despite an ankle injury that slowed him his second year.

NO. 92: HUNTER HILLENMEYER

A mainstay defender for the Bears at linebacker between 2003 and 2010, Hunter Hillenmeyer never played a down in the NFL for any other team. That was despite being drafted in the fifth round by the Green Bay Packers out of Vanderbilt. Green Bay cut him and Chicago picked him up.

After a stint on special teams to get used to the NFL, the 6-foot-4, 238-pound Hillenmeyer moved into the starting lineup wearing No. 92. The trio of Brian Urlacher, Lance Briggs, and Hillenmeyer was acclaimed as the best linebacking corps in the league.

During his eight seasons in Chicago, Hillenmeyer was in on 382 tackles. He made 90 tackles in 2009 alone, but one game into the 2010 season he suffered a concussion, was sidelined for the season, and never played in the NFL again.

In retirement from football, Hillenmeyer writes a column for the financial services website TheStreet.com while studying for an MBA.

Rob Fada (1983–84) introduced No. 92 to a Bears roster. Fada was a guard who played 19 games in Chicago. Raymond Morris (1987) was a linebacker who had one sack in three games. Troy Johnson (1988–89) notched one sack in 23 games in his two Bears seasons. Linebacker Barry Minter (1993–2000) spent the bulk of his career with the Bears, collecting 473 tackles. One season he was in on 125 tackles, another year 106. A back injury sidelined Minter and then he was replaced by Brian Urlacher.

Ted Washington (2001–02) was a colossal nose tackle checking in at 375 pounds. He won a Super Bowl with New England and earned one of his four Pro Bowl selections representing the Bears. Hunter Hillenmeyer followed Washington at No. 92. Stephen Paea (2011–14) was born in New Zealand and grew up in Tonga. He played rugby, not football, until he moved to the United States at age sixteen for high school. Playing football at Oregon State made him a second-round Bears draft pick as a defensive tackle. In his first NFL game, Paea sacked Minnesota Vikings (and longtime Philadelphia

Eagles) quarterback Donovan McNabb in the end zone for a safety. He later played for other NFL teams.

Linebacker Pernell McPhee (2015–16) won a Super Bowl with the Baltimore Ravens, and was in on 52 tackles in his first year with Chicago. He remained with the Bears going into 2017 training camp.

NO. 93: ADEWALE OGUNLEYE

At 6-foot-5 and 260 pounds, Adewale Ogunleye definitely filled out his No. 93 jersey after joining the Bears in 2004. A three-time Big Ten all-star at Indiana University, Ogunleye was not drafted out of college because he tore up a knee as a senior, but forced his way onto the Miami Dolphins roster with his play.

After a few years in Miami and a Pro Bowl selection on his resume, he came to the Bears in a trade for receiver Marty Booker. Ogunleye moved right into the defensive line and stayed there until 2009. He recorded 10 sacks in 2005 and nine in 2007.

A broken leg sidetracked Ogunleye in his final season with the Bears. He tried to make a comeback with the Houston Texans, but played in only four games. Ogunleye retired in 2010 with 67 career sacks.

After leaving the pro game, Ogunleye went into business. When he realized he didn't know enough about running companies, he obtained a masters degree from George Washington University and entered the real estate world. He needed a break from football anyway.

"When I first got done I couldn't watch the game," he said. "I couldn't watch TV. It was tough. I was so programmed to watching the game a certain way that I couldn't watch it as a fan. I was dissecting every play."

End Oliver Williams (1983) was the first Bear in No. 93. He was drafted by Chicago, but mostly played elsewhere. Will Johnson also wore No. 89. Guy Teafatiller (1987) was a defensive tackle who got into three games. Trace Armstrong (1989–94) was an All-American defensive lineman drafted out of Florida. The Bears started his 15-year NFL career, and Armstrong later played with the Miami Dolphins and Oakland Raiders, making one Pro Bowl appearance (in 2000 with the Dolphins). He was also president of the NFL Players Association between 1996 and 2003.

Ervin Collier (1995) was a defensive end who didn't get into a game. Paul Grasmanis (1996–98) made just a few defensive line starts after being drafted out of Notre Dame, but played more in Philadelphia. The 6-foot-5, 302-pound Phil Daniels (2000–03) was a very solid player for the Bears (nine sacks in 2001), and also played well for the Seattle Seahawks and Washington Redskins.

Adewale Ogunleye came next at No. 93. Thaddeus Gibson (2011) played two games on the defensive line for Chicago and has also been part of six other NFL teams and two Canadian teams. Between a substance abuse suspension and a knee injury, Nate Collins (2012–13) didn't play too much for the Bears before moving on to the Winnipeg Blue Bombers. Arizona State's Will Sutton (2014–16) remained a nose tackle with the Bears until signing with the Minnesota Vikings in May of 2017.

NO. 94: KEITH TRAYLOR

You've got to say this for Keith Traylor: For a guy who moved around as often as he did in his seventeen years of playing in the NFL, he timed some of those moves brilliantly. That's why he ended up with three Super Bowl rings—two from his affiliation with the Denver Broncos and one earned while playing for the New England Patriots.

Alas, No. 94 for the Bears, another one of those nose tackles who take up more than one parking space, did not win such jewelry in Chicago. Traylor stood 6-foot-2 and played at 340 pounds. When he teamed up with Ted Washington and his 375 pounds during his Chicago stay, nobody was going to be running on the Bears without a locomotive clearing track.

Traylor was a helpful run-clogger in Chicago between 2001 and 2003. In his first season with the Bears, the defense permitted just 82.1 yards rushing per game. In a remarkable career, of note for longevity as well as mobility, Traylor played for the Bears, Broncos, Patriots, Oakland Raiders, Green Bay Packers, Kansas City Chiefs, and Miami Dolphins. He saw the nation NFL style.

Traylor played in 229 career games, and was known as much for steering the run in other directions as making the tackle himself. Somehow, he grabbed two interceptions, although he certainly wasn't a downfield coverage man. Traylor returned one of those interceptions 67 yards, but not at what would be called a sprint pace.

"I just followed the ball," Traylor said describing the play. "When it landed, I said, 'Oh, I got it. What should I do now?' I was looking for someone to pitch it to, but no one showed up. I did the best I could. I was trying to get there [the end zone], but they got me."

Linebacker Mike January (1987) was the first Bear to wear No. 94, and he appeared in just three games. Dick Chapura (1987–89) was a defensive tackle with three sacks in 1989 before moving on to other teams. John Thierry also wore No. 91. Defensive tackle Shane Burton (1999) played for four teams and had three sacks in his one-season Chicago visit. Ty Hallock

(1999–2000) was a linebacker and fullback in Chicago, though mostly played fullback elsewhere. Keith Traylor came next wearing No. 94.

Being born in the Congo made Alain Kashama (2004) an unlikely NFL defensive end. He played three games with the Bears before being traded to Seattle, and then played more in Canada. Brendon Ayanbadejo (2000, 2005–2007), who is part Nigerian, was a devastating special teams player for the Bears. Ayanbadejo was chosen for the Pro Bowl three times because of his special teams performance (twice with the Bears).

Defensive tackle Marcus Harrison (2008–09) got most of his NFL action with the Bears. Charles Grant (2010) was mostly a New Orleans Saints star and didn't even get into a Bears game in his last NFL stop. Defensive tackle Nick Reed (2011) played seven games for Chicago. Defensive end Chauncey Davis (2011) appeared in six games for the Bears after six seasons in Atlanta. Cornelius Washington also wore No. 90. Linebacker Leonard Floyd joined the Bears in 2016, when he was drafted in the first round (No. 9 overall) by the Bears in the draft.

NO. 95: RICHARD DENT

Defensive end Richard Dent left so many dents in the bodies of ball carriers that he was elected to the Pro Football Hall of Fame. A major component in the Bears' Super Bowl-winning defense in 1985, Dent was a terror to be faced by quarterbacks.

A four-time Pro Bowl selection, Dent, who was the first Bears player to wear No. 95 when he joined the team in 1983, stood 6-foot-5 and weighed 265 pounds. An eighth-round pick out of Tennessee State, it came across that Dent was an after-thought in the draft, but he proved any skeptics wrong. He stayed with the Bears through 1993, left for the San Francisco 49ers where he collected another Super Bowl ring despite being injured much of the year, and then returned to Chicago in 1995.

In the Bears' Super Bowl victory over the New England Patriots, Dent was chosen as the Most Valuable Player. He was credited with 1.5 sacks and two forced fumbles in that game. Immortalized for posterity, Dent was also a soloist on the Super Bowl Shuffle video.

Still hoping to squeeze some extra playing time out of his aging and frequently injured body, Dent signed on with first the Indianapolis Colts and then the Philadelphia Eagles before retiring in 1997.

Dent ran up 137.5 sacks and managed to pick off eight passes from the defensive end spot. The secret to Dent's pass-rushing success was speed and enough of it to skip around tackles determined to block him.

After a wait that seemed longer than proper to him, Dent was inducted into the Hall of Fame in 2011.

Like so many aging ex-football players, Dent is aware he suffered undiagnosed concussions and deals with recurring aches.

"My foot bothers me, circulation, shoulders, elbow, back, hip, head trauma and memory loss," he said. "I don't have any regrets about it. The game gave me many opportunities. I'd play the game again the same way. I'd have played it for free, but they were giving us checks."

Post-Dent, the next Bear in 95 was Pat Riley (1995). Not to be confused with the basketball Pat Riley, this one played in only one game for Chicago. Linebacker Dana Howard (1996) was twice a University of Illinois All-American and twice the Big Ten Defensive Player of the Year. He played three games for the Bears, but was sidelined by a broken finger. Mark Thomas (1997–98) twice had 4.5 sacks in a season for Chicago and spent nine years in the NFL. Russell Davis (1999) played only the first of his nine pro years with the Bears and won a Super Bowl with the New York Giants in his last NFL season. Defensive end Troy Wilson (2000) came out of little Pittsburg State of Kansas, didn't stay long with the Bears, but did stick around the league and won a Super Bowl with the San Francisco 49ers.

Defensive lineman Karon Riley (2001) traveled around the NFL a bit and also played Arena football. Defensive lineman Keith McKenzie (2002) played for five NFL teams in short bursts and then became an assistant coach, most recently at his alma mater Ball State. Defensive end John Stamper (2002) got into four Bears games. In the best of the four years he played with the Bears, defensive tackle Ian Scott (2003–06) made 44 tackles, including two sacks.

Defensive tackle Anthony Adams (2007–11) gave the Bears five solid seasons wearing No. 95, complementing four seasons in San Francisco. In 2009, Adams had a high of 44 tackles with two sacks, mirroring Scott's best year. Linebacker Cheta Ozougwu (2012–13) played in nine games. Larry Grant (2013) started out as a running back in high school and became a linebacker while starring at Ohio State after being a junior college All-American. Grant played two games for the Bears. The stay of defensive end Ego Ferguson (2014–15) with the Bears was marred by injuries, surgeries, and a drug suspension.

NO. 96: ALEX BROWN

A defensive end out of Florida, Alex Brown was a popular player and a contributor as soon as he showed up in Chicago. Brown was a two-time college All-American, but only a fourth-round draft pick in 2002. At 6-foot-3 and 260 pounds, Brown was agile and seemed to have a honing device implanted that allowed him to seek out quarterbacks. He occupied a spot on the Bears' defense from 2002 to 2009.

Given his notoriety and honors won with the Gators, Brown felt certain he would be an early draft pick by an NFL team. He was amazed he dropped down on so many teams' lists.

"Back in 2002, the first three rounds of the draft were all on the first day," Brown said. "I heard that I'd be going late in the first, or maybe in the second, but for sure I wouldn't make it past that first day. I thought I was the best defensive end in the draft."

Brown even thought the Bears might take him—although earlier.

"I was real hell-bent on making sure that he [Chicago general manager Jerry Angelo] didn't make a mistake," Brown said. "I always thought that I don't want people to say he made a mistake by picking me. I ended up in a great spot and everything felt good when I got to Chicago."

It was a great spot for both Brown and the Bears.

Brown played all but one season of his NFL career with the Bears, finishing up with the New Orleans Saints. However, Brown signed a one-day contract to retire as a Bear. The vast majority of Brown's tackles and sacks came with Chicago and when he retired he had been in on 411 tackles and recorded 43.5 sacks. He also forced 15 fumbles and picked off five passes, evidence he was a disruptive defensive force in several ways.

Now in business in the Chicago area, Brown stays in touch with football by doing some radio commentary. He and former teammate Dez Clark have co-hosted their own sports show on the air.

The first Bear in No. 96 was Keith Ortego, who also wore No. 89. Greg Fitzgerald (1987) was a defensive end who got into three games. Tim Ryan (1990–93) was a defensive tackle out of Southern Cal who gathered 4.5 sacks in four seasons with the Bears, his whole NFL career. Linebacker Percy Snow (1993) got into 10 games with the Bears after a College Football Hall of Fame career at Michigan State. Al Fontenot (1993–96) was a defensive end out of Baylor who had a high of 4.5 sacks for Chicago before moving on to the Indianapolis Colts and San Diego Chargers.

Tyrone Williams (1997) spent six years in the NFL, three games in Chicago, before winning a Grey Cup championship in Canada. Having the right last name did not bring Chris Draft (1998) terrific luck on NFL draft day, as he fell to the sixth round coming out of Stanford as a linebacker. The Bears kept him around for one game, probably not even breaking a sweat in No. 96. But Draft played for six other teams and ended up with 667 tackles.

Defensive end Clyde Simmons (1999–2000) came to Chicago at the end of his 15-year career. Earlier, Simmons was a two-time Pro Bowl pick. Still, he accumulated seven of his 121.5 total sacks for the Bears in 1999. He has been an NFL coach since 2012, currently with the Cleveland Browns. Defensive tackle Henry Taylor (2001) played one game for Chicago. Alex Brown took over No. 96 after that.

Barry Turner (2010) was a defensive tackle out of Nebraska who appeared in two Bears games. Mario Addison (2011) played in four games for Chicago, but has been much more important to other squads, especially the Carolina Panthers. Defensive tackle Zach Minter (2013) came out of Montana State and played two games in Chicago before passing through other NFL teams and settling in with Canadian league teams. Jeremiah Ratliff also wore No. 90.

Linebacker Terrell Manning (2014) managed to sign with nine NFL teams while only getting into 11 games by 2016, three of them with the Bears. Defensive tackle Jarvis Jenkins (2015) had a pretty good one year with Chicago, making 32 tackles, including four sacks. Defensive tackle Akiem Hicks (2016) was in on 54 tackles, including seven sacks for the Bears, and remains with the team in control of No. 96's destiny.

NO. 97: CHRIS ZORICH

A 6-foot-1, 282-pound defensive tackle, Chris Zorich has led a Chicago-centric life. He was born in Chicago, went to high school in Chicago, became an All-American at Notre Dame 90 miles away, and then spent all but one season of his NFL career with the Chicago Bears.

Zorich was a second-round draft pick by Chicago in 1991, and stayed with the Bears through 1997 before playing a single season with the Washington Redskins—appearing in just five games there. He was chosen for one Pro Bowl (as an alternate), in 1993, for the Bears. During that 1993 season, Zorich collected seven sacks. In all, he was in on 211 tackles during his career.

Touted as an academic, as well as athletic, success story, Zorich's life was energetically covered by the Chicago media. He was raised by a single mother and developed a reputation early as a football player who gave back to the community. Long into retirement he has maintained a generous profile. He created the Chris Zorich Foundation to aid disadvantaged families. He has also been a motivational speaker and earned a Doctor of Jurisprudence degree from Notre Dame.

However, in 2013, Zorich ran into legal troubles for not filing his federal income tax return for several years and was sentenced to probation. His foundation was also having difficulties.

In 2015, Zorich became athletic director of two-year Prairie State College in Chicago Heights.

Linebacker Bobby Bell (1987) introduced No. 97 to Bears fans. Bell played parts of two seasons in the NFL, but only three games with the Bears. This was obviously not the Kansas City Chiefs Hall of Famer. Sean Smith (1987–88) was a 280-pound defensive end out of Grambling who played in 19 Bears games. Chris Zorich moved in as No. 97 next. A 325-pound defensive tackle out of Iowa, Mike Wells (1998–2000) had an eight-season NFL career.

Christian Peter (2002) was one of the most controversial NFL draft picks ever. The New England Patriots cut the former Nebraska defensive star only a week after the draft when he had gotten into trouble with the law for the eighth time. Four of those incidents involved violence against women. A year later, the New York Giants signed Peter as a free agent under the condition he undergo counseling, anger management sessions, and alcoholism treatment. By the time he reached the Bears he had played five years in the NFL. During his stay in Chicago, Peter issued a public apology for his earlier-in-life actions. Peter made 18 tackles in 12 games for the Bears.

Years later, married with children and describing himself as long-since rehabilitated, Peter was consulted by the NFL when it was instituting a domestic violence policy for players. He has said he knows he is lucky that he was given a second chance by society and said he is not the same person he was in college.

Defensive tackle Michael Haynes (2003–05) was a Bears first-round draft pick out of Penn State. While never a full-time starter in Chicago, Haynes played well inhabiting No. 97, especially in 2004 when he had 31 tackles, including two sacks. Mark Anderson (2006–10) was a fifth-round draft choice out of Alabama whom the Bears used as a third-down rusher. In only one start in 2006, Anderson set a team rookie record with 12 sacks. Anderson later played with three other NFL teams. A hip injury wiped out the rookie season of linebacker J. T. Thomas (2011–12). He played every game for Chicago the next year. He is currently with the New York Giants.

Defensive tackle Landon Cohen (2013) passed through nine NFL teams, making 14 tackles in his sole year with the Bears. However, he moved on to the CFL and won a Grey Cup title with the Ottawa Redblacks. Linebacker Willie Young (2014–16) was still wearing No. 97 going into the 2017 season. He has been a recent sack machine for the Bears, often without even starting. He recorded 10 quarterback sacks in 2014, and a combined 14 in the following two seasons.

NO. 98: BRYAN ROBINSON

A 304-pound tackle out of Fresno State, Bryan Robinson was a mainstay defensive player for the Chicago Bears between 1998 and 2003, and probably the best player to wear No. 98 in its relatively short time in Chicago action.

The big man was born in Toledo, Ohio, and played one season in the NFL with the St. Louis Rams before becoming a Bear. A good run-stopper who totaled 24 sacks in his career, Robinson had as many as five in one season for Chicago.

A solid player, Robinson is particularly fondly remembered by Bears fans for one huge play. In the same week that the great Walter Payton passed away from liver disease, the Bears lined up to face their chief rival Green Bay Packers. The game was on the road, but the Bears held a 14–13 lead as time clicked off the clock in the fourth quarter. The Packers' Ryan Longwell lined up for what amounted to a gimme 28-yard field goal attempt.

Only Robinson burst through the blockers and knocked away the kick to preserve the Bears' triumph.

Robinson remained in the NFL through 2010 and appeared in a Super Bowl game for the Arizona Cardinals.

In 2016, Robinson was found dead in a Milwaukee hotel room from no apparent cause. A medical examiner later announced Robinson was suffering from heart disease. He was forty-one.

Defensive lineman Tyrone Keys (1983–85) was the first Chicago player to wear No. 98, and was a member of the Super Bowl champs. Brian Glasgow (1987) also wore No. 82. Defensive end Jon Norris (1987) played in only three games, but did have two sacks. Linebacker Greg Clark (1988) came out of Arizona State and, after his 15 games with the Bears, played for five more NFL teams.

Defensive tackle Carl Simpson (1993–97) spent five of his six NFL years with the Bears with a career high 4.5 sacks in '97. Bryan Robinson wore 98 next. Defender Shurron Pierson (2004) got into six games for Chicago. Nose tackle Dusty Dvoracek (2006–08) had so many injuries he almost never got into the lineup his first two seasons with the Bears. Darrell McClover also wore No. 58.

Defensive end Corey Wootton (2010–13) out of Northwestern recorded his first sack on a hit that gave Hall of Famer Brett Favre a concussion and ended his career two games earlier than planned. Wootton had 11 sacks for the Bears in all. Brandon Dunn (2014–15) bounced back and forth between the active roster and the practice squad for the Bears before heading to the Houston Texans.

The 6-foot-4, 300-pound Mitch Unrein (2015–16) made three other NFL stops before joining Chicago after coming out of the University of Wyoming. Athleticism runs in Unrein's family. Two of his brothers played college football, a sister was an All-American swimmer, and Unrein's wife, Corey Cogdell, won an Olympic bronze medal in trap shooting. Unrein was still with the Bears entering 2017 training camp.

NO. 99: DAN HAMPTON

The nickname "Danimal" was a compliment. It was applied to Hall of Fame defensive lineman Dan Hampton during his time with the Bears because he was so tough. Hampton wore No. 99 between 1979 and 1990, and in the middle of his stay in Chicago the Bears won a Super Bowl.

The 6-foot-6, 265-pound Hampton played his college football at Arkansas, where his home was. A first-round NFL pick after an All-American career for the Razorbacks, Hampton was an All-Pro six times. One of Hampton's distinctions was being an All-Pro at both defensive end and defensive tackle.

Hampton played all 157 of his games with the Bears and compiled 82 sacks (unofficial). In one astounding performance, the Bears collected 12 sacks in a game against the Detroit Lions with Hampton being a major contributor.

"I was so pleased to be a part of such a great dynasty," Hampton said. "But when you do things the right way, you'll be successful."

The only thing that ever slowed down Hampton was his knees. Even by football standards, he endured a lot with ten knee operations. He was an equal-opportunity employer of doctors, with five surgeries on each knee.

Hampton has been a broadcast football analyst in a variety of forums for more than twenty years. Active with various charities, Hampton did run afoul of drinking and driving laws, being stopped three times in a six-year period, but not since 2002.

Elected to the Pro Football Hall of Fame in 2002, Hampton also works as a motivational speaker.

Jim Daniell (1945) must have been a guy who thought outside the box since he put on No. 99 at a time when almost no one else wore such a number. A tackle out of Ohio State, Daniell's choice of number made him a pioneer of sorts. Nobody else on the Bears wore that number until Dan Hampton took it over in 1979.

Tim Ryan also wore No. 96. Jim Flanigan also wore No. 68. Joe Tafoya (2001–03) was a backup defensive end who played for other teams, but retired after a foot injury in 2008. The real first name of defensive tackle Tank Johnson (2004–06) is Terry, even if at 6-foot-3 and 315 pounds he is built like a tank. Johnson almost missed playing for the Bears against Indianapolis in Miami because he was confined to the state of Illinois due to legal matters. He got clearance to go and made four tackles. Afterwards, Commissioner Roger Goodell hit Johnson with an eight-game suspension. When he had another run-in with the law, the Bears cut him.

The Bears were one of five NFL teams Darwin Walker (2007) played defensive tackle for; he got into 11 games in Chicago.

Former first-round pick (No. 4 overall), defensive end Gaines Adams (2009) tried on Bears No. 99 and showed it off in public in 10 games. In 2010, Adams died of cardiac arrest due to cardiomyopathy (an enlarged heart). He was twenty-six years old.

Marcus Harrison also wore No. 94. Shea McClellin also wore No. 50. Linebacker Lamarr Houston (2014–16) was hoping to regain form in 2017 after missing all of 2016 with a knee injury. In 2015, Houston had eight sacks for Chicago.

ABOUT THE AUTHOR

Lew Freedman is the author of nearly one hundred nonfiction books, mostly about sports. He is a veteran newspaperman and the winner of more than 250 journalism awards. Freedman has worked on the staffs of the *Chicago Tribune*, *Philadelphia Inquirer*, *Anchorage Daily News*, and currently writes for the *Cody Enterprise*. He and his wife Debra live in Cody, Wyoming, and Columbus, Indiana.